PINKERTON'S WAR

The Civil War's Greatest Spy
and the Birth of the U.S. Secret Service

JAY BONANSINGA

LYONS PRESS
Guilford, Connecticut
An imprint of Globe Pequot Press

In Loving Memory of Guy Stickler
1961–2009

ALSO BY JAY BONANSINGA

Nonfiction
The Sinking of the Eastland:
America's Forgotten Tragedy

Fiction

Perfect Victim	*Bloodhound*
Shattered	*Headcase*
Twisted	*The Killer's Game*
Frozen	*Sick*
Oblivion	*The Black Mariah*
The Sleep Police	

To buy books in quantity for corporate use
or incentives, call **(800) 962-0973**
or e-mail **premiums@GlobePequot.com.**

Lyons Press is an imprint of Globe Pequot Press.

Text design: Sheryl P. Kober
Layout artist: Kirsten Livingston
Project editor: Kristen Mellitt

Library of Congress Cataloging-in-Publication Data is available on file.

ISBN 978-0-7627-7072-4

Printed in the United States of America

10 9 8 7 6 5 4 3 2 1

CONTENTS

[If] the incidents seem to the reader at all marvelous or improbable, I can but remind them, in the words of the old adage, that "Truth is stranger than fiction."

—ALLAN PINKERTON

PROLOGUE

Incident at Eaton Walker's

SUMMER 1846

The life's work of Allan Pinkerton, one of America's greatest detectives, began thirty-eight miles northwest of Chicago, where the Fox River slices through a vast, rolling patchwork of hardwood forests and rugged pastures. In the mid-nineteenth century most of this territory lay wild and unsettled. Only a few scabrous villages dotted the land—one of which was the quaint little river town of Dundee, Illinois.

Clinging to the banks of the Fox like a stubborn patch of ironweed, its dirt roads and clapboard buildings lining the shore, Dundee was founded as a dairy farm community in 1840 by a Scotsman named Alexander Gardiner. In less than a decade, it had become an outpost for western travelers, as well as a hub for commerce in northern Illinois.

The town also served as a perfect dwelling place for recent Scottish emigrants Allan Pinkerton and his new bride, Joan.

Pinkerton was only twenty-four when he and his wife arrived in Dundee in 1843. A barrel maker by trade, hardworking, frugal, tough as cowhide, Pinkerton immediately felt at home in Dundee with his fellow Scotsmen and simple tradespeople. He became the town cooper and reveled in the area's scenic wonders.

"Before you, looking upstream, you would see at your feet the rapid river," Pinkerton once wrote of Dundee. "And above this, stretching and winding away into the distance like a ribbon of burnished silver, the river would still be seen, gliding along peacefully with a fair, smooth bosom, wimpling fretfully over stony shallows . . . until the last thread-like trail of it is lost in the gorges beyond."

For his new home Pinkerton chose a spot on a grassy knoll about three hundred yards upstream from the wooden bridge that led into the center of town. With his own hands he built a single-story log cabin, with a workshop attached in the rear. He erected a hand-painted sign above the gate that said, ONLY AND ORIGINAL COOPER OF DUNDEE.

Joan Pinkerton fell in love with the place. She cared for the home, raised chickens, and cultivated a garden of fruits and vegetables. "Our time in that little shop," Mrs. Pinkerton would recall many years later, "with the river purling down the valley . . . and Allan, with his rat-tat-tat on the barrels, whistling and keeping tune with my singing, were the bonniest days the Good Father gave me in all my life."

An idyllic setting for the immigrant couple, it remained so for nearly three years. Then, in the summer of 1846, on a sweltering July afternoon, Allan Pinkerton found himself drawn into a fateful turn of events.

—◦—

It started with a knock on the shop door. Pinkerton put down his hammer, wiped the sweat from his brow, and went to open the door.

"Mr. Pinkerton, sir," said a young dungareed boy, his words indelibly preserved in Pinkerton's memory and later written in the 1880 essay "How I Became a Detective."

"What is it, lad?" Pinkerton stood in the doorway, barefoot, dressed in his work clothes—blue denim overalls and a coarse hickory shirt. Squarely built, compact, and broad-chested, Pinkerton sported a thick, dark beard. His eyes were dark and deep-set under prominent brows, and he had a piercing, judicious gaze.

The boy blurted, "Mister Hunt needs to see ya."

Pinkerton frowned. He knew the name well. H. E. Hunt owned a general store on Dundee's main road. "Mister Hunt is it?" Pinkerton wiped his hands on his pant legs.

"Said it was important, sir."

Pinkerton shrugged, let out a sigh, then followed the boy down the narrow dirt road that wound along the river. The sun was high, and the heat pressed down on Pinkerton's thick neck as he strode along the water. By the time he reached the plank porch in front of the general store, his shirt would have been soaked through with sweat.

"Come in here, Allan," the merchant said, standing in the doorway of his general store. Pinkerton followed the man down the cool aisles of flour sacks and fabric bolts stacked to the ceiling. The store likely smelled of coffee beans and new linens—not an unpleasant place for a mysteriously "important" encounter.

Hunt led Pinkerton into the rear office, where another man, I. C. Bosworth, waited nervously in the shadows. Bosworth was another merchant in town. The two men often served in the unofficial capacity of civic leaders. Their grave expressions steeled Pinkerton.

"We want you to do a little job in the detective line," Hunt finally announced.

"Detective line?" Pinkerton replied with a frown. "My line is the cooper business."

"Never mind now," Bosworth said. "We *know* you can do what we want done. You helped break up the coney men on Bogus Island, and we're sure you can do work of this sort."

Pinkerton shook his head, a tad exasperated. The "coney men" (as counterfeiters were called in the nineteenth century—probably a bastardization of the word "coining") referred to an incident that had occurred earlier that year. Pinkerton had been harvesting timber for his barrel staves on a small, as-yet-unnamed island up near Algonquin when he stumbled upon a suspicious campsite. He returned the next night and hid in the reeds, discovering what he was certain was a band of counterfeiters using the island as a meeting place for the dispersal of "bogus dimes and the tools used in their manufacture." Pinkerton came back the next evening with Luther Dearborn, the Kane County sheriff, and the coney men were arrested and carted away. The story circulated throughout the county and made Pinkerton a minor celebrity for a few months. By July he had told the story so many times he had grown weary with the telling.

At last the cooper said, "But what is it you wish done?"

Hunt explained that there seemed to be another counterfeiter in the village, this time working with paper bills of all denominations. Nineteenth-century America had been scrambling for a consistent currency, and several bank chains had been circulating their own bills. The confusion had led to a rash of counterfeit paper.

"What makes you think there's a counterfeiter here?" Pinkerton asked Hunt.

"Stranger in town's been asking the whereabouts of Old Man Crane."

Pinkerton nodded. He had heard of Crane. The old buzzard was a legendary ne'er-do-well who lived in the neighboring county of Lake. According to locals, Crane "bore a hard character" and was suspected by many to be engaged in the distribution of worthless money from the east. "But what do *I* know about counterfeiting?" Pinkerton protested. "I never saw a ten-dollar bill in my life."

"Come now, Allan, we're wasting time. The man is down there now at Eaton Walker's harness shop, getting something done about his saddle."

Pinkerton was nonplussed. "But what am *I* to do about it?"

The two merchants shot each other a glance, then looked back at the cooper. Hunt said, "Just do your best."

After a moment, Pinkerton let out a long sigh. Then he turned and strolled through the exit and into the brilliant light of day, beginning, in earnest, a career that seemed an odd choice for a man of his background.

Born in 1819 in a hardscrabble area of Glasgow known as the Gorbals, Allan Pinkerton was the youngest of eleven kids. A scrawny, bookish boy, he grew up in a very difficult period for working-class families in Scotland. The country had been through a series of wars with France, followed by years of a stagnant economy and rampant unemployment. After the death of his father, William Pinkerton, in 1830, young Allan dropped out of school and worked as an errand boy, a harness maker, and a pattern drawer for the local dressmaking industry.

In his later writings, Pinkerton would recall the stunning poverty of his childhood and the joyous celebrations when his mother, Isabella, would bring home a single egg for the family tea. But it was Pinkerton's initiation into the brotherhood of barrel makers that would ultimately drive him out of Scotland.

Pinkerton learned the cooper trade from his Uncle John and soon joined the burgeoning union movement. Years of bending staves and hammering iron hoops hardened his muscles and turned his wiry form to brawn. He kept up with his reading as well, feeding his ravenous appetite for learning. By the time he turned twenty, he had developed progressive political leanings. He joined the Glasgow Universal Suffrage Association in 1839 and began to attend public demonstrations. He marched in the street, channeling his youthful energy into righteous anger toward the Crown, hollering for the right to vote for all men and women over the age of twenty-four.

The Scottish press called them "Chartists" after the charter of axioms by which they operated, which included equal rights, better working conditions, and unionized labor forces. The Chartists became a turbulent movement of radical liberalism. But infighting sabotaged the organization. As the months passed, Pinkerton drifted toward the leftist fringe, and by 1841, had gotten himself mixed up in a series of violent uprisings. "I had become an outlaw with a price on my head," Pinkerton wrote years later in a letter to his son. The young radical began to flirt with the idea of emigrating.

Around this time Pinkerton attended a concert at a public house near Glasgow Cross. Dressed in his finery, sitting in the front row next to his mother, he gaped in awe at the handsomeness of a young soprano named Joan Carfrae. A bookbinder's apprentice from Paisley, she was a tiny girl with soulful brown eyes. Pinkerton was instantly smitten. "I got to sort of hanging around her, clinging to her so to speak," Pinkerton wrote later, "and I knew I couldn't live without her."

By the spring of 1842, Pinkerton had reached a crossroads. Hounded by the law, desperately infatuated with Miss Carfrae, he made one of the most crucial decisions of his life. He would marry Joan and move to America. The couple wed on March 13 in the High Parish Church in Glasgow, and four weeks later they slipped out of the country unnoticed by all but their closest family and friends.

If they thought they were leaving all their troubles behind, they were wrong.

"The Atlantic crossing in April 1842 was no honeymoon," writes Pinkerton biographer James Mackay. "It was the Pinkertons' misfortune to make the hazardous voyage during some of the worst storms on record." The battered ship ultimately foundered off the coast of Halifax, and the passengers and crew were forced to row ashore in lifeboats. As soon as they reached land, they were attacked by Indians and robbed of their few belongings. A few days later the stranded travelers were picked up by a merchant vessel and taken to Montreal.

For a few months Pinkerton made barrels to finance the rest of the journey. Finally, in the winter of 1842, the Pinkertons took a schooner through the Great Lakes to Detroit, then traveled overland in a "ramshackle wagon drawn by an old spavined horse" to Chicago. There, in that stinking, moldering frontier town, settled only a couple of decades earlier—a place where, as Mackay has noted, the "cows roamed at will, and often passed the night on sidewalks"—the Pinkertons stayed with an old Chartist friend named Robbie Fergus. Allan made beer barrels from dawn to dusk for fifty cents a day in order to get back on his feet.

In time Pinkerton set his sights on Dundee as a proper home. Perhaps the Scottish origins of the community drew him there. Or maybe the tranquil landscape called to him. But whatever the reason, by springtime the following year, the Pinkertons had relocated to the little "fair and lovely spot" on the Fox River, the place where Allan Pinkerton would soon learn the delicate business of being a detective.

Eaton Walker's harness shop sat on Dundee's main road, nestled in a copse of overgrown maple trees. The building's facade was a pleasing plank porch flanked by square timbers, set off by curtained front windows. As most of the repair work was done in the rear, the front of the shop served as a sort of rustic gentlemen's club—not unlike the fabled pickle barrel conclaves in small-town stores of that era. On any given summer afternoon, one might find at least half a dozen townspeople lingering there, discussing anything from the burning issues of the day to the local weather.

July 15, 1846, was no different. "There was the usual quota of town stragglers loafing about the shop, and looking with sleepy eyes and open mouths at the little that was going on about the place," Pinkerton recalled in his memoir *Professional Thieves and the Detective.*

Approaching from the east, Pinkerton padded along on the hardpacked dirt road, still barefoot, still clad in his sweaty hickory shirt and jeans. He realized that he probably looked like a real bumpkin—no hat, a vexed expression on his ruddy face, his beard still mottled with the sawdust of the cooperage. Right then, stricken with a bolt of inspiration, Allan Pinkerton began to reinvent himself.

Acting the part of an awkward country buffoon, Pinkerton approached a splendid horse hitched outside the shop—in Pinkerton's words, a "fine, large roan, well built for traveling." He pretended to silently admire it.

All the while, Pinkerton's eye was on the horse's apparent owner.

The stranger stood well over six feet tall and looked to weigh in excess of two hundred pounds. In his mid-sixties, he had dark hair and chiseled features, and a pair of the "keenest, coldest eyes" that Pinkerton had ever seen.

Pinkerton said nothing to the man at first but simply feigned interest in the horse.

After a while, the stranger leaned down and asked Pinkerton in a soft voice so that no one else could hear, "Stranger, do you know where Old Man Crane lives?"

Replying in the same low, conspiratorial tone, Pinkerton said, "Cross the river to the east, take the main road through the woods until you come to Jesse Miller's farmhouse. Then *he* will tell you." Pinkerton paused here, glancing over his shoulder for maximum effect. He further lowered his voice. "But if you don't want to ask, hold the road to the northeast and inquire the direction to Libertyville. When you get there you will easily find the old man, and he is as good as cheese!"

The stranger smiled, then whispered, "Young man, I like your style, and I want to know you better. Join me over the river in the ravine. I want to talk to you."

"All right," Pinkerton said. "But you better let me go ahead. Then you follow on, but not too closely. I'll be up in some of the gorges, so we can talk entirely by ourselves."

The stranger's smile widened. "I'll make it worth something to you."

Pinkerton gave a nod and walked away. Then he circled around the back of the shop, heading toward the footbridge across the river.

All at once the young cooper was buzzing with adrenaline and mixed emotions. He had barrels to make, and little time for playing detective. On the other hand, he was convinced now that this stranger was indeed a counterfeiter, and Pinkerton had always believed that the law must prevail. He headed across the river and into the woods.

In *Professional Thieves and the Detective,* he writes:

There I was, hardly more than a plodding country cooper, having had but little experience save that given me by a life of toil in Scotland, and no experience of things in this country save that secured through a few years of the hardest kind of work. For a moment I felt wholly unable to cope with this keen man of the world, but as I was gaining the top of the hill I glanced back over my shoulder, and noticed that the horseman was following my instructions to the letter. I reasoned that, from some cause, I had gained an influence over this stranger, or he thought he had secured one over me. By being cautious and discreet, I had obtained a sufficiently close intimacy with him to cause the disclosure of his plans, and possibly his capture. My will had been touched, and I resolved to carry the matter through.

This moment of truth in the cool shadows of the forest would not only change a young cooper's destiny but would go on to alter the shape of law enforcement in this burgeoning country. In those swaying, fragrant shadows above the Fox River, the Era of the Detective was born.

Pinkerton's maiden voyage into that strange new territory known as undercover work went surprisingly well. Gaining the horseman's trust, Pinkerton proceeded to purchase counterfeit bills with funds provided by Hunt and Bosworth. The final transaction occurred in Chicago, where Pinkerton had arranged a raid by the deputy sheriff of Cook County. The counterfeiters were arrested and indicted in Kane County on Pinkerton's deposition before the grand jury.

Pinkerton could have returned to the obscurity of his cooperage at that point, living out his years as a simple tradesman who had once briefly flirted with detective work. He could have basked in the momentary glory of catching the counterfeiters and then gone back to, as Pinkerton puts it, the "hardest kind of work" on his tranquil little hillside above the Fox. But the experience of going into that dark unknown and coming back with the taste of justice in his mouth galvanized the idealistic immigrant.

Was it his background as an agitator in the Gorbals? Or was it something else that resonated? Pinkerton had grown up a fighter, a survivor, and it is likely the very process of detective work gave him something for which he hungered in the hinterlands of America: *mastery*. Mastery over his environment, over others, over his own destiny.

Pinkerton began taking assignments on a regular basis from Hunt and Bosworth, as well as from the leaders of neighboring communities. "I suddenly found myself called up from every quarter to undertake matters requiring detective skill," he wrote years later.

Toward the end of 1846, Sheriff Dearborn offered Pinkerton the part-time post of deputy sheriff of Kane County, and the brawny cooper enthusiastically accepted. He continued to make barrels when he wasn't apprehending thieves, serving court orders, or settling minor disputes. The imprimatur of local government also gave Pinkerton a boldness and a sense of himself the likes of which he had never known. His progressive politics reemerged, and he became a staunch supporter of the abolition movement. He and Joan opened their home to runaway slaves heading north to Canada via the Underground Railroad.

In 1847, in the wake of Luther Dearborn's retirement, Pinkerton ran for county sheriff on the abolitionist ticket. Local church leaders, led by the fire-and-brimstone preacher M. L. Wisner, began a systematic campaign to discredit the humanist deputy. By his own admission, Pinkerton had never "had a great deal of time for organized religion," and now his liberal propensities further deepened the animosity between cooper and clergy. A few days after announcing his candidacy, Pinkerton suffered through a series of scandalous letters published in the local newspaper, the *Western Citizen*, accusing the barrel maker of everything from bootlegging to circulating blasphemous literature. Pinkerton fought back with bare-fisted righteousness, but he eventually lost the election and became a pariah in his own community.

By late November, the cooper faced another crossroads. Joan had given birth to their first child, William, and the barrel-making business had begun to decline. As he approached his thirties, Pinkerton grew restless. No longer the freckled, stocky kid from the Gorbals, he had physically calcified like a stubborn oak—the lines on his sun-weathered face deepening, and that bear-like, heavily muscled body turning to middle-aged bulk. He had taken to wearing suits and chewing on small cheroot cigars, which enhanced his tough exterior. He had outgrown his small, sylvan village in every way and was ready for a new challenge.

Perhaps this was why the telegram from Chicago that arrived on Allan Pinkerton's doorstep that autumn seemed so propitious. That night, Pinkerton saved the news until he and Joan were settled down for dinner. The conversation that ensued is taken from biographer Arthur Orrmont's book *Master Detective Allan Pinkerton* (the dialogue extracted from Pinkerton agency files).

"Telegram today from the Sheriff of Cook County, fellow named Church," Pinkerton announced to his wife that night, broaching the subject carefully over the supper table.

"Aye," Joan said with a casual nod. She very likely knew that this was a life-changing subject. The petite lass with the soulful eyes was a quiet, stabilizing influence on her dynamo of a husband. She would be the silent partner—an unsung confidante and adviser—throughout the coming storm of events.

"Wants to offer me a position," Pinkerton went on. "Said I would be a sort of special agent, a deputy in fact, charged with doin' police work of various kinds."

"Aye." Joan's face revealed nothing at first.

"The salary ain't much, but the future of it looks fairly bright," Pinkerton continued. "Might eventually get the chance to take over for Mr. Church, who's up in his sixties already. Could leave the cooperage with Schultz. He's a good man. Liable to buy me out." Still no reaction from the stoic woman across the table. "Question is," Pinkerton said at last, "would you want to leave Dundee?"

Joan said nothing. She narrowed her eyes at him, perhaps with just a trace of a smile on her tulip-shaped lips.

Pinkerton asked her what was wrong.

She let out a sigh. "It's just that yer talkin' straight English, without a hint of Scots. And whenever ya get excited, as I know you are now, your burr is always thick enough to cut with a carvin' knife. Or used to be."

Pinkerton gave her a look. "My dear, pardon me for saying so, but this is a very serious matter. It means our future lives. Don't be joking with me."

"I'm not joking, Allan. If you'll let me finish, I was going to add this— it seems at last you've stopped bein' a Glasgow cooper and become a Chicago blue."

Joan beamed at him.

Allan embraced the woman. He held her tightly, appreciatively, for several moments, then said to her, "You won't miss Dundee too much?"

She touched his cheek. "Not if I have you to miss it with me."

The die had been cast.

The next day Pinkerton accepted Church's offer without reservation.

———

Chicago was a town born out of mud, tears, and blood. Situated in a desolate bog in the throat of Lake Michigan, cleaved through by a sluggish, foul-smelling river, the place attracted only the heartiest of souls. The first permanent resident was the son of a black slave, Jean Baptiste DuSable, who would one day see his reeking homestead acquire a nickname derived from the Indian word for stinking onion: "Checagou."

The first white encampment—Fort Dearborn—was built in 1803 as an outpost for fur traders and explorers. The fort served as a critical stronghold, connecting the Great Lakes with the Mississippi Valley. It was the meanest terrain imaginable. "Those who waded through the mud frequently sank to their waist," reported one fur trader, "and after reaching the end and camping for the night came the task of ridding themselves of the bloodsuckers."

In August 1812, Pottawatomie warriors attacked and slaughtered the few settlers surrounding the area's main garrison. For the next four years, the decaying bodies of men, women, and children lay unburied in the shifting muck of the marsh. The lingering trauma of the massacre, though, very likely bolstered the settlement's growth.

The government stepped in—securing the area, building more ramparts—and by 1833 the town was incorporated. The population grew in leaps and bounds, and just four years later Chicago was designated as a city.

John Lewis Peyton, a journalist of this era, wrote of the cow-ridden city: "There was no pavement, no macadamized streets, no drainage, and the three thousand houses in which people lived were almost entirely small timber buildings, painted white, and this white much defaced by mud."

The main streets, covered with heavy boards resting on cross sills, only added to the filth and stench. Standing water under the planks rotted and teemed with insects, putrefying with the runoff of horse dung and cow droppings. "A frightful odor was emitted in summer," Peyton marveled, "causing fevers and other diseases foreign to the climate."

Crime festered—as profusely as the bacteria—and the need for organized law enforcement soon became paramount. Early settlers relied on a town crier, who would skulk through the encampments late at night with a lamp and a bell, searching for lost children. Later, the city established an official constabulary, charged with the removal of obstructions, the maintenance of public health, and, in the words of a reporter from the *Chicago Democrat*, "the removal of all idle and suspicious persons . . . and the protection of property thereof."

Constables usually ruled with bare-knuckle justice, dragging offenders off to the "calaboose"—a log cabin stockade at the corner of Madison and Michigan Avenues—or running ne'er-do-wells out of town "on a rail" (a colonial practice of carrying miscreants out of town in disgrace on a fence rail).

In the 1840s, Chicago's first police agency grew out of the "City Watch," a term for the head constable's office. All officers then reported to the mayor, with whom the real power resided. Early police struggled with the ballooning population and the inevitable rise in the "dangerous classes." Gamblers, whiskey men, whoremongers, and petty criminals ruled the night, and the police could not keep up. "When a burglary was committed," writes Chicago historian Richard Lindberg, "the only reasonable way to apprehend the robber was to engage a private thief catcher."

Arriving in Chicago at this pivotal time, Allan Pinkerton transcended this role.

Over the course of a single decade, Pinkerton would become the critical link between the lawlessness of the frontier and the new science of investigation—his method a sui generis combination of brute force and spontaneous invention.

But nobody, not even Pinkerton, could have imagined the critical role the young Scotsman would play, at the height of his career, in the theater of national events.

PART I
THE CALLING

Death knocks at the portals . . . and the gates fly open at his magic touch.

—ALLAN PINKERTON

CHAPTER ONE

Tinderbox

AUGUST 1857

Around 5:30 p.m. on a muggy Chicago summer night, Allan Pinkerton was strolling down a scarred boardwalk along Adams Street. He was on his way home from the offices of the newly established Pinkerton National Detective Agency, located in the heart of the city, at the corner of Washington and Dearborn Streets, and he was not thinking one whit about slavery or secession or angry mobs or the stirrings of war, when he heard a voice call out: "Mr. Pinkerton!"

It was a local abolitionist named Justice D'Wolf, peering out his half-ajar gate with a look of alarm.

"What is it, sir?" Pinkerton inquired, stepping up to the threshold.

The urgent news that Mr. D'Wolf was burning to impart, as well as the subsequent dialogue, was later recounted by Pinkerton himself to the *Chicago Daily Tribune.*

"Couple of Negroes," D'Wolf began, "they just told me they're trying to run off a slave who ain't a slave!"

"They're what?"

"Some gentlemen at the Commercial House . . . they got the wrong idea about a Negro boy staying there. I'm goin' up there soon to set it right, but I think a detective oughtta be involved."

"Alright, sir . . . I'll go and see about it when I have a chance," Pinkerton said, and then, with a tip of his hat, the muscular Scot turned on his heels and walked on a bit more purposefully.

He needed to check in at home first before going off on any impromptu detective work.

A casual observer might not have noticed the toll that the last nine years of crime fighting had taken on Pinkerton's bearing as he continued along Adams Street. The job had changed him, toughened him like a hide that had been tanned. First, as a deputy sheriff patrolling Chicago's treacherous outlying areas, and then, in 1849, as the first full-time detective for the city's newly organized police force, he had carved out—often through sheer force of will—an impressive niche for himself. Writes James Mackay: "Never afraid to tackle criminals on his own, he soon acquired a formidable reputation for rough justice."

On many levels—at work, at home, in his dealings with others—Pinkerton had become, in a word, *more*. More alert, more secretive, more industrious, more demanding, more visionary, and above all, more fearless.

His steely nerves could be observed even in his posture, the bullish way he now carried himself. Pinkerton walked with a forward inclination like the prow of a squat, sturdy ship cutting through perilous ice. He favored Cuban cigars and businesslike attire during this period: the three-piece suit of a professional and a trademark vest that barely contained his fireplug of a body. The dark, bushy fringe of whiskers on his chin accentuated his unyielding presence.

Pinkerton often strode with one arm tucked behind his back, hidden under his great coat. It gave him a slightly Napoleonic air. In fact, this idiosyncrasy had actually saved his life back in 1853. Out of the darkness one night an anonymous assassin—riled by Pinkerton's growing reputation—had snuck up on the detective and sent two large caliber slugs into the unsuspecting lawman's back.

The arm had absorbed the mini-balls, preventing a mortal wound.

He was now holding this same arm, stiff with scar tissue, in this customary manner, as he strode down the uneven, dew-slick planks of the sidewalk. Plumes of cigar smoke wreathed his head as he marched along, more than likely lost in thoughts of business and family.

Lately Pinkerton had been worried that he was spending too much time away from Joan and the children. Since the day he had left the police department and gone freelance in 1852, he had worked virtually around the clock. He worked cases either by himself or closely supervising a small group of associates. And almost inadvertently he had become a pioneer in the frontier of law enforcement, systematically perfecting techniques that he would employ from this point on.

On a regular basis Pinkerton would disguise himself as a construction worker, rail-yard bull, or transient gambler, and would penetrate the dark corners of Chicago's back rooms and dens of iniquity previously inaccessible to a constable or regular police officer. He had investigated and captured a plethora of pickpockets, embezzlers, horse thieves, bank vault sneaks, mail defrauders, burglars, hooligans, grifters, and railroad bandits.

"His early record of running malefactors to earth and making them confess, disgorge, and repent their crimes would be phenomenal in any period," writes historian Richard Rowan of Pinkerton's formative years as Chicago's first detective, "but to his contemporaries, who recalled the very recent lawless years of pioneering, there was downright wizardry in what this self-taught master of investigation went about quietly accomplishing."

But now the work had begun to consume him.

The stakes of his personal life had also been raised. Shortly after he, Joan, and William had settled into a cozy, little two-room clapboard house on Adams Street—a home in which the Pinkerton clan would reside for several years—Joan gave birth to twins. The boy was named Robert and the girl Joan. Another girl, Mary, came along in 1852. Pinkerton—already a stern, demanding patriarch—insisted on naming the children himself. As his daughter Joan would recall many years later, "My dear little mother never had any choice in naming us—my father announced the name of the new arrival and that ended the matter."

Tragedy may have also driven Pinkerton deeper into his work. In early 1854, his beloved baby Mary died of an illness, leaving Pinkerton and his wife heartsick. Less than a year later, Pinkerton lost his mother, and then his elder daughter, Joan, from fever.

The lack of a sewer system in Chicago at this time caused outbreaks of cholera and rheumatic fever on a regular basis. The Pinkerton children were among the thousands of casualties in the mid-nineteenth century due to poor sanitation. For Pinkerton, death—or the nearness of it—became a constant nagging companion.

After checking in at home that night—and finding that all was well—Pinkerton decided to take another stroll: west on Adams toward Sherman Street.

Curiosity had gotten the better of him.

At this point in his career, with his reputation growing among Chicago's law enforcement community as the consummate private investigator, Pinkerton saw little conflict of interest in his zeal for the abolitionist movement. Pinkerton hated slavery.

Throughout the 1850s, Pinkerton would provide safe passage for nearly a hundred families of color through the Underground Railroad, harboring them in his home, helping usher them to freedom in Canada or far-flung areas of the North—even though the Fugitive Slave Act of 1850 had made it a federal offense to assist runaway slaves. The clapboard cottage on Adams Street became a safe-house "bursting at the seams" with runaways.

Many of Pinkerton's secret "guests" were brought by John Jones, a famous Free-Negro leader, whose subjects were often escaped slaves liberated by the infamous militant abolitionist John Brown. As a left-leaning man of the North, Pinkerton most likely admired and sympathized with Brown, but he also drew the line at armed insurrection—a remedy Brown vehemently advocated.

Still, Pinkerton had always been unequivocal about his feelings toward slavery: "The institution of human bondage," he wrote later in life, "always reclined [sic] my earnest opposition." And this opposition, apparently, trumped the law. "While Pinkerton's right hand caught lawbreakers," writes one journalist of the day, "his left hand broke the law. But his conscience was as clear as that of any Quaker patriot out on the long Underground route."

The Commercial House hotel was a squat, brick edifice set close to the boardwalk at the corner of Sherman and Van Buren. By the time Pinkerton arrived on that humid August evening, the frontage teemed with hundreds of angry men—black and white—hollering and waving clubs and rocks. The men wanted the black boy given up. They believed rumors that had been circulating throughout the day that the boy was being transported illegally as a slave.

The situation was quickly deteriorating. The hoteliers were keeping the mob at bay—for the moment, at least—but violence was in the air. Pinkerton ordered the crowd to calm themselves and disperse—all to no avail.

Inside the hotel, Pinkerton found the boy in question—a skinny sixteen-year-old named Samuel Gantz—huddling terrified in a room with his middle-aged white benefactor Samuel Thompson. After an hour of questioning, Pinkerton pieced together the pair's story.

Apparently, Mr. Samuel Thompson, a farmer from Juniata County, Pennsylvania, had saved the young boy fourteen years earlier from a cruel slave owner. The boy had become an apprentice to Thompson, and the two of them were en route to Thompson's new farm in Monmouth, Illinois. Pinkerton checked with a U.S. marshal he knew in Chicago (who had been a resident of Monmouth), and the man vouched for Thompson.

But regardless of his due diligence, Pinkerton also knew that getting the man and the boy out of town was not going to be easy. Chicago in 1857 had teeth and would bite you at the slightest provocation. But Pinkerton, in his own way, knew how to negotiate the thorniest situations. He was a student of human behavior in extremis. Self-taught, hyper-vigilant, prepared for the unexpected, he was a man of his time—an era of great upheaval and social change.

The mid-nineteenth century was a time of innovation. The advent of the postage stamp was not the only novelty changing lives. Celestial photography, artesian wells, player pianos, typewriting machines, surgical anesthetics, pneumatic tires, sewing machines, printing telegraphs, artificial limbs, ophthalmoscopes, magazine-loaded firearms, nitroglycerine, electrolysis, paraffin, elevators, and photographic film rolls all were introduced in this era—alongside the early incarnation of the American detective.

The father of the modern detective, however, was most likely a French criminologist, born in 1775, named Eugène François Vidocq. A former thief, who spent time in prison for forgery, Vidocq turned informant in his mid-thirties and discovered a new calling, the application of his criminal knowledge to catch criminals.

In 1811, Vidocq organized a plainclothes unit known as Brigade de la Sûreté (Security Brigade) to infiltrate criminal lairs, "to procure information . . . to go to the theaters, the boulevards, the barriers, and all other public places . . . the haunts of thieves and pickpockets." Vidocq's undercover work revolutionized law enforcement and soon became legend. An uncanny man-hunter, a polymath mind, Vidocq later employed dazzling displays of deductive reasoning in his crime scene investigations.

Inspired by Vidocq's exploits, Edgar Allan Poe created a fictional version of the French investigator in 1841 with the story "The Murders in the Rue Morgue." Poe's fictional Auguste Dupin, who appeared in several other tales, was an almost preternatural version of Vidocq, a man who could read a crime scene like Braille (another nineteenth-century invention). Many years later, in the late Victorian era, Sir Arthur Conan Doyle would spin yet another incarnation of the legendary Vidocq, an eccentric investigator named Sherlock Holmes.

It is not beyond the realm of possibility that Allan Pinkerton had studied the life and career of Eugène Vidocq, as well as perhaps perused the pages of Poe's fictional creation. Vidocq's memoirs were published in 1828 and were widely available in Europe and America. By the 1840s other private policing agencies were coming into existence—in places like St. Louis and New York—staking their own claims to the patent. And Pinkerton was not above perpetuating a few legends of his own.

The myth that Pinkerton invented the private detective was, in the words of one historian, "reinforced by the bold emblem of [Pinkerton's] company, a wide-awake human eye . . . which, in due course, gave rise to the expression 'private eye' as a nickname for private investigators."

Some biographers believe that Joan Pinkerton was the first to suggest the famous slogan, after her husband told her his idea for the company symbol.

"I've got it!" Joan allegedly blurted one night at the Adams Street house. "'We never sleep.'"

Allan must have looked at her then with a mixture of amusement, love, and admiration. As historian Arthur Orrmont writes, "She was thirty-one now and there were traces of gray in her hair, but Joan Carfrae Pinkerton was just as slim and attractive as she had been on that night thirteen years ago when he had walked her home to the Gorbals. And . . . twice as clever."

Finally, after giving her idea some thought, pursing his lips with that patented Scottish skepticism, Pinkerton said, "Well now, I'll have to give that some consideration. It might do . . . an' then again it might not."

Of course, as usual, Joan was on to something.

—◦—

But on that volatile night in August 1857—as Allan Pinkerton walked into a tinderbox of racial tensions—the niceties of company slogans, the tropes of fiction, and the memoirs of legendary lawmen were all about to be cauterized by the flames of reality.

—◦—

Justice D'Wolf—Pinkerton's abolitionist friend—arrived at the Commercial House that evening just after dusk. He found the detective huddling with the black boy and Thompson in the lounge, and tense plans were made. It was decided that the boy and his caretaker would be ushered quickly off the premises via the hotel's surrey and then taken to the Burlington train station.

But when Pinkerton and his subjects emerged from the hotel, the crowd had grown in size and agitation. Deep-rooted animosity and rage flickered on faces illuminated by torchlight. The wagon was backed awkwardly toward the frontage, as Pinkerton called out to the crowd: "This boy is a free indentured ward of this honest farmer! The young man is in no danger! He will be treated in the proper manner! Please disperse at once!"

The thinking here was that the presence of Pinkerton and D'Wolf—two known abolitionists—would be an adequate buffer to sooth the savage throng.

The thinking was decidedly wrong.

Gantz and Thompson lurched onto the wagon, as the crowd surrounded the conveyance. Pinkerton stepped in between the mob and the wagon and shouted out a plea for temperance, which was instantly drowned by the angry chorus, now whipped into a mad, righteous frenzy. Pinkerton was backed toward the wagon by the profusion of the crowd. He stepped onto the running board and pleaded for calm.

Before Pinkerton could register what was happening, a man lunged out of the horde and seized at the horse's bridle. The horse reared up, and the driver panicked. The whip came down, and the wagon erupted into motion.

The crowd roared, and Pinkerton held tightly to the rail as the carriage charged. Stones flew. Bricks, torches, and enraged epithets pelted the surrey. Gantz and Thompson ducked down into the bowels of the coach.

"STOP!" Pinkerton ordered, but the driver was furiously whipping the horse now, as the gauntlet of bystanders along Sherman Street launched another salvo of rocks at the speeding wagon.

The surrey raced down Sherman to Harrison. Shots rang out. Wooden wheels drummed on the boarded road. Pinkerton drew his revolver and hollered at his charges: "Stay down!"

Angry men gave chase on foot. The wagon slammed around the corner at Harrison Street, nearly tipping as it sped northward. Bullets traced through the thick summer night. Pinkerton ordered the driver to turn right at Wells. The wheels groaned as the surrey keened around the corner, raising wood chips and dust. Soon the assault diminished, as the carriage put distance between itself and the mob.

Five blocks rushed past the wagon in a blur of lantern light and wood smoke. At Madison Street the wheels gave away. The wagon banged against the macadam and skidded to a halt in a cloud of dust and debris.

"This way—quickly!" Pinkerton leaped off the coach and led the frantic passengers down a dark alley.

The shadows of tall brick buildings swallowed the terrified escapees as they felt their way through the passageways redolent with the stench of garbage and dung cast off from the thoroughfares. But Pinkerton had a plan. He hastened the farmer and boy westward through the darkness and the filth.

By this point in his career, Pinkerton had come to know these back alleys well. They reached the train station within minutes, and Pinkerton commandeered the idling Burlington with a flash of his metal badge. He hurried the boy and the farmer onto the train. He hid them in the saloon car, and he found the conductor, urging the man to embark early. Monmouth was only 184 miles to the west. They could be there before morning. The conductor was skeptical, thinking it possible only if the boilers could be stoked in time.

No such luck.

As the engines hissed and complained, another angry crowd of black men began gathering outside the train. More shouting and threats of violence, and stones being pelted at the iron bulwark. The situation was becoming hopeless. This was a moment of truth for Pinkerton.

It was also highly apropos that the incident would come to a head on a train.

The railroad had proven to be much more than a mere conveyance for Allan Pinkerton. Railroad companies would become the Pinkerton Agency's most lucrative customers, the backbone of the business. They would also transport the detective onto the national scene in unexpected ways.

It was another Scot, James Watt, who patented the first steam locomotive in the late eighteenth century. In America, as the frontier opened up in the 1800s, and the West was explored, mapped, and settled, it would be the railroad that would circulate life blood to the young nation.

From 1830 to 1840, twenty-seven hundred miles of iron capillaries spread across the land. By the 1850s the number had increased fivefold. The largest railroad line in the world at this time was the Illinois Central.

By 1855, a rash of robberies, derailments, and rail-side crimes compelled the Illinois Central to hire the brash Scottish detective from Chicago to provide security. Pinkerton rose to the occasion—he had already been cultivating other railroad clientele such as the Rock Island Railway and the Galena and Chicago Union line—developing protocols for protecting in-transit payrolls, preventing banditry, and tracking down train robbers. But most importantly, Pinkerton's affiliation with the Illinois Central Railroad would bring him into contact with individuals who would one day play key roles in the detective's destiny.

George B. McClellan, chief of the Illinois Central's Engineering Department at the time of Pinkerton's hiring, would soon befriend the burly detective.

McClellan, who would march into history six years later with scabbard rattling as a celebrated Union general, was a cultured scion of great wealth. He had been an excellent student, graduating second in his class at West Point. A veteran of the Mexican-American War, McClellan cut an imposing figure with his patrician nose, elegant mustache, cat-like eyes, and aristocratic bearing.

At first blush, McClellan and Pinkerton might strike one as an unlikely duo, but Pinkerton found much to admire in the ambitious railroad executive. "Both were obsessive," writes James Mackay, "with a passion for order and a mania for preserving even the most trivial scraps of paper."

Pinkerton also had the pleasure of one other significant acquaintance during this time. The attorney who drafted the original contract between the Illinois Central and Pinkerton's organization was based downstate but did much business in Chicago. He was a skilled litigator, who had tried thousands of cases over the last eighteen years: taxes, foreclosures, disputed wills, assaults, and debts to slander, murders, divorces, and even horse thefts. He had also once served as a U.S. congressman and was now considering another run for office.

Abraham Lincoln and Allan Pinkerton, according to all accounts, made similar impressions on each other when they first spoke, most likely in the Illinois Central Railroad headquarters in Chicago. It is possible they recognized each other as kindred spirits—not just because of their shared political leanings but for more inchoate reasons—their humble origins and work ethics, their shared affinity for the simple chalk line of logic, the geometric split of a rail, the watertight seam of a barrel.

McClellan, in his underestimation of these two self-taught savants, saw the spark of admiration between Lincoln and Pinkerton somewhat differently: "They each were typical of good people who were rather primitive in their appearance and habits."

But Lincoln and Pinkerton—destined to cross paths again very soon—shared more than a home state and impoverished, hardscrabble childhoods. Each man was a skeptic, each a progressive thinker with abolitionist leanings and a strong belief in science. And each had run up against the church.

Lincoln had long believed that the influence of the church had been used against him in politics. During his 1846 campaign for U.S. Congress, he had been forced to issue a handbill, which attempted once and for all to define his beliefs, formed as a young man fond of philosophical debate:

I have never spoken with intentional disrespect of religion in general, or any denomination of Christians in particular. It is true that in early life I was inclined to believe in what I understand is called the "Doctrine of Necessity"—that is, that the human mind is impelled to action, or held in rest by some power, over which the mind itself has no control; and I have sometimes (with one, two, or three, but never publicly) tried to maintain this opinion in argument. The habit of arguing thus, however, I have entirely left off for more than five years.

Like Lincoln, Pinkerton knew all too well these compulsions of the human mind (as well as the inability of some to control them). And even at this early stage in his career, Pinkerton was more than willing to square his shoulders and look at this phenomenon—metaphysical or not—directly in the face.

But there was nothing metaphysical about Pinkerton's gradual descent into the quagmire of Lincoln's political causes—exemplified by the stalemate at the train station on that sweltering, ill-fated August night.

—～—

At some point that night, hunkering down with that trembling boy in the train car, it is likely that Pinkerton once again faced the fact that this was becoming the central conflict of his life. This was a country being rent by the institution of slavery.

Fortunately, before the scene at the depot had a chance to completely erupt, a pair of policemen arrived at the train yard. The two officers informed Pinkerton that they had orders to take the lad and Mr. Thompson into custody. Pinkerton realized that this was the best course of action.

With guns at the ready, the officers accompanied Pinkerton and his party to the neighboring guard house for safekeeping.

As the night dragged on, with Pinkerton nearby, standing guard, the Gantz boy made a courageous decision. He realized on some level that it was up to him to diffuse this explosive situation.

With first light, the boy requested a brief dialogue with the rioters. He came out and calmly explained that he was better off with the farmer, that he was in no danger, and that he was free. The collective anger, much to Pinkerton's relief, began to subside.

—～—

No charges were levied as a result of this incident. A public examination of the affair was conducted in the Common Council Room before Mayor Milliken, with Pinkerton giving his expert testimony, as well as the boy and Thompson speaking their piece, and the charges of inciting a riot were dropped.

At the end of the hearing, Pinkerton was slapped on the wrist by the mayor for what the *Chicago Daily Tribune* called "assimilating political beliefs" into the incident. Pinkerton was appalled at the accusation and defiantly said that his abolitionism was well known and that, as a detective, his principles were not for sale. The next day, the *Tribune* summed up the smoldering fuse of tensions in this country with both candor and thinly veiled condescension.

"We cannot blame the colored men of this city for the jealousy with which they watch anything that looks like an attempt to take one of their color back to slavery," wrote an anonymous editor. "That bitter, cursing, terrible slavery, which so many of them have suffered. They are, many of them, ignorant and easily deluded in a matter of this kind."

Pinkerton saw things differently. Not only did the detective still harbor the left-wing sentiments he had acquired as a young man in Scotland, but slavery, for Pinkerton, was, in the words of Mackay, "an abomination that had to be rooted out by whatever means possible." Pinkerton saw the plight of black people as a symptom of *white* ignorance. Black people were certainly the objects of constant scorn and derision, as well as, more importantly, underestimation.

Over the coming months, as the storm front of rebellion formed on the nation's horizon, Pinkerton would risk practically everything to put these principles into practice.

Chapter Two

Blood on the Wind

Late September 1859

Massive steel wheels churning, the locomotive snaked its way across the vast, verdant pastures of central Tennessee. The engine huffed and chugged—sending up puffs of black smoke as dark as ink.

The train, the pride of the Louisville and Nashville line, was thundering toward Columbia, a small hamlet in the piney woods deep below the Mason-Dixon Line. The passenger cars clattered along noisily, filled with anonymous figures.

In the rear of one coach sat a middle-aged man, his expression fixed. To the untrained eye he could be anybody—a businessman, perhaps, or a gentleman farmer on his way to market, or even a minister.

Harper's New Monthly Magazine described the man as having a full beard now, a compact and muscular frame, and "a rather grave and dignified demeanor, which, with the usually plain and somewhat clerical cut of his coat, surmounted by a white 'choker,' gives him more the appearance of a country parson than of a man thoroughly cognizant of all the arts, wiles, and iniquities of a demoralized age."

Allan Pinkerton rose from his bench as the train whistled into the Columbia depot.

Air brakes hissed, and the iron beast shuddered to a halt. It was early autumn in Tennessee, and the afternoon sun would have been hammering down on Pinkerton as he stepped off the train and found his way across the dusty patchwork of boardwalks and storefronts to the local bank.

In this era, crossing state lines during an investigation was unheard of by law enforcement departments. Up until the late 1850s, a local sheriff or constable in hot pursuit of a criminal would be forced to yank the reins and give up at the county line. Writes Mackay: "The states, jealous of their rights and ever watchful against Federal encroachment (a matter which would be at the heart of the dispute that caused the Civil War), did not cooperate in such matters as law enforcement, yet the rapid development of the railroads meant that criminals could roam over vast areas, perpetrating crimes far apart."

Murder, rape, arson, robbery, assault, horse thievery, and general lawlessness plagued the Mississippi River valley and the backwater areas throughout the South. By the late 1850s Pinkerton had broadened his company vision to encompass the entire nation, his operatives free to cross state lines—a pioneering approach that would take the U.S. government another half century to adopt for its Bureau of Investigation (BOI), which would ultimately come to be known as the FBI.

On this particular day in September 1859, Pinkerton had business with a bank president in Columbia, a man named Lowry who had contacted Pinkerton earlier in the month with a mystery to unravel. One of the bank's cashiers, a man named Jackson Carter, had been murdered while working late at night. The next morning, Carter had been found with his head bashed in, the lock on the bank's rear door forced open. Lowry suspected a local man named John Slocum.

Among the pieces of evidence collected at the scene was a charred scrap of paper that appeared to be an IOU for a large sum, which Slocum owed to Carter.

$$\sim\!\!\!\sim$$

"That's fairly good circumstantial evidence," Pinkerton commented to Lowry later that day, meeting with the banker in his private office. "Good enough to get Slocum in for questioning."

The tense exchange that followed is from Arthur Orrmont's reconstruction, Pinkerton's case files providing the source.

Lowry looked troubled. He shook his head. "Slocum's highly thought of in this town, and some of his best friends are my depositors. I'd lose 'em all if I suggested such a thing on present evidence."

Pinkerton puffed his Cuban for a moment. "How has Slocum been acting in recent months? Has he been acting normally?"

"No," the banker said, "and that's another thing. He hardly sticks his nose out his door any more, and folks say he's become a regular recluse."

Pinkerton pondered the situation for a moment. "Well, then . . . if he won't come to us, we'll have to go to him."

Lowry narrowed his eyes. "How in tarnation you going to manage that? Slocum won't even let tradesmen into his house. It's gotten so he can't keep his help. Lost three housekeepers in as many months."

Pinkerton murmured something, which Lowry, at first, did not hear. The banker had to lean forward. "What was that?"

"Servants," Pinkerton said.

"I'm not following," the banker said at last. "Servants, you say?"

"Jock and Mary Littleton," Pinkerton replied somewhat cryptically.

"And who might they be?"

Pinkerton looked at the man. "Before I answer that question, Mr. Lowry, I'll have to ask one of my own. What are your feelings on the slavery question?"

This unexpected turn in the conversation would have taken aback many a banker in a small Southern town in the mid-1800s. But Lowry simply shrugged and said, "I incline toward abolition, Mr. Pinkerton, but I wouldn't want to see the states go to war over it."

Pinkerton gave a satisfied nod, as though he were a schoolmaster qualifying a student for advanced study. "That's good enough, Mr. Lowry."

The detective went on to explain that the Littletons were escaped slaves, and they were fine, upstanding people. Pinkerton had assisted the twosome in their flight and had helped them get to an Underground Railroad safe house in Huntsville, Alabama, where they were currently hiding. Over the intervening months, Pinkerton had gotten to know the couple beyond "hello" and "thank you, sir," and at some point the idea had taken root in Pinkerton's brain that they could very possibly acquit themselves well as operatives.

"If I could bring them here, to take over Slocum's household," Pinkerton said finally, "it would help a great deal in ultimately getting them over the line."

He was referring, ostensibly, to the Mason-Dixon Line—originally drawn between Pennsylvania and Maryland by Charles Mason and Jeremiah Dixon in 1767 as a resolution to a border dispute between the two colonies—a boundary that ultimately became the cultural dividing line between the North and the South.

On a deeper level, Pinkerton could have meant "over the line" between slavery and freedom—between the past and the future—between what-has-been and what-could-be in some new place such as Canada.

"They could also function," Pinkerton added without missing a beat, "as our undercover operatives in bringing Slocum to justice."

———

Pinkerton's daring gambit—a strategy that might have at first appeared reckless and irresponsible to the flustered banker—fell right in line with the detective's evolving approach to penetrating hidden worlds. With the same ingenuity with which he had harvested hickory logs back on the Fox River, the detective now used the raw materials of society as grist for undercover work.

In Chicago, the headquarters on Washington Street had a special wardrobe room full of disguises, a collection, as Pinkerton noted in his writings, "kept in a state of ever increasing variety by frequent attendance at rummage sales." Wigs, costumes, uniforms, false mustaches, and various identification papers filled the shelves, meticulously cataloged and labeled.

Pinkerton had used the same eccentric, patchwork-quilt approach to staffing his operation. Shortly after opening the firm, he decided to hire a manager to supervise his five detectives, two clerks, and secretary. An impressive man named George Bangs was the perfect choice.

Described by one historian as "tall, handsome, elegantly dressed, and patrician, proud of his descent from *Mayflower* pilgrims," Bangs shared Pinkerton's monastic work habits and relentless attention to detail. Bangs had an almost photographic memory. He was also an efficient business-man and a natural detective who could "make connections and unravel a mystery in no time at all."

Bangs would become Pinkerton's right-hand man.

At some point in 1854—although historians differ as to the time-line—Pinkerton bought out his original partner in the business, a young attorney named Ruckner.

Perhaps the confusion among biographers regarding the timeline is partially due to the secretive nature of Pinkerton's work. In the 1853–54 Chicago City Directory, Pinkerton is still listed as a "Deputy-Sheriff," residing at "16 Edina." It is possible that this is either an error (perhaps allowed to pass uncorrected as a security measure) or a false address in the interests of discretion. Two years later, in the 1856–57 directory, he is listed under private police agencies as "Detective A. Pinkerton," his business address "corner Dearborn and Washington."

The Pinkerton name would gradually become far more than a titular designation of private practice or entrepreneurial enterprise. During the nation's growth spurt in the mid-1800s, Pinkerton traveled the country, acquiring new agents, searching for the best and brightest operatives he could find. These highly skilled yet invisible paladins would one day come to be known simply as "Pinkertons"—or "Pinks"—and would in many ways embody the abstract line between order and chaos, lawlessness and civilization.

"I am overwhelmed with business," Pinkerton told a friend from Dundee during this period, and the volume of work would necessitate the employment of bold, cunning, resourceful individuals who could blend in with the populace, travel in all quarters, and effect a wide variety of covers.

Two Englishmen were early acquisitions: Pryce Lewis and John Scully. Lewis, in the words of Mackay, was "in his mid-twenties, always well dressed, handsome, intelligent and possessed of great Old World charm." Scully was a close friend of Lewis's, a little coarser in nature but a resourceful young man nonetheless. What Pinkerton did not know about Scully, however, was that the young agent was also an avid drinker—and somewhat weak-willed—a combination of traits that would one day lead to utter catastrophe.

Another early hire was a ragged, rural-born young man named John H. White. Pinkerton must have foreseen the need to use a lad such as White to penetrate rough-and-tumble underworlds, because Pinkerton later observed that White "looked more like a con-man than a detective."

The fact was, none of these individuals had any previous experience in law enforcement, but Pinkerton—ever the shrewd judge of character—saw heart and verve in all of them. "The detective should be hardy, tough, and capable of laboring in season and out of season," Pinkerton once wrote of his criteria for operatives, "to accomplish, unknown to those around him, a single absorbing objective."

Moreover, Pinkerton had an uncanny ability to find prodigies, sometimes in the most unlikely places.

On a visit to New York, for instance, Pinkerton recruited a young man who would turn out to be one of the most valuable human assets the agency would ever enjoy. Thirty-one-year-old Timothy Webster was a British-born dandy, employed as a patrolman with the New York Police Department. With striking, angular features, finely trimmed beard, long hair, and cultured manner, Webster felt that his prospects in New York were limited in the brutish world of beat-patrols. When offered a position at the Pinkerton Agency, he jumped at the chance to come to Chicago and prove himself in this exciting new vocation known as private detective work.

The final piece to the personnel puzzle, however, came to Pinkerton in an unexpected way.

One day in 1856, a Chicago woman named Kate Warne happened to glance at an advertisement in the *Chicago Tribune*. The notice featured an illustration of a human eye, with the words PINKERTON NATIONAL DETECTIVE AGENCY wrapped around the top lash. But what truly captured her imagination was the phrase beneath the eye: WE NEVER SLEEP.

At that point in her life, Kate Warne most likely struggled with sleep herself.

Married four years earlier, Warne had recently lost her husband in a wagon accident. The tragedy had left the childless woman, barely into her twenties, lost and alone in the bustling, rough-hewn city. As historian Margaret Bzovy writes, "The year 1856 did not offer much employment for women, and [Warne] detested the idea of becoming a washerwoman."

On a whim, as Bzovy writes, Kate Warne put on her finest "long, crisp, dark navy blue gown," then headed uptown to the address prominently displayed on the advertisement.

En route, the slender, chestnut-haired woman would have turned very few heads as her long skirt swished and dragged along the boardwalk. "Her features," Pinkerton would write years later, "although not what could be called handsome, were decidedly of an intellectual cast . . . her face was honest, which would cause one in distress to instinctly [sic] select her as a confidante."

The offices of the Pinkerton Agency were on the second floor of a multistory building on Washington. Warne entered and climbed a narrow staircase. At the end of a long hallway, she found a glass door with the trademark eye logo painted across the pane. She opened it and found herself in a vestibule dominated by a matronly woman in a stiff white collar, shuffling papers. The woman asked Warne the purpose for her visit.

According to Bzovy's account, Warne told the woman, "I'm here to inquire about a job."

The receptionist eyed Warne. "Why don't you take a seat and I'll go and ask Mr. Pinkerton if there could be any openings."

Warne sat on a chair near the door while the receptionist vanished down a hallway. After a few moments she returned and said, "You can go meet with Mr. Pinkerton now, it's the main office just to the left."

Warne carried her bag, the newspaper still under her arm, around the corner and down the hall to the first door. Inside the main office she found Allan Pinkerton standing beside his secondhand rolltop desk. As Bzovy writes, "He had a large oval face with a long brown beard and receding hairline. His eyes were oval, dark brown with a kindly, attentive look."

"Please," Pinkerton said with a smile, motioning to a side chair, "sit down."

Warne did so and came right to the point. "What I need, Mr. Pinkerton, is a job."

Pinkerton nodded. "It just so happens we have a position for a woman to keep records. Do you know the common methods of filing?"

Warne glanced at the sizable piles of documents crowding the rolltop desk. "Mr. Pinkerton, I must confess I never was schooled in the filing of papers." She looked at him. "But I am not here to take such a job."

Pinkerton stared at her. "What job, may I ask, are you here to take?"

She smiled. "I want to be a detective."

After a pause Pinkerton smiled, clearly amused. "Madam, I never hire women to become detectives."

"May I ask why not?"

Pinkerton sighed. "For one, such a position is not suitable for their sensitive demeanor."

"With all respect, sir, I think I'm just the person you need."

Pinkerton was still smiling. "And why is that?"

Warne held his gaze. "Because no one would ever consider a woman to be a detective."

At this point perhaps Pinkerton's smile faltered slightly. He would later learn that Kate Warne had always wanted to be an actress, but as Bzovy writes, "Her parents would never permit her to expose herself to what they believed was below her level. Detecting would be almost like going on stage . . . and the idea thrilled the nature of her acting ability."

Pinkerton told her to go on.

"Well," Warne continued, playing all her cards now, "she could attend social gatherings and obtain information easily without anyone considering she was working for the law. And she could worm out secrets in many places which would be impossible for male detectives to gain access to."

Pinkerton was not smiling anymore.

He was thinking.

"The more he considered it," Mackay writes, "the more he liked it."

Pinkerton spent a sleepless night weighing the pros and cons of such a gamble.

The next day Pinkerton put his first full-time female detective—arguably the first in American history—on his payroll.

Pinkerton read incessantly. He loved Dickens's work—especially *Martin Chuzzlewit*, a satirical, picaresque novel that paints America in the 1840s as a backward wilderness filled with hucksters. Dickens, an avowed abolitionist himself, also published many ghost stories, another genre Pinkerton would have found not only irresistible but useful.

The second half of the nineteenth century saw a tremendous rise in a belief system known as Spiritualism. A quasi-monotheistic religion, Spiritualism augments its tenet of a supreme being with the belief that spirits of the dead reside in a "spirit world" and can communicate and interact with the living through "mediums." The high mortality rate of the 1800s (half of all children perished before the age of ten) may have contributed to its appeal. By the 1850s, Spiritualism had millions of followers in America. Pinkerton, despite his natural skepticism toward such matters, knew how to capitalize on these mass superstitions.

It is distinctly possible that, on that muggy Tennessee afternoon in 1859, as Pinkerton considered an unorthodox approach to Lowry's dilemma, the machinery of Fate was once again in motion for the detective. Pinkerton did not know it then, but the Slocum case—which would unfurl over the next few sweltering weeks—would become an important precedent for a series of investigations that would lead him into the darkest shadows of the Civil War.

―――

"I won't stand in your way," the Tennessee banker, Lowry, told Pinkerton with a sigh, after considering the unorthodox stratagem of engaging runaway slaves in a murder investigation. The two men were standing outside the bank in the blistering heat.

Pinkerton gave a nod.

"But may I ask how this Negro couple can help get Slocum for us?" Lowry asked. "By this time he's had more than enough opportunity to destroy any papers that connect him with Jackson Carter."

"True," Pinkerton said, chewing his cigar, the plan hatching in his mind. "But you're forgetting Slocum's state of mind. It's showing signs of heavy strain." Pinkerton likely paused for dramatic effect, turning to look the banker in the eye. "We can strain it even further . . . to the point of breakdown."

―――

Being strained to the breaking point was not an unfamiliar concept to Pinkerton, as the stress of his business life continued to intensify. Chicago had become, according to the *Daily Tribune*, a "volcano of crime"—with fifty-three burglaries reported during a single week in 1859—which prompted the newspaper to suggest in an editorial that a vote be taken among the citizens to employ Pinkerton to "clean up the city."

The vote never occurred, but with the distractions of multiple railroad cases in play, as well as another new baby daughter at home (born in 1857)—a sickly child named Mary, after her paternal grandmother, but known to the family simply as Belle—Pinkerton began to entrust new assignments to his lead operatives.

He sent his "best man" (Pinkerton's words) to Columbia, Tennessee, to execute a strange new paradigm for "sweating a suspect" that Pinkerton was about to concoct.

Timothy Webster heartily accepted the mission.

―――

Born in 1821 in Newhaven, Sussex County, England, Webster emigrated to the United States at the age of twelve. His family settled in Princeton, New Jersey, where Webster went to finishing school. While still in his teens, he met a plucky, adorable girl named Charlotte Sprowles, whom he eventually married in 1841. The couple had four children.

Webster's quick wit and cobra-like calm served him well as a young man in the teeming crucibles of the eastern cities. In 1853 he joined the New York Police Department as a patrolman, and according to Mackay, he "performed skillfully" in the months before his fateful meeting with Pinkerton.

An early glass "Ambrotype" photograph—for which subjects had to sit still for many minutes due to the long exposure—reveals something of Webster's character. With his long, sculpted face at complete repose, his beard finely trimmed without a hair out of place, he doesn't so much stare into the lens as engage it in combat. He looks older than his years. His light-colored eyes—either pale blue or green—appear alert and unbearably sad.

———

Timothy Webster set out for Columbia, Tennessee, a few days after Pinkerton had returned to Chicago. On board the rattling Louisville and Nashville coach car, he rode anonymously—a single, dapper gentleman from the North—down through Indiana, past Louisville, and into the wilds of central Tennessee.

Meanwhile, Lowry was reluctantly making arrangements to safely convey the slave couple, the Littletons, to the small Tennessee town in order to offer their services as butler and housemaid for John Slocum.

———

Columbia, Tennessee, in the late 1850s, was a small but bustling village of merchants and plantation homes. Situated on the Duck River, about forty-five miles south of Nashville, the town was known as the "Mule Capital" of the South—a center for the breeding and sale of work mules. Tobacco fields and rolling hills of white pine bordered the village, stretching into the patchwork quilt of distant plateaus.

The Columbia Hotel was a centrally located inn, ideal for the temporary quarters of a detective supervising a very special operation.

Shortly after arriving and checking into the hotel, Timothy Webster called a secret meeting with Lowry and the Littletons. Treating the black couple with the respectful accord of collaborators, Webster explained in his subtle British accent that he would be giving them specific instructions to carry out over the next week as Slocum's housekeepers, and they were to stay in close contact.

He also informed them that the "Boss"—an appellation Webster had begun to use for Allan Pinkerton—would soon be returning to Columbia to appraise the situation.

That night, the local sheriff showed Webster the murdered man's effects. Among the items was a half-empty bottle of strong cologne, which the late cashier had used in profusion. Inspiration struck Webster, and he pocketed the vial.

The next morning, Webster met with the Littletons. "I would ask that you discreetly scatter drops of this scent over Slocum's linen, handkerchiefs, and towels," he instructed the couple.

"Yessir," Jock Littleton said with a nod, taking the vial of cologne.

"And that's only part of it," Webster said. "There's much more I would like you to do."

The Littletons listened closely as Webster gave them further instructions.

———

Over the next several days, as they performed their normal duties as housekeepers for the paranoid, nerve-wracked John Slocum, the Littletons took every opportunity to secretly insert foreign agents into Slocum's crumbling environment.

They sprinkled the ghostly fragrance on pillowcases and bedsheets, in drawers and closets. They also dabbed spots of scarlet dye—Pinkerton's idea, outlined in a telegraph message to Webster—on the petals of white flowers in the garden and on the pristine fabric of handkerchiefs.

"The initials 'J.C.' might also be traced in this same bloodlike dye on various objects," Pinkerton wired to Webster, "but not so clearly as to make Slocum wonder if a ghost would have written in so legible a hand."

The eerie stains and odors almost immediately began to gnaw at the psyche of John Slocum.

———

"His nerves are in a terrible state, sir," Jock Littleton reported to Webster a couple of days later at the hotel. Also in the room, the bank manager nervously paced and listened.

"*Are* they now?" Webster thought about it for a moment. He had one additional maneuver he wanted to execute.

"Yessir," Mary Littleton piped in. "Mister Slocum's taken to eating his meals in the library now, and he sleeps behind locked doors."

Lowry spoke up. "But what if you frighten him into a fit? Or else he may go clean crazy and try and kill himself!"

Webster responded calmly: "He can't take much more of this punishment, you're right there. But the next thing he'll do is make a run for it, away from Columbia, and I'll be right behind him."

Webster turned to the black couple: "I want you to step up the operation with one additional task." He looked at Jock Littleton. "Would it be possible for you to install a tube?"

"A what, sir?"

Webster explained what his boss had advised in a second telegraph message.

———

Although no record exists of what John Slocum experienced in the wee, dark hours those next seven nights, sealed and locked inside his lonely chamber, one thing is fairly certain. According to multiple accounts of the case, Slocum heard moaning—uncanny, sinister, ghostly moaning— seeping out of the very grain of the house. The sound whispered in the air around the fidgeting suspect, tormenting him, pushing him to the edge of sanity.

By this point, Pinkerton had returned to Columbia to supervise the final stages of the audacious operation. He and Webster had provided the Littletons with a voice tube that was, according to biographer Sigmund Lavine, "similar to those used in the foyers of apartment houses [in the early twentieth century]." The couple had rigged the tube between the library and an outer room, and per Pinkerton's instructions, they had begun a relentless campaign of taunting the sleepless suspect with disembodied moaning.

In his writings Pinkerton claims that a criminal's crime "haunts him continually, and when the burden of concealment becomes at last too heavy to bear alone . . . he must relieve himself of the terrible secret which is bearing down on him." Hence the agonizing groaning rose and fell for seven nights, unabated, unrelenting.

"We keep him awake half the night, groaning through that tube, Mr. Pinkerton," Jock Littleton reported a week later. "During the day, we don't see much of him as he spends most of his time in the library with the door locked. My wife thinks he sits there and broods."

"I think she's right," Pinkerton replied. "Try and keep an eye on him at all times, for we don't want him to leave town unless he is followed."

"Yessir."

"Meanwhile," Pinkerton added, "make those groans more ghastly."

The Littletons obliged. And they must have done an exemplary job of conjuring unimaginable noises from beyond the grave, because two days later, without much warning, the case came to an abrupt climax.

Pinkerton jerked awake in the darkness of his hotel room. Writes biographer Sigmund Lavine: "It was pitch black, and he fumbled for several minutes before he found a match to light the lamp."

Pinkerton pulled on his trousers, went to the door, and threw it open.

"It's happened, Boss!" Timothy Webster, already dressed in his smart attire, stood outside the door. "Littleton just came by to say Slocum's all packed and ready to catch the five-ten to Nashville."

"The devil you say!" Pinkerton glanced at his pocket watch. It was already two minutes past 5:00. "Just enough time to catch the train, if we hurry. Be sure to bring along that bottle of Carter's cologne."

Pinkerton grabbed his remaining pieces of clothing, his gun, and his hat, and hurried out of the room, as biographer Richard Rowan describes, "tucking his shirt in" as he went.

The depot sat within shouting distance of the Columbia Hotel.

It would have taken the two detectives only a few minutes to race through the predawn gloom to the station. As they approached the soot-stained rolling stock of the Nashville Special, the whistle of the engine, acknowledging a flag signal, warned them of how little time they had left.

Pinkerton and Webster hopped onboard the rear foot-rail of the caboose just as the train jerked in a storm cloud of steam and smoke.

"Boss, we're in trouble," Webster whispered to Pinkerton before the burly Scotsman even had a chance to cross the rear vestibule.

"What is it?"

"With Slocum shut up in that house all the time, I was never able to get a good look at him. Maybe, after all, he isn't even on the train."

Pinkerton had no time to pause and assess the situation dispassionately. Right then, he acted as he always did in high-pressure, high-stakes moments of truth: with a crafty, artisan-like flourish—a barrel maker knowing instinctively just how far a hickory rod can be bent until it breaks.

"Don't worry," Pinkerton said, leading Webster through the hatch. "First, let's find out from the conductor who got on at Columbia."

The train picked up speed. It is likely that Pinkerton and Webster had to use the hand-straps for purchase as they discreetly, silently traversed the coaches, seeking the conductor.

They finally found him. Rowan writes: "The conductor, a new man, did not know Slocum, but could point out the three passengers who had come aboard at Columbia." One of the men, perhaps a tobacco farmer on his way to market, appeared far too young to be Slocum.

Two other middle-aged men sat "chatting rather stiffly" in the center coach. Either man could have matched Slocum's general description, but, as Rowan writes, "the pale man next to the window appeared far more nervous and embarrassed."

Pinkerton and Webster settled down on a vacant bench a few rows behind the two men. The train, by this point, had built a head of steam and was clattering swiftly northward toward the outskirts of Nashville.

"Let's have the cologne," Pinkerton whispered. Webster slipped him the bottle of amber liquid, and Pinkerton doused a handkerchief with the offending fragrance. With a glance and a nod, Pinkerton rose.

He calmly strode several rows until he reached the two middle-aged gentlemen, at which point he paused and feigned a sneeze. Blowing his nose with the redolent handkerchief, Pinkerton waved the scent into the air.

Almost instantly the pale man next to the window "exclaimed something in a muffled, stricken tone," which Pinkerton could not decipher. Writes Rowan: "So sure was [Slocum] of his own hallucination, he did not even trouble to glance around." Before Pinkerton could excuse himself, Slocum sprang to his feet.

The suspect pushed his way out into the aisle, nearly knocking Pinkerton over.

By this point, the commotion had drawn the attention of other passengers. Slocum lumbered toward the forward hatch right as the train careened around a curve at top speed. The frantic suspect clawed at the door, but gravity and vertigo foiled his attempts to open it.

Pinkerton joined the man at the door and said, "I'll try and help."

Pretending to put his weight into the effort, Pinkerton acted as though the door was stuck. He did not want Slocum to slip away. But another waft of the ghostly scent fueled Slocum's adrenaline, and the man finally got the hatch open. Wind rushed in, as Slocum awkwardly negotiated the coupler and vestibule, plunging into the smoker car.

Pinkerton paused.

The scream of iron wheels filled the coach.

Webster joined Pinkerton at the hatch. "What's next?" Webster whispered.

"I'm going to follow him into the smoker," Pinkerton said under his breath. "If he comes rushing out, grab him. He might try to leap off the train."

Webster gave a nod.

Pinkerton entered the smoker car. Inside the coach, which was crowded with empty tables, Slocum had collapsed onto a seat near a raised window, breathing the rush of air heavily "with his cravat undone." Pinkerton took a seat opposite the man, wiping his hands in the damp handkerchief.

"Train's making good time," Pinkerton commented, locking eyes with the man.

Slocum could not form a reply. Mouth agape, the odor now wafting again, the suspect could only stare. Orrmont writes: "In the small, almost airless smoker, the smell of Jackson Carter's scent was almost over-powering."

Pinkerton spoke up. "What's the matter, sir? Is there something wrong?"

In a paroxysm of terror, Slocum sprang to his feet and let out a cry.

In a blur the man lunged back the way he had come.

———

Timothy Webster, standing outside the smoker door, tried to dodge the crazed individual barreling back into the coach, but he passed too quickly.

Slocum's forward momentum knocked the British detective to the deck.

The door hung open, the noise of the rails and the wind whirling, as Slocum reared back onto the precipice between the two cars.

He turned and prepared to jump off the coupler.

"SLOCUM, DON'T!"

Pinkerton's booming voice pierced the thunder of the train, as Slocum let out another cry. Grabbing the emergency stop-cord, Pinkerton yanked with all his might—as John Slocum jumped.

The brakeman lurched. Levers jammed. A whistle shrilled. Air brakes hissed.

Passengers pitched forward in their seats as the train scraped and shrieked. It took nearly a half mile for the great locomotive and its chain of freight to grind to a stop.

—◆—

They found Slocum in a gully.

Clinging to life, battered and bloody, the murderer had evidently tumbled down an embankment and landed in a washed-out furrow.

Pinkerton and Webster were the first to reach the dying man. "He was fearfully injured," writes Richard Rowan, "and yet, still conscious. All the frenzy had gone out of him."

"Easy," Pinkerton soothed as he crouched down in the weeds next to Slocum.

Webster stood respectfully nearby, his handsome head likely bowed in reflection. It is not improbable, considering Webster's uncanny rapport with Pinkerton, that the young protégé sensed something deeper about to transpire than a mere deathbed confession.

Others approached—the trainmen, curious passengers—but the culvert seemed to fall into a hush, the hissing, puffing noise of the engine fading into the morning sizzle of crickets. The first rays of dawn peered over the horizon.

Slocum was trying to say something. Pinkerton and Webster had to lean closer to hear what the feeble, choked voice was trying to convey.

"That—perfume—" Slocum uttered with blood-slick lips, his eyes unfocused.

"Do you mean Jackson Carter's cologne?" Pinkerton suggested softly, yet firmly, staring into the glazed eyes of the murderer.

"Y-yes—y-you—*knew*—Carter—?"

The detective nodded somberly. "I liked that scent myself. Matter of fact . . . got some of it with me."

At this point, as Rowan writes, a "cloud seemed to sweep over Slocum's eyes," and as Pinkerton watched the man very carefully, it became more and more clear to the detective that this was no crazed lunatic. This was an ordinary man who had strayed off the path, who had simply allowed the baser instincts of fear and greed to get the better of him.

Pinkerton, as Arthur Orrmont puts it, "did not fight the pity he felt, but he had a job to do."

The detective softly inquired, "Isn't there something about Jackson Carter you'd like to tell me?"

The murderer closed his eyes. A moment passed, and the onlookers might have thought the man had slipped away, when Slocum suddenly opened his eyes one last time and gazed up at the detective. Slocum's eyes were suddenly clear, lucid. "I know I'm—dying—justice I reckon—I killed Carter—a quarrel—had owed him—made it look like a robbery—I tried to—tried to . . ."

Slocum's voice faltered, his eyes closing again, his lips moving impotently.

Very softly, almost mercifully, Allan Pinkerton said, "Your conscience has troubled you but now you'll feel much easier in your mind because—"

Pinkerton never finished his thought. Slocum's face had turned, in the words of Rowan, "the color of clay."

Rowan writes: "He sighed once, and lay still; and all of them helplessly standing or crouching around him saw that the slayer of Jackson Carter was dead."

⁓

Pinkerton and Webster returned to Columbia with the body. They communicated the sad news to Slocum's relatives and then met with Lowry to close the case. The trainmen had all agreed to sign affidavits confirming Slocum's confession. The Littletons were sent to freedom.

Chances are, though, during the course of this strange operation, Timothy Webster learned a lot more about his boss than he did about the superstitious torments of the guilty. It is likely that Webster saw a side of Pinkerton—despite his midnight tortures of Slocum—that deepened the bond between the two detectives.

Webster, who would soon become practically a surrogate younger brother to the burly Scot, was a man of refined sensibilities and resolute nerve. He would have been mightily impressed by Pinkerton's complex empathies for his prey.

Years later Pinkerton would write:

I must admit that among the thousands of hardened criminals with whom my detective experience has brought me into contact, there have arisen many instances where I have in my own mind felt a deep commiseration with, and sympathy for, numbers of this outlaw class. I have no manner of apology for their guilt, and there is no man on earth who would be more relentless than myself in running them to the ground, and assisting in placing them where they must pay the full penalty of their misdoing. Of this everybody is well aware; but I repeat, there are instances, many of them, where these people have become reckless, desperate criminals, not from choice, or any natural depravity or bent in that direction, but from what must have seemed the most luckless of all possible circumstances.

Pinkerton's own luck—not to mention his destiny, as well as the fate of the entire nation—was about to take another turn.

As he and Webster were preparing to leave the bank offices in Columbia, Lowry remembered something. "By the way," the banker said, "a telegram came for you, Mr. Pinkerton. I'm sorry, I nearly forgot it."

Pinkerton took the document, unfolded it, and began to read the brief dispatch.

Webster saw the expression on the Scotsman's face harden.

CHAPTER THREE

An Extremely Grave and Urgent Matter

MONDAY, OCTOBER 17, 1859

The case of John Slocum had been resolved with the murderer's dying confession. But the circuitous series of events that would draw Allan Pinkerton into the tangled web of national politics soon after began developing on the eve of the transmittal of that telegram Pinkerton received in Tennessee.

Most likely sent to Pinkerton by John Jones, the Free-Negro leader in Chicago, the wire conveyed the following facts in urgent lines of text:

JOHN BROWN'S RAID AT HARPER'S FERRY TO SEIZE FEDERAL ARMS A TRAGIC FAILURE. STOP. AT THIS MOMENT BROWN AND HIS MEN BESIEGED BY OVER-WHELMING U.S. MARINE FORCES UNDER COMMAND OF COLONEL ROBERT E. LEE. STOP.

The fiery abolitionist, Captain John Brown—the same man whom Pinkerton had admired for years, whom Pinkerton had aided with food and shelter and clothing and funds, whom Pinkerton had even embraced warmly during a visit by Brown to the Adams Street house—was now embroiled in a bloody insurrection. Brown and his band of twenty-one men—sixteen whites and five blacks—fought furiously for forty-eight hours to hold off the overwhelming forces.

At dawn on Tuesday, October 18, 1859, Brown and his few surviving guerrilla warriors were taken prisoner. They were transported to Charles Town the following day and imprisoned there. Within two weeks, Brown was tried, found guilty of treason, and sentenced to death.

Pinkerton scholars disagree over many of the details of Allan Pinkerton's response to these troubling events, as well as his actions over the course of this tumultuous six-week period. Some biographers believe that Pinkerton immediately marshaled his operatives—wiring more than thirty agents in various Southern states to leave their present assignments and meet in Charles Town—in order to, in the words of Orrmont, "free John Brown, whether or not Northern officials approved."

The likeliness of such a drastic scheme—to penetrate the Charles Town jail and break John Brown and his compatriots out—seems questionable. "Of this there is absolutely no proof," writes James Mackay.

Part of the dearth of evidence here is due to the fact that Pinkerton—a meticulous note taker and record keeper—lost all of his files in the Great Chicago Fire of 1871.

What is generally considered incontrovertible, however, is that Pinkerton spent the thirty days between the sentencing and the execution of John Brown trying everything in his power to save his friend.

Pinkerton raised money in Chicago for a defense fund. He wrote letters. He sent telegrams to political leaders urging clemency. He even persuaded George McClellan "to use his considerable influence, through his Southern Democratic connections, on Brown's behalf, to win a stay of execution, if not a reprieve."

It was all to no avail. On the morning of December 2, 1859, Brown—surrounded by fifteen hundred soldiers in case of any last-minute attempts to save the abolitionist's life—took his last steps up the scaffold. Watching from the ranks of the Richmond rifle company, as the drums rolled and the crowd hushed, was a man who would soon carve his own name in infamy: John Wilkes Booth.

Before the hood was lowered over Brown's head, the controversial figure took one last glance at the stunning Blue Ridge Mountains. The hood came down. A hatchet snapped the rope on the trap door and Brown exited this world and entered the realm of legend.

Interestingly, many years later, Pinkerton wrote these cryptic lines (which may explain the stubborn folklore of an attempted jailbreak): "Had it not been for the excessive watchfulness of those having him in charge, the pages of American history would never have been stained with the record of this execution."

The eye that never slept widened at this point. Pinkerton's operation expanded its scope, becoming a powerful spyglass scanning both the North and South, contracting protective services for numerous railroads and express lines, most of which were navigating the treacherous borders of a conflicted country. Pinkerton was now a driven man—burning with a righteous purpose.

At home he became even more distracted and, as one biographer put it, "tyrannical." Pinkerton was almost a ghostly figure, seldom seen by his children, who were now being raised almost solely by the long-suffering and loyal Joan. Allan Pinkerton worked constantly—perhaps a remnant of his Calvinist upbringing. "He was a man who could get by on two or three hours sleep at most," writes James Mackay, "a tireless worker, with reckless courage and a formidable grasp of detail."

Considering the events that were about to unfold, it seems almost providential that the "Boss" was integrating into his growing team of operatives such unlikely candidates as freed slaves and women with no formal investigative background. Kate Warne would turn out to be especially valuable to the operation in the coming months, quietly and skillfully proving herself to Pinkerton.

Warne used her natural inclination toward performance to pose as secretaries, jilted lovers, wives of imprisoned criminals, and all varieties of aristocratic women. Her chameleon-like features and articulate use of language enabled her to cross the spectrum of society. Within a year, she had done so well in the field that Pinkerton decided to hire more women and make Warne the head of what came to be known as the Female Detective Bureau. To put this innovation into context: Regular police departments did not employ women in any capacity until 1891. And it wasn't until 1903 that women were first employed as investigators in New York City.

Kate Warne played a key role in a celebrated case, late in 1859, involving a series of robberies on the Adams Express line. A popular rail courier of the day, operating on both sides of the Mason-Dixon Line, the company was missing $40,000 from two separate payroll deliveries between Augusta, Georgia, and Montgomery, Alabama.

The president of Adams Express, Edward S. Sanford, had heard so much about the ingenious thief-catcher from Chicago that he sent a letter to Allan Pinkerton outlining the mystery and closing with the simple query, "Can you identify the thief?"

Not one to pass up a challenge—despite the fact that even Sherlock Holmes might find such a long-distance assignment fairly ludicrous—Pinkerton proceeded to deduce solely from the facts of Sanford's letter that the guilty party was most likely a gentleman named Nathan Maroney, the manager of the Montgomery Express office.

Once again Pinkerton's instincts proved impeccable. Part of his conclusion was due to the lack of damage to the train car and the container from which the money had turned up missing. Another factor was the amount of private time Maroney had with the shipment itself. A man of Maroney's modest wages would find the temptation irresistible.

These became the linchpins of Pinkerton's self-taught deductive approach—motive and opportunity—an approach that would become de rigueur among modern investigators. The key to the Adams Express affair, however, would be proving Maroney's guilt, and that was where Kate Warne came into the picture.

Over the next several weeks, disguising herself in the decadent beaded bustles and silken finery of a Southern belle, Warne ingratiated herself into the daily activities of Maroney's wife, who was on an extended vacation in the great cities of the northeast.

Posing as a woman known as Madame Imbert—the spouse of a real-life forger whom Pinkerton had caught years earlier—Warne befriended Mrs. Maroney, gained the woman's trust, and eventually learned where the stolen money had been hidden (the couple's cellar in Alabama).

"Mrs. Maroney is planning a trip to Montgomery," Warne wired to her boss as the case was about to break. "I would make sure she is shadowed."

After the money was recovered, the news of Pinkerton's investigative prowess zipped along the wires, making headlines in all the major eastern cities. In England, journalists began calling the Pinkerton National Detective Agency "the American Scotland Yard." The symbol of the human eye—ever vigilant—became emblematic of Pinkerton's burgeoning reputation among lawbreakers.

"The choice of the open eye was singularly apt," writes James Mackay. "In time it would become Allan's nickname in underworld circles, and the almost supernatural notion of the eye that somehow saw everything became a powerful deterrent to wrong-doers."

Pinkerton, however, was not the only man from Illinois gaining international renown at this time.

Another Illinoisan of simple means and values—a man who would soon march into a whirlwind—was about to avail himself of the special services of "The Eye."

———

Lincoln's political comeback began in 1854, in Peoria, Illinois, while Pinkerton was still in the embryonic stages of his own private crusade.

Warmed by the Indian-summer dusk, framed by Romanesque columns, the portico of the Old Peoria Courthouse echoed with the high-pitched, righteous voice of an orator who might have felt right at home next to Cicero, standing before the ancient Senate, arguing for the Republic.

"There can be no moral right in connection with one man's making a slave of another," the speaker crowed in his Kentucky twang to the thousands present that night. "No man is good enough to govern another man without that other's consent."

Over the years, the somewhat clumsy manner of the presenter's style had drawn much criticism, even from his early admirers. "His voice was unmusical and high-keyed," writes historian Richard Carwardine. The speaker's law partner, William Herndon, called the voice "shrill-squeaking-piping, unpleasant." Another eyewitness to the orator's public pronouncements put it this way: "He swung his long arms sometimes in a very ungraceful manner. Now and then he would, to give particular emphasis to a point, bend his knees and body with a sudden downward jerk, and then shoot up again with a vehemence that raised him to his tip-toes and made him look much taller than he really was."

But in Peoria that night—as the greater nation was about to learn—it was the *substance* of what the man said that truly sank a hook into the crowd.

"Repeal the Missouri Compromise—repeal all compromises—repeal the Declaration of Independence—repeal all past history, you still can not repeal human nature," Abraham Lincoln told the audience. "It still will be the abundance of man's heart that slavery extension is wrong; and out of the abundance of his heart, his mouth will continue to speak."

Lincoln was referring to the repeal of the Missouri Compromise, established in 1820, which prohibited the spread of slavery above the 36th parallel. This uneasy negotiation between proslavery and antislavery factions had held until the passage of the Kansas-Nebraska Act in 1854, which lifted these limitations on new territories to the west.

The old tensions between free states and slave states were being stirred up again. The buzzing of this ideological hornet's nest had lured Lincoln back into the political arena. After serving out his single term in Congress, he had returned to his law firm in Springfield in 1849 to mind his business as an increasingly successful prairie lawyer, but destiny had other plans for him.

When Lincoln's fellow Illinoisan, the stalwart Democrat and U.S. Senator Stephen A. Douglas, engineered the Kansas-Nebraska Act, the urge to counterattack proved irresistible for the agnostic philosopher from Springfield. Lincoln found Douglas—a short, heavy-set, master-politician—to be the perfect intellectual foil, a bête noire toward whom Lincoln could focus and organize his opposition to the spread of slavery.

A former justice on the Illinois Supreme Court and a onetime manager of a slaveholding plantation in Mississippi, Douglas was a brilliant debater known as "The Little Giant." On that fortuitous night in Peoria, Douglas had happily shared the portico steps with Lincoln, providing a famous rebuttal and setting the stage for future debates.

The clash between these two rhetorical masters—opposites in both worldview and physical stature—would lead to a legendary Senate race in 1858, highlighted by the famous Lincoln-Douglas debates across the state of Illinois. Douglas would go on to narrowly defeat Lincoln, but the die had been cast: Lincoln's firebrand status as an antislavery man was solidified by his elegant, powerful, well-crafted arguments in the hamlets and river towns along the Mississippi.

◆

One of the more famous photographs of Abraham Lincoln—a daguerre-otype, its incredibly detailed, almost ethereal image imprinted upon a metal plate—was made on February 27, 1860, in Mathew Brady's studio in New York.

Brady, considered at the time America's greatest photographer, would go on to become the pictorial chronicler of the Civil War. But in this early portrait, he captured something otherworldly in the lank and determined pose assumed by Lincoln.

In the picture, taken just before his famous Cooper Union speech, Lincoln stands bolt upright, burning his dark gaze into Brady's optics. With his black mortician's coat and raven hair, his left hand resting on a book that looks suspiciously like a well-thumbed Bible, he seems to personify resolve.

That night, addressing the throngs in the academy's great hall, Lincoln humbly threw down the gauntlet. "Your purpose, plainly stated," he told the crowd, addressing the imminent threat of Southern secession, as well as the growing schism between proslavery and antislavery forces, "is that you will destroy the Government, unless you be allowed to construe and enforce the constitution as you please. . . . You will rule or ruin in all events."

The speech lasted more than an hour and was regularly interrupted by loud applause from the mostly Republican audience. At points, Lincoln even mocked the speech patterns and syrupy Southern accents of politicians who promoted "populahhh soverrrrreigntay," the euphemistic phrase for new states being free to vote up or down on slavery within their own boundaries. This was the fiery, verbally limber, combative Abraham Lincoln, and the speech propelled him to the Republican nomination for president of the United States.

The *New York Tribune* called the Cooper Union speech "one of the happiest and most convincing political arguments ever made in this city."

James Mackay writes: "One wonders whether the former cooper of Glasgow and Dundee, Illinois, was present on that momentous occasion."

The Republican National Convention—held in May in Chicago, and almost certainly watched closely by Pinkerton—found itself deadlocked. Eastern states could not produce a large enough bloc of delegates for Lincoln until western states pushed the number over the edge.

Lincoln barely won the nomination on a third ballot.

———

Allan Pinkerton supported his old business acquaintance and kindred soul with great gusto. Left-leaning Chicagoans saw Lincoln as a potential figurehead to carry the torch of abolitionism into the new decade. "The Republican party in its early days was the new broom in American politics," writes one historian, "opposed to slavery if not openly commit-ted to abolitionism, and containing many radical elements whose left-wing views were pretty much in line with [Pinkerton's] own outlook."

Lincoln campaigned with the same righteous intellectual fervor he unleashed at Cooper Union in February, and despite his attempts to appease Southern states with his willingness to allow slavery to continue where it existed, he made a multitude of new enemies. The central prob-lem was Lincoln's insistence that, as president, he would fight tooth and nail to prevent slavery from spreading to new territories "which had not yet attained statehood."

In the November election Lincoln garnered only two million votes out of nearly five million cast. Only twenty-four thousand of these votes came from slave states. But due to the split on the opposing ticket—two candidates, Douglas and John Breckinridge, ran as Democrats—the gen-eral vote broke down in the Electoral College in Lincoln's favor.

The dominoes began to fall. With Lincoln heading to the White House, Republican leaders smelled rebellion in the air.

In December, party moderates traveled to Springfield to ask if Lin-coln would be willing to work out a deal not unlike the Kansas-Nebraska Act. Lincoln responded with another fiery speech five days before Christ-mas, "effectively closing the door" to any possible compromise. He would not allow slavery to spread under his watch.

Anger and resentment swept across the South. On the very same day of Lincoln's December 20 speech, South Carolina formally seceded from the Union. Other like-minded state legislatures also whispered about secession. Fissures in the bedrock of the beleaguered country were begin-ning to appear.

Mississippi followed South Carolina's lead, officially seceding on January 9. Texas would soon follow suit. In the hills and the hollows of the South, excitable anti-government loyalists simmered with rage. In the dark alleys of border towns, drunken men muttered vengeful, pro-fane tirades about the new chief executive. Even southern counties in free states such as Illinois roiled with rumors of, in Pinkerton's words, "armed rebellion" among the citizens "sympathetic to the South."

It is likely that Allan Pinkerton would have been watching these events with grave concern. With his preternatural ability to intuit the slightest hint of imminent foul play, Pinkerton would have been hyperalert in these turbulent months.

But even a man of Pinkerton's wakefulness can be taken by surprise.

———

In his declining years, Pinkerton wrote voluminously of this anxious period following the election of the sixteenth president of the United States.

The detective noticed the apocalyptic signs all around him and was well aware of their implications. "The low mutterings of the storm that was soon to sweep over our country, and to deluge our fair land with fratricidal blood, were distinctly heard," he wrote in his 1883 memoirs.

He also saw troubling portents in the surprisingly ecstatic reaction to Lincoln's victory among some of the more radical elements:

> *In many portions of the South, this result was hailed with joyful enthusiasm. The antislavery proclivities of the successful party was instantly made a plausible pretext for secession, and the withdrawal of slaveholding States from the Union was boldly advocated.*

Horace Greeley, the famous liberal newspaper editor, described one Southern enclave as a hotbed of disturbing euphoria: "Men thronged the streets, talking, laughing, cheering. . . . [They were] like a seedy prodigal, just raised to influence by the death of some far-off, unknown relative, and whose sense of decency is not strong enough to repress his exultation."

The border states, such as Maryland, which was a slaveholding state, quickly became thickets of tangled, clashing loyalties. Cities like Baltimore, with its mèlange of cultures, began to foment treasonous talk.

———

With its strategic location near the Chesapeake Bay, Baltimore was already nearly a half century old in 1861, with a storied history as a stronghold for American revolutionaries. The narrow, gas-lit streets—many of them cobblestoned—crisscrossed labyrinths of gothic buildings. Omnibuses and jitneys teemed at all hours. The thunder of trains regularly filled Calvert Station, connecting the eastern seaboard with the rapidly growing west.

Baltimore bustled with nightlife, with commerce, and quite often, with crime. Edgar Allan Poe, the acknowledged creator of the modern detective story, died his sad, mysterious death in a Baltimore hospital, gripped in an unexplained delirium, only eleven years earlier. Politically, the town sided mostly with the South. A mere two percent of the Baltimore vote went to Lincoln, and the disgruntled denizens of the town's dark back rooms and opulent gentlemen's clubs soon began furtively scheming.

All of which points to a great irony in the fact that Pinkerton, at first, saw nothing that would directly connect Abraham Lincoln to the letter he received on the morning of January 19 from a man named Samuel Felton.

———

Pinkerton had been absently perusing the newspapers that morning, perched at his trusty rolltop desk at the Washington Street headquarters in Chicago.

He had been reading article after article on the "doings of the malcontents of the South," and despite his hyper vigilance, as well as a mounting sense of danger, he saw nothing at the moment to worry about. "I entertained no serious fears of an open rebellion," he wrote later of that day, "and was disposed to regard the whole matter as of trivial importance." He had turned his attentions to other documents—the "manifold duties" facing him at the time—when the office boy appeared in the doorway with a letter.

Pinkerton accepted the delivery, unsealed the missive, and began to read.

"My dear Pinkerton," the letter began, written in the personal hand of the President of the Philadelphia, Wilmington and Baltimore Railroad. Pinkerton had done his usual meticulous work for the line in the past, and Samuel Felton, the railroad's chief executive, trusted the detective unreservedly. "An extremely grave and urgent matter has arisen which I must discuss with you, here in Philadelphia," Felton wrote. "It concerns the railroad. Time is short and your presence is vital. You would oblige me greatly by coming east as quickly as you can."

Did Pinkerton recognize the import of the letter at this point? Most likely not—despite the alarming developments across the South in the wake of Lincoln's election. After nearly ten years of rapid growth, the detective agency occupied practically every waking hour for Pinkerton.

He found it difficult to delegate. He believed that he should not give his operatives assignments that he would not be willing—and able—to undertake himself.

All too often, Pinkerton would take over an investigation that wasn't proceeding to his liking. Or he would intervene if he thought a case was proving to be too arduous for his employee. "Allan ran his business like he ran his family—with a rod of iron," Mackay writes. The strange thing, however, is that, "for all his domineering ways, Allan inspired an almost fanatical loyalty in his staff."

But his resources would soon be tested to its limits in the brushfire of events sparked by Felton's letter.

"Let me repeat," the letter concluded, "I believe this matter to be extremely grave, not merely for the PW&B—but for the country as well."

Pinkerton did not have to ponder the proper response for long.

He called the office boy and then arranged to have a simple, single-line telegram wired to Samuel Felton in Philadelphia: COMING AT ONCE.

Chapter Four

Into the Breach

January 21, 1861

Northeasterly winds whipped across the upper tier states, buffeting the eastern seaboard with stinging temperatures. The mercury dipped into the teens across the Midwest, and snow flurries waxed and waned. Powdery gusts sliced across the railroad track as the Pittsburgh, Fort Wayne, and Chicago rumbled eastward.

On the long, cold trip to Philadelphia, Pinkerton rode in a coach alongside four of his "best operatives"—Timothy Webster, Kate Warne, his dapper assistant Harry Davies, and a Brit expatriate named John Seaford.

No record exists of what they discussed on their way to see Samuel Felton that day, but Pinkerton certainly would have had no idea how the meeting with Felton would soon converge with events of national import unfolding at that precise moment 136 miles to the east.

The wintry weather in Washington, D.C., could not compare to the emotional chill spreading across the Senate chamber that morning. Only days earlier, Florida, Georgia, and Alabama had joined South Carolina and Mississippi in secession; and rumors were circulating that Louisiana would soon follow.

By 9:00 a.m. the standing-room-only crowd in the Senate chambers had flooded into the cloakrooms and lobby to hear the dreaded farewell addresses of five senators who had announced their resignations. The final address came from a tall, gaunt, brooding senator from Mississippi.

"We are about to be deprived in the Union of the rights our forefathers bequeathed to us," boomed Jefferson Davis. He finished by urging his fellow senators to work for peaceful relations between the federal government and the departing states.

Interference with these states, Davis concluded, would "bring disaster on every portion of the country." With that Davis and his four colleagues "solemnly walked up the center aisle and out the swinging doors."

Historian William C. Davis writes: "Absolute silence met the conclusion of his six-minute address. Then a burst of applause and the sounds of open weeping swept the chamber."

The headquarters of the Philadelphia, Wilmington & Baltimore Railroad would have had a somber cast that day as Pinkerton shook hands with Samuel Felton. In the richly appointed room with its velveteen-backed chairs and great maps of the eastern United States in gilded frames, showing the lacework of rail lines connecting the coast, Samuel Felton, a tall, thin, bearded man, revealed his suspicions to Pinkerton and his team.

"In the event of war," Felton began, "it is clear that the PW&B will be of great strategic importance. Our line provides the only direct rail connection between the federal government in Washington, and the major cities of Boston, New York, and Philadelphia in the North."

Pinkerton remained silent, listening intently.

"Cut the PW&B," Felton said, "and you cut an important part of the Union in two. Cut the PW&B, and Northern reinforcements could not reach the capital in time to defend it. Within a few days the city would fall to the South. Think of it—Washington, Congress, perhaps the president himself—in the hands of the South army."

At last Pinkerton spoke up. "And you believe if war breaks out the secessionists will try to cut the railroad?"

"There are rumors to that effect, yes." Felton turned and pointed to the map on the wall behind his desk. "Our lines run here, from Philadelphia, through Wilmington, and on to Baltimore. From Philadelphia to Wilmington we're safe in Union territory and there's no danger. But between Wilmington and Baltimore the country is alive with secessionists. Our loyal people claim that some of them already have formed into bands of so-called cavalry troops, and these troops are drilling secretly with arms, and in the event of war they mean to blow up our railway bridges and sink our ferryboats."

At this point, Felton sat back down at his desk, perhaps letting out a sigh, as the anxiety weighed heavily on him. Pinkerton took his seat in front of the desk and waited for Felton to give him the bottom line.

"We do know this much," Felton said finally. "Between Wilmington and Baltimore—and in Baltimore itself—there are many dangerous Southern sympathizers." He looked at Pinkerton. "Can you find out who they are, and what they're planning?"

Pinkerton very calmly replied, "I'll start my investigation today."

—⁓—

Pinkerton spent the next few days in Philadelphia poring over Felton's reports. He met with the superintendent of the railroad, H. F. Kenney, to learn as much as possible about the daily operations of the line, and also to propose an approach to the business of intelligence-gathering.

Kenney thought the small village of Havre de Grace might be especially vulnerable.

Thirty miles northeast of Baltimore, situated at the mouth of the Susquehanna River, Havre de Grace was the point at which ferry boats shuttled trains across the muddy waterway to Delaware and all points south and east. "Serious damage might be done to the company," Pinkerton wrote in his journal, "should the ferries be destroyed."

Other weak spots galvanized the detective. Perryman, another small hamlet directly across the Susquehanna from Havre de Grace, offered saboteurs a banquet of possible targets, including trestles, causeways, and ferry ports. Large railroad bridges in Wilmington, Delaware, connecting Philadelphia with the Southern trunk lines, also seemed particularly vulnerable. Pinkerton worked each night on his recommendations. Toward the end of January, he returned to Felton's office to present his seven-page proposal.

With Felton's approval, Pinkerton would assemble a team of highly skilled operatives, and he would take them to Baltimore—as well as outlying areas—"to infiltrate the secessionist organizations, in order to monitor their plans and movements closely."

In his document Pinkerton stressed the complexity and time-consuming nature of attaining, in his words, "a controlling power over the mind of the suspected parties." Most importantly, Pinkerton put a great deal of emphasis on the need for absolute secrecy.

Although Pinkerton, at this stage, had no inkling of what he would be up against in and around Baltimore that winter—or the fact that the Felton job would plunge his team into the direst of circumstances—the taciturn Scot would have been well aware of the demands that were about to be placed on his organization.

With nearly seven years under his belt as a private investigator, Pinkerton had now become a man of science, embracing new technologies. His work for railroads had allowed him unlimited free travel and discreet access to every corner of the country. He had taken great advantage of the telegraph system—even in its early incarnations—as a means of communication with his teammates. He used elaborate codes in letters, telegrams, and reports.

He had even become an enthusiastic, pioneering user of primitive photography. By the middle part of the nineteenth century, practically every town of significant size in America had its own "daguerrian artist," or professional portrait photographer. In his first decade as a detective, Pinkerton had collected and systematized a virtual rogues' gallery of mug shots at his Washington Street headquarters in Chicago. He routinely circulated photos of fugitives to other law enforcement organizations— along with detailed descriptions—long before the Federal Bureau of Investigation was even born.

"For someone who had been born when the Industrial Revolution was in its infancy, and who had little formal education," marvels James Mackay, "Allan was quick to embrace the latest technology as it developed, and adapt it to the task of detecting or preventing crime."

Even his use of disguises—which, may, at first, seem obvious or melodramatic—was pioneering. These techniques of "assuming a role" or "shadowing a suspect," in the words of one historian, "would later be used so devastatingly in combating industrial terrorism and organized crime." But they would reach an early apogee of sorts in this assignment Pinkerton was about to undertake for Samuel Felton.

At this point—once he secured Felton's blessing—Pinkerton would open a case that would remain shrouded in secrecy for more than twenty years.

In Springfield, Abraham Lincoln—attempting to spend his last few days on routine domestic business before embarking on the journey of a lifetime—received death threats with alarming frequency. In mid-January, Mary Lincoln innocently opened an unmarked parcel sent from South

Carolina only to find a painting depicting her husband "with a rope around his neck, his feet chained and his body adorned with tar and feathers." For Mary Lincoln, a woman prone to fits of anxiety and rumination, the painting must have seemed a gruesome harbinger.

"For Lincoln," writes presidential historian Doris Kearns Goodwin, "the hours of his remaining Springfield days must have seemed too short. The never ending procession of office seekers and the hard work of packing left little time or space for the most important task of all—the composition of his inaugural address."

Distractions abounded. Townspeople thronged the Lincolns' gracious, two-story house on Eighth Street practically around the clock. In response, Lincoln would simply lean out the door and wave politely.

The Lincolns decided to rent out their house while away in Washington, hence much of that January was spent selling off their furnishings and putting items into storage. Toward the end of the month, another parcel arrived on the Lincolns' doorstep, one that featured no disturbing artwork but still contained invisible portents of peril.

The letter came from the Indiana legislature, inviting Lincoln to visit on his way to Washington. Similar offers followed from lawmakers in Ohio, Pennsylvania, New York, New Jersey, and Massachusetts.

Oblivious to the dangers inherent between the lines of each invitation, Lincoln began planning his preinaugural victory tour.

———

At this same time, in Chicago and Philadelphia, in anonymous hotel rooms and apartments, carpetbags flipped open in preparation for journeys that would ultimately both precede and follow Lincoln's progress toward Washington.

It is very likely—among the toiletries and extra changes of clothing packed by Pinkerton's operatives—that disguises went into these bags as well. Wigs, costumes, accessories favored by aristocratic sons and daughters of the South, all of these items went into the cloth grips with grave purpose.

In a boardinghouse in Philadelphia, a slender brown-haired woman packed as though for a funeral. She folded a black scarf into her bag, an elegant bustle, a dark gown, and one last item that would prove critical in the coming days.

The small black brooch, known as a mourning cockade, and usually worn to funerals, had become the secret lavaliere of Southern sympathizers—a signal to secessionists that the wearer was a friend. Made of black and white silk, the cockade featured ornate folds of fabric like the petals of a flower, gathered in the middle by a silver metal bullion star. It would be the final flourish of a very elaborate disguise.

Closing the carpetbag, Kate Warne made her exit quietly, heading to the depot for the short trip to Baltimore—unaware that her mission would soon bring her into close contact with the president-elect.

Allan Pinkerton had spent the previous week scouting the backwater burgs surrounding Baltimore.

A threat to the life of Abraham Lincoln the furthest thing from his mind, the burly detective concentrated instead on possible sabotage of the railroad. He discreetly rode in a PW&B coach across the frozen wetlands and inlets, assessing the general mood in the small towns at each stop, looking for signs of insurrection.

In Wilmington, Delaware, he saw the evidence, in his words, "of great political excitement," but nothing that would indicate hostile interference with the railroad. He got back on the train and rode it southward into Maryland.

At Perryman, the detective got off the train and strolled the boardwalks, listening, observing. "I found the same excitable condition of affairs," Pinkerton would write later, "but nothing of a more aggressive character than at Wilmington. Men indulged in fierce arguments, in which both sides were forcibly represented, but aside from this, I discovered no cause for apprehension, and no occasion for active detective work as yet."

The next stop, however, gave Pinkerton pause. On the other side of the Susquehanna River, where the little port city of Havre de Grace stretched along the weedy banks, the detective smelled bitter rancor on the winter winds. Did he hear something disturbing in the taverns there? Did he see something in the dark faces of dockworkers?

As Pinkerton drew nearer and nearer to Baltimore, the fever of discontent rose accordingly. The secessionist movement had gained widespread support in this area, and Baltimore was a nexus of insurgent activity. Pinkerton arrived at Baltimore's Calvert Station—a lavish Italian Gothic building erected only ten years earlier—with his senses sharpened. He strolled the side streets, listening, observing, taking mental notes.

At one point, according to published accounts, the detective paused outside a dark tavern and heard the following fragment of drunken conversation: "No damned abolitionist should be allowed to pass through the town alive!"

The time for Pinkerton to launch his operatives into this unstable borderland had finally come.

—⁓—

Saddened by the prospects of leaving the place in which he had lived and worked for nearly three decades, Abraham Lincoln said his farewells during that first week in February.

He traveled to Farmington to say good-bye to his beloved stepmother, Sarah. He then visited his father's grave. He came back to Springfield and met with his faithful law partner, William Herndon.

"If I live," Lincoln said somewhat ominously to Herndon, "I'm coming back some time, and then we'll go right on practicing law as if nothing had ever happened."

Lincoln's staff had set his departure date for February 11.

Several railroad companies had offered to put executive cars at the disposal of Lincoln's entourage, and a program of special trains was arranged to take the lanky president-elect through Indianapolis, Columbus, Cincinnati, Cleveland, Pittsburgh, Buffalo, Albany, New York, Trenton, Philadelphia, and Harrisburg.

"There was a strange lull in the North," writes James Mackay of those last days before Lincoln's departure.

For Pinkerton and his team, that first week in February would turn out to be the final quiet before the storm.

—⁓—

Each night, in the freezing temperatures, by the pale light of a diamond-chip February moon, Samuel Felton secretly drilled two hundred of his most trusted railroad workers (per Pinkerton's instructions). This private army would guard and fortify the lines between the Susquehanna River and Baltimore.

By day, the men fireproofed the bridges and trestles, applying as many as eight coats of whitewash, salt, and alum. Tensions among the men crackled like static electricity in the air. Felton feared the worst.

On February 8, in Montgomery, Alabama, six states—Georgia, Florida, Alabama, Mississippi, Texas, and Louisiana—joined South Carolina in the drafting of the Constitution for the Provisional Government of the Confederate States of America. The following day, the new rogue government elected Jefferson Davis, the senator from Mississippi and the former U.S. secretary of war, as president.

The Confederacy immediately moved toward potential armed conflict, mobilizing an army of more than a hundred thousand men and raising $15 million through export taxes on cotton. Despite the hubris inherent in these provocative acts—a Southern population of a mere five and a half million free citizens going up against the Union's twenty-three million—the symbolism must have emboldened sympathizers on both sides of the Mason-Dixon Line.

Battle lines were being drawn, and Abraham Lincoln became a marked man among the many secret societies active across the border states.

Pinkerton's elite group of undercover agents—each carrying the secret tools of their trade, the accoutrements of their assumed roles—took separate trains from Philadelphia to their respective assignments.

Timothy Webster traveled alone to Perryman, the ramshackle little town which clung to the banks of the Susquehanna north of the city.

With the aplomb of a thespian making a grand entrance onto a stage, the foxy Brit descended the running board of the train and immediately vanished into his new persona. He became a Southern dandy, an ardent secessionist with designs on joining a secret militia. A naturally quiet and thoughtful individual, Webster became gregarious and flamboyant in his "hatred" of the North.

"Webster's talent for sustaining a role of this kind," Pinkerton would later write, "amounted to positive genius." With his graceful bearing, shoulder-length hair, and carefully groomed beard, he played the part of the "prince of good fellows to perfection. In a lifetime of detective experience I have never met one who could more readily adapt himself to circumstances."

The other operatives arrived, one by one, at their appointed posts.

Kate Warne, attired in the fancy frills and feathered bonnet of a Southern belle, disembarked at Baltimore's Calvert Station. She checked herself into a hotel under an assumed name and began her systematic sweep of the city. She took copious notes regarding what she saw and heard as she sauntered the opulent districts.

John Seaford, the staunch, cunning Brit operative, journeyed to a small town on Baltimore's outskirts called Magnolia, a place where Pinkerton had observed sentiments "among men of all classes" in favor of "resistance and force." George Bangs, Pinkerton's right-hand man, currently running the New York bureau of the agency, closed up shop and departed immediately for Baltimore. Hattie Lawton, one of Warne's top female agents, arrived in Perryman to provide covert assistance to Webster.

Harry Davies, Pinkerton's suave and handsome assistant, came to Baltimore shortly thereafter, transforming himself into a debonair Frenchman by the name of Joseph Howard. If Timothy Webster was the favored "younger brother" of Pinkerton's investigative "family," then Harry Davies was the sophisticated cousin, almost Webster's doppelgänger. Davies, according to Pinkerton, "possessed the advantage of extensive foreign travel, and the ability to speak, with great facility, several foreign languages." Davies's finest creation, the character of "Joseph Howard," made his theatrical entrance on a cold February night.

Ambling conspicuously into the gas-lit labyrinth, Davies (in the guise of Howard) became, per Pinkerton's instructions, "an extreme secessionist" from Louisiana. Davies checked into a first-class hotel called the Barnum, registering his alias as a resident of New Orleans. "This was done," Pinkerton writes, "because he was well acquainted with that city, having resided there for a long time, and was consequently enabled to talk familiarly with prominent individuals of that city whom he had met."

The final role to be assumed—perhaps the most important of all—debuted at a building on Baltimore's bustling South Street.

The Relay House sat at a wide, graveled intersection in the heart of Baltimore's business district, with magnificent views of neighboring cathedral belfries and the distant maze-like streets. The building also had ideal features for an undercover operation's command center. Surrounded on all sides by either streets or alleys, the edifice had four separate exits, through which intelligence agents could come and go, unseen, at all hours.

On February 10, 1861, one day before Abraham Lincoln departed Springfield for the last time, a man going by the name of Hutchinson, hailing from Charleston, South Carolina, stood at the window of his newly rented office at the Relay House, a letter in his hand.

"What do you make of this, Bangs?" the burly, bearded Hutchinson softly inquired of his associate, who stood across the room.

Allan Pinkerton had chosen the alias of Hutchinson in order to blend into the local business community. He had chosen the office not only for its strategic location but also because it was situated across the hall from a notorious secessionist named J. H. Luckett, whom Pinkerton had only just begun to soften up at the local public houses. "The normally teetotal Pinkerton, in line with his assumed persona of a bluff, jovial Scotsman," writes James Mackay, "began frequenting the pubs and taverns of Baltimore, identifying the Copperheads [northern Democrats] who made no secret of their hatred of Lincoln and the Union. Soon Pinkerton was ingratiating himself with Luckett over drams."

George Bangs stepped forward and held out his hand. "May I?"

Pinkerton handed over the letter. The terse message, written by the master mechanic of the PW&B Railroad, had arrived only minutes earlier, and Bangs read it over carefully:

> *Mr. Hutchinson;*
>
> *I am informed that a son of a distinguished citizen of Maryland said that he had taken an oath with others to assassinate Mr. Lincoln before he gets to Washington, and they may attempt to do it while he is passing over our [railroad]. I think you better look after this man, if possible. This information is perfectly reliable. I have nothing more to say at this time, but will try and see you in a few days.*

Bangs handed back the letter and said, "It could just be another rumor like the one about the bridges. No names are given. And the writer doesn't offer any proof. Frankly it doesn't seem—"

"Wait a minute," Pinkerton interrupted. "If you were planning to murder safely a person traveling by train, how would you do it?"

Bangs thought it over, then smiled sheepishly. "I should have seen it. The best way would be . . . to blow up a bridge while the train was passing over it."

Pinkerton nodded. "Of course it is. The plan is probably to blow up a specific bridge, but someone couldn't keep quiet about it." He paused, thinking. "That someone probably exaggerated and that's how Felton learned his property was in danger and sent for us."

Bangs agreed.

Then Pinkerton added, "Let's hope we're as lucky finding out what those society horsemen in Perryman really have in mind."

———

"They were extremely lucky," writes historian Sigmund Lavine—thanks to the work of a few daring detectives, whose actions, until many years later, were "shrouded in a veil of mystery."

PART II
THE BALTIMORE PLOT

Let the consequences be what they may, whether the Potomac is crimsoned in gore and Pennsylvania Avenue is paved ten fathoms deep in mangled bodies, the South will never submit to such humiliation and degradation as the inauguration of Abraham Lincoln.

—A GEORGIA NEWSPAPER EDITORIAL,
CIRCA 1861

CHAPTER FIVE

A Strange and Almost Weird Presentiment

FEBURARY 11, 1861, 7:05 A.M.
A chilly drizzle strafed the frozen planks of Springfield's Western Railroad Depot. The gray morning sky hung low, as more than a thousand people thronged the platform, bumbershoots and parasols sprouting.

The man they had come to see arrived shortly after 7:00 a.m. with his oldest son by his side (the rest of his family was planning on joining him en route the next day). The tall, sinewy man carried a single trunk—which he had packed himself—tied with rope and labeled simply: "A Lincoln, White House, Washington, D.C."

Before departing, the president-elect shook hands with well-wishers inside the depot house, thanking them for their thoughts. "His face was pale," wrote the *New York Herald*, "and quivered with emotion so deep as to render him almost unable to utter a single word."

Eventually words *would* come, because he was Abraham Lincoln. A few minutes before 8:00, he followed his escort—most likely his dear friend, Norman Judd, a railroad attorney and head of the Illinois Republican State Central Committee—to the private coach.

He stood on the running rail, took off his hat, turned to the crowd, and "requested silence." Then, his voice tight with emotion, he spoke these words:

My friends, no one who has never been placed in a like position can understand my feelings at this hour, nor the oppressive sadness I feel at this parting. For more than a quarter century I have lived among you, and during all that time I have received nothing but kindness at your hands. Here I have lived from youth until now, and I am an old man; here the most sacred ties of earth were assumed; here all my children were born, and here one of them lies buried. To you, dear friends, I owe all that I have, and all that I am. All the strange checkered past seems now to crowd upon my mind. Today I leave you. I go to assume a task more difficult than that which devolved upon Washington. Unless the great God who assisted him shall be with me and aid me, I must fail; but if the same Omniscient Mind and Almighty Arm that directed and protected him shall guide and support me, I shall not fail—I shall succeed. Let us all pray that the God of our fathers may not forsake us now. To Him I commend you all. Permit me to ask that with equal sincerity and faith you will invoke His wisdom and guidance for me. With these few words I must leave you, for how long I know not. Friends, one and all, I must bid you an affectionate farewell.

Pinkerton, later in his life, would go back to these words often and marvel at their eerily prophetic quality. "A strange and almost weird presentiment of grief and suffering," Pinkerton observed, "give his utterances a pathos that becomes profoundly impressive when linked with subsequent events." But on that wintry morning, no one could have imagined what those subsequent events would entail.

Abraham Lincoln, with one last deferential bow, turned and vanished inside the private coach. "Three cheers were given," reported the *Herald*, "and a few seconds afterwards the train moved slowly out of the sight of the silent gathering."

Accompanying Lincoln on the special train as it set out on the journey's first leg were seven additional close friends and associates.

Judge David Davis, a three-hundred-pound bear of a man with "a big brain and big heart," was delighted to be along. This trusted consultant had twisted political arms the previous May on the floor of the Republican convention. Also present was a handsome, bearded campaign adviser, Ward H. Lamon, one of Lincoln's law partners. John G. Nicolay, Lincoln's private secretary—a neat, punctilious man who shadowed the president-elect's every movement—was also on board.

Elmer Ellsworth, also at hand on the trip, was a clerk in Lincoln's law office. During the last few years, Ellsworth had become almost a surrogate son to Lincoln.

Captain John Pope, one of the three military men riding along in the coach that day, would, in the coming months, become a Union general. The two other military officers present on the trip, Colonel Charles Sumner and Major David Hunter, were called, "brave and impetuous" by Pinkerton.

Not a single bodyguard was in attendance.

Not long after Lincoln's departure, eight hundred miles to the east in Baltimore, Pinkerton's faithful assistant and special agent, Harry Davies, a.k.a. "Joseph Howard," entered one of the Barnum Hotel's private parlors for a secret meeting.

Built in 1825, situated in the heart of Baltimore on Monument Square, the Barnum had a reputation as the hostelry of the elite. In 1827 John Quincy Adams spent several days here, providing a stamp of distinction that grew over three subsequent decades.

The building rose six stories above the cobblestone crossroads, a massive landmark of stone and ornamental cornices and balconies. Inside, chandeliers and velvet cordons greeted guests on their way to opulent rooms and private parlors. "The most comfortable of all hotels of which I had any experience in the United States," Charles Dickens once wrote of the Barnum, "where the English traveler will find curtains to his bed, for the first and probably the last time in America."

On that bitter February evening, Harry Davies arrived at the Barnum to find Marshal George P. Kane, head of the Baltimore police department, waiting for him. Kane, a known Copperhead, had invited "Joseph Howard"—the polished, genteel dandy from New Orleans—to a clandestine gathering of Southern sympathizers that night.

Evidently Davies's performance over the past few days—informed by his avowed contempt for Lincoln and the North—had wooed the city's underground society of "Fire-eaters" (Northern slang for proslavery extremists). In Pinkerton's words, "Harry's romantic disposition and the ease of his manner captivated many of the susceptible hearts of the beautiful Baltimore belles, whose eyes grew brighter in his presence, and who listened enraptured to the poetic utterances which were whispered into their ears under the witching spell of music and moonlight."

The city's police force, as Pinkerton had learned, "was entirely composed of men with disunion proclivities." Shocked by Kane's brazen conflict of interest, Pinkerton writes: "Their leader was pronouncedly in favor of secession, and by his orders the broadest license was given to disorderly persons and to the dissemination of insurrectionary information." With each passing day, Davies had drawn nearer and nearer to Kane's inner circle, until the invitation to attend one of the meetings at the Barnum had finally been proffered.

Davies followed Kane through the grand and lavish lobby and then down a sumptuous corridor to a private parlor reserved for a group calling itself "the Palmetto Guards."

Upon entering the chamber, Davies was taken aback. So many familiar faces crowded the dimly lit, smoke-hazed meeting room. These were men Davies had seen behind store counters, behind the desks of legitimate businesses, even wandering the alleys—men of all ages and social standings—gathered to fan the flames of their common hostility.

Davies mingled before taking a seat to enjoy the evening's presentation.

The president of the Palmetto Guards, a wild-eyed Italian named Cypriano Fernandina, rose from his seat and strode to the front of the room to deliver his keynote address. Fernandina worked days as the Barnum's hotel barber, but, as Pinkerton observed, "treason and conspiracy had elevated him to the station of a military captain whose orders were to be obeyed, and a leader whose mandates compelled respect."

Davies listened closely to Fernandina's speech, which began softly, advocating the doctrine of states' rights and denigrating abolitionists as blights on the country's future. The barber's passions began to stir as he came to the subject of Abraham Lincoln.

Livid with rage, Fernandina paused to catch his breath. He reached into the inner breast pocket of his fancy coat and brandished a long, gleaming knife.

"This hireling Lincoln shall never, never be president," Fernandina growled in his heavy accent, displaying the dagger for maximum dramatic effect. "My life is of no consequence in a cause like this, and I am willing to give it for his!"

The room grew silent. Hands clenched. All faces, glimmering in the lamp light, and, according to Pinkerton, "eyes glistening with the fires of hate," fixed themselves on the barber. Davies watched and listened.

"As Orsini gave his life for Italy!" Fernandina boomed, waving the blade, referring to the Italian revolutionary who had made an unsuccessful assassination attempt on Napoleon III just three years earlier, "I am ready to die for the rights of the South and to crush out the abolitionist!"

Davies feigned enthusiasm, cheering along with the rest of the conspirators. But deep inside the undercover operative, the realization was dawning that railroad bridges were the least of Pinkerton's worries.

Abraham Lincoln was in grave danger.

Thirty-four large-caliber blasts shattered the winter air outside Indianapolis as the special train carrying the president-elect rumbled into the depot. The noisy salute would have shaken the inside of Lincoln's private coach, and perhaps would have made Judd and Lamon and the others jump. But it's likely that Lincoln barely reacted. He had been in a sullen, pensive mood the entire way to central Indiana, despite the festive enclosure.

Dark furniture decorated the private coach carrying Lincoln. A "rich tapestry carpet" adorned the floor of the car, and crimson curtains provided privacy. The paneled exterior of the coach, festooned with colorful flags and streamers, drew the attention of onlookers along the way, but did nothing to raise the spirits of its most important passenger.

For most of the journey to Indianapolis, Lincoln "sat alone and depressed . . . forsaken by his usual hilarious good spirits." Was it the gravity of his mission? Did he sense the dangers lurking around every bend?

The train thundered to a hissing halt inside the Indianapolis depot.

Lincoln gathered his things, including his notes for that evening's speech, which he would deliver from the balcony of the Bates House. It would be, writes Doris Kearns Goodwin, "one of the few substantive speeches he would make during the long journey."

Did Lincoln pause at the coach door before exiting? He would have heard the boisterous, enthusiastic noise outside the door, and he would have had to marshal his spirits. Nearly twenty thousand people—friend and foe alike—waited for him to appear.

He was public property now, and there were some—scattered among the supporters, hiding in the shadows—who wanted their money back.

———

"You're talking about murder," Allan Pinkerton said under his breath, in the guise of John Hutchinson, in the dim light of Guy's Restaurant around 3:30 in the afternoon on February 12.

At the table sat five other gentlemen: J. H. Luckett, the secessionist from the South Street building, whom Pinkerton had befriended over the past few days; Harry Davies, who had introduced his friend "Hutchinson" as a secessionist from South Carolina; a Captain Trichot, one of the Palmetto Guards' top officers; a young Lieutenant Hill, one of the Palmetto's rising stars; and of course, Captain Cypriano Fernandina, the dark-eyed, fanatical leader.

The restaurant, only a few doors down the street from the Barnum, served a wide range of clientele, both rich and poor, powerful and disenfranchised—most of them secessionists. Pinkerton, alias John Hutchinson, would become a regular. And this night, at this table, over brandies and cigars, the hook would be sunk.

"Murder of any kind," Fernandina replied at last, speaking softly, burning his smoldering gaze into the eyes of his new ally Hutchinson, "is justifiable and right to save the rights of the Southern people."

Pinkerton would have provided very little in the way of a reaction at that point. The canny Scot most likely gave a nod and began to carefully coax information from the barber. But Fernandina would have been cautious. He was not a stupid man. Pinkerton observed later: "He was a man well calculated for controlling and directing the ardent-minded."

Even Pinkerton found himself vulnerable to Fernandina's withering gaze. The detective noted with some chagrin: "I, myself, felt the influence of this man's strange power, and wrong though I knew him to be, I felt strangely unable to keep my mind balanced against him."

In the silence following Fernandina's stunning assertion, a voice spoke up: "Are there no other means of saving the South except by assassination?" The question came from Captain Trichot.

The barber turned and glowered at the man. "No . . . as well you might attempt to move the Washington Monument yonder with your breath as to change our purpose. He must die—and die he shall." And then almost as an afterthought, the barber added, "And if necessary we'll die together."

"There seems to be no other way," the young Harry Davies concurred. "And while bloodshed is to be regretted, it will be done in a noble cause."

Fernandina glanced with approval at Davies. "Yes, the cause is a noble one, and on that day every captain will prove himself a hero. With the first shot the chief traitor, Lincoln, will die, and then all Maryland will be with us."

Pinkerton spoke up. "But . . . have all the plans been matured? A misstep in so important a direction would be fatal to the South, and ought to be well considered."

"Our plans are fully arranged," the barber replied with a "wicked gleam," as Pinkerton recalls in *Spy of the Rebellion*, shimmering in his almond eyes, and Pinkerton could see that the man would not elaborate. "If I alone must strike the blow," Fernandina added, again for dramatic effect, "I shall not hesitate or shrink from the task. Lincoln shall certainly not depart from this city alive."

Fernandina left it at that, and the men refilled their goblets.

Pinkerton needed details. He needed to gain the Italian's trust. But trust comes with a price. For an undercover operative, the cost of trust is time. Current circumstances, unfortunately, did not endow Pinkerton with much in the way of time.

At this point in the meeting, however, Pinkerton noticed something interesting—across the table. The mousy, young Lieutenant Hill sat rigid in his chair, the only man in the room who did not have the look of bloodlust in his eyes. The boy looked jittery, unnerved.

As the meeting adjourned and the men filtered back out into the streets for a night of reverie, Pinkerton decided to accompany Hill—with Davies in tow—on an impromptu pub crawl. Pinkerton realized that Hill may very well be the soft spot in the core of the conspiracy.

"I determined to select this man for the purpose of obtaining the information I so much desired," Pinkerton wrote of Hill. "Being of a weak nature and having been reared in the lap of luxury, he had entered into this movement more from a temporary burst of enthusiasm and because it was fashionable, than from any other cause. Now that matters began to assume such a warlike attitude, he was inclined to hesitate before the affair had gone too far."

At Pinkerton's suggestion, Harry Davies would become, over the next few days, a "bosom friend" and "inseparable companion" to the nervous young conspirator.

"Hill," Pinkerton writes, "soon proved a pliant tool in our hands."

On February 13 Lincoln's preinaugural train rumbled into Cincinnati.

For the most part, the fog of melancholy had lifted from Lincoln's shoulders. One observer noted that he had "shaken off the despondency which was noticed during the first day's journey, and now, as his friends say, looks and talks like himself."

The jovial change in atmosphere surely lightened the dispositions of most of those accompanying the president-elect. All except one must have shared in the festivities awaiting them in that great town on the Ohio River.

A brief telegram tempered the frivolity for Norman Judd. A Chicago resident and a close friend of both Lincoln's and Pinkerton's, Judd had been involved in some of the contractual work between Pinkerton and the railroads. With his open, boyish face set off by a thick goatee, he may have given the impression of impulsiveness or naïveté, but Judd suffered from neither. A shrewd, skilled attorney, he was methodical and cautious. He would have been very protective of Lincoln's time.

The brief message, sent by Allan Pinkerton, received by Judd en route, read simply:

I HAVE A MESSAGE OF IMPORTANCE FOR YOU. WHERE CAN IT REACH YOU BY SPECIAL MESSENGER?

Keeping the development to himself, Judd wired back to Pinkerton that the message should be delivered, for the Hon. Norman Buel Judd's eyes only, in Cincinnati.

The next evening, alone at the Relay House headquarters, Pinkerton responded to Judd's reply with a second message. In this telegram the detective explained that he had reason to believe there was a plot afoot to murder the president-elect on his passage through Baltimore.

Pinkerton promised to advise Judd further as the presidential party progressed through Cleveland, Pittsburgh, and Buffalo.

"This information Mr. Judd did not divulge to anyone," Pinkerton wrote in his memoir years later, "fearing to occasion undue anxiety or unnecessary alarm."

Although accounts in the historic record differ as to the timeline of events following this second telegram, it is highly likely that Pinkerton received an unexpected visitor that same night.

───

A knock on the door of the temporary office roused Pinkerton from his writing desk.

He went over to the door, opened it, and found his top operative standing there, face damp with sweat, lungs heaving hard from a long ride.

"I've discovered what the plotters are up to," Timothy Webster uttered between breaths.

They sat at a table in the parlor next to Pinkerton's office, and Webster proceeded to relate what had happened to him earlier that day.

Webster, who had still been in Perryman until this point, had insinuated himself into what Pinkerton described as the "most sinister of all the cavalry regiments." Webster's ruse—aided by the strength of his personality, his charisma, and his jovial charm—won him the finest horse available to members of the unit. He also garnered the confidence of the regiment's captain.

That day, after the regiment had finished its usual drills, the captain pulled Webster aside and requested his presence at the captain's house that evening.

At the appointed time, Webster arrived at the two-story home to find guards standing watch outside and the windows shrouded with heavy quilts. He told the guards who he was, and the men ushered him inside.

On the second floor, the handsome, long-haired Webster came upon a hushed meeting-in-progress behind shaded windows. The captain introduced Webster to three "members of a secret league in Baltimore," as Pinkerton refers to them in his writings, and the men made room for Webster at the table. They treated Webster cordially. They needed a man of his bearing and confidence to join their mission.

Within minutes, Webster realized that this group of conspirators had their sights set on killing the president-elect.

"On the twenty-third of February, Mr. Lincoln will pass through Maryland," Webster explained to Pinkerton. "On that date, somewhere within the state, Captain Fernandina and the Palmetto Guards will attempt to assassinate him."

Webster went on to explain that the leaders of his regiment planned to provide support for the assassination team. As soon as the deed was done—most likely in Baltimore—the news would be transmitted via telegraph "along the line of the road" to the regiment.

Once the members of the regiment received word of Lincoln's death, they would cut all the telegraph wires.

They would proceed to destroy the bridges and tear up the track "in order to prevent for some time any information from being conveyed to the cities of the North, or the passage of any Northern men toward the capital."

Lastly Webster described for Pinkerton how the conspirators brought their secret meeting to a close: with excited, boisterous backslapping. Repressing any natural revulsion he might have felt at the time, Webster told his new friends how happy he would be to aid them in their heroic mission. They warmly congratulated him.

In the stillness of the office parlor, Pinkerton thought about this for a moment. "We'll need more information if we're to convince Mr. Lincoln of the danger, and if we're to protect his life. Where will the attempt take place? At what time of day? And how does Fernandina plan to use his men?"

Webster shook his head. "Boss, unfortunately I don't know any of the details. Nobody in Perrymansville does. While our troop is part of the general conspiracy, I found out tonight that we're not to have anything to do with the assassination itself. That's being planned here in Baltimore. Marshal Kane's aware of the plot, I can tell you that. And Fernandina's the ringleader."

Webster nervously looked at the clock. He had to get back to the regiment before suspicions were aroused. He had told his fellow cavalrymen he was riding into town "for amusement" but would be back soon.

Pinkerton had already started thinking about his next move. He wrote an urgent message for the office courier to deliver immediately to "Joseph Howard" at the Fountain Hotel.

Minutes later, according to historian William Wise, "Agent Webster left by one door, as Agent Davies entered by another."

"You will have to get to the inner circle of their league," Pinkerton informed Davies in the stillness of the parlor that night. "There's nothing more to be learned in Perryman. Get Hill to put you right on the inside. He can do it, with Kane and the Italian also ready to vouch for you."

The young, elegant Frenchman nodded. He had, by this point, become more than a mere confidant of the unstable Lieutenant Hill—the two young men drank together, went to the theater together, and even frequented houses of prostitution together. Hill had become exceedingly dissipated and unstable, at times "thoughtful and morose" and then, without warning, breaking out into "enthusiastic rhapsodies."

The previous night, at a brothel known as Anne Travise's House, Hill had drifted off into a sort of opiate stupor and had murmured to Davies: "Rome had her Brutus, why should we not have ours? I am destined to die, Howard, shrouded with glory. I shall immortalize myself by plunging a knife into Lincoln's heart." But Davies could not help wondering whether these words were proof of something, or simply boastful, intoxicated rambling.

Pinkerton saw that Davies needed assurance. "Harry, why don't you tell them that you want to share in the immortal glory of freeing the South from her Yankee tyrant."

"They are all very solemnly sworn, sir," Davies replied. "Hill has told me that much."

"Then you will have to take the oath too."

Davies hesitated. "I suppose it's really no worse than calling myself Joseph Howard, a hot rebel straight up from New Orleans."

Pinkerton smiled. "I'm counting on you."

"If it means the president's life—"

"None can judge that better than yourself."

After a moment's hesitation, Davies said, "If they swear me in, sir, I'm in."

CHAPTER SIX

The Drawing of the Red

FEBRUARY 14, 1861, 7:01 P.M.
Music swelled. Shoe leather shuffled and scuffed. The cream of Ohio society glided in "full evening dress" across the floor of a crowded ballroom in Columbus.

All heads turned toward the front of the room, where a long-limbed man in a funereal-black coat maneuvered awkwardly across the dance floor with a dignitary's wife. All around the room, throughout the rapt crowd, eyes twinkled. Abraham Lincoln, his spirits lifted, now looked the part of a triumphant president-elect.

Earlier that day, Lincoln had received a telegram from Washington. The electors had met to count the votes and make the election official, and the process had proceeded without incident. For weeks, Lincoln's associates had worried that secessionists would intercede, perhaps violently, but now the election had entered history, and Lincoln could breathe a sigh of relief.

Immediately following the news, a great celebration broke out in the streets of Columbus. Lincoln, now joined by Mary and the children, enjoyed a sumptuous reception at the governor's mansion, followed by a gala dance. At the ball, Lincoln showed, in the words of Doris Kearns Goodwin, the "good humor, wit, and geniality" his friends had come to expect. The ballroom, filled with VIPs, responded in kind.

Salmon P. Chase, the Ohio senator who had founded the national Republican Party, waltzed happily alongside the man from Springfield, and for years afterward, eyebrows had raised at the rumors that Lincoln had taken Chase's lovely daughter, Kate, for a spin across the boards.

"The image of Lincoln dancing with the twenty-year-old beauty, tall, slim, and captivating, was spoken of in hushed tones for many years afterward," writes Doris Kearns Goodwin. "In fact, the charismatic young belle could not have danced with Lincoln that evening, for she was absent from the city when the Lincolns arrived."

One man in attendance that evening, however, may have had difficulty keeping his mind on the frivolous matters of dance partners.

Norman Judd had not yet told a soul of the troubling telegrams from Allan Pinkerton. Did he need more detail before he apprised Lincoln of the dangers lurking in Baltimore? Cognitive dissonance may have paralyzed Judd during these celebratory days.

Lawyers are natural skeptics. They require documentation, signatures, precedent, corroboration, options, and contingency plans. Judd, perhaps, would have worried about piercing the membrane of merriment surrounding his fellow lawyer and friend with such speculative warnings. After all, politics is a dirty business, and in this tense, dysfunctional period it had never been dirtier.

It is possible, though, that Judd had no conception of the raw, unfettered hate being leeched out of the shadowy extremes of the opposition.

~~~

As Abraham Lincoln whirled in the candlelight of the Columbus ball, his mind sanguine and focused on an optimistic future, a letter writer in some far-flung county, most likely below the Mason-Dixon Line, completed a brief yet potent missive addressed to the newly elected chief executive.

The author of the short epistle, a man named A. G. Frick, would never be apprehended. His name would be known to history solely for this one-page letter, dated February 14, 1861. It is possible—in fact, highly probable, given the sequence of subsequent events—that Allan Pinkerton studied the letter (after it arrived in Washington) and may have followed up with an investigation.

Although the correspondence—if one could call it that—had nothing to do, specifically, with the Baltimore plot to assassinate Lincoln, the ink-spattered lines of Frick's letter reveal the threat spreading like a malignancy across the country, metastasizing in Baltimore, Maryland:

Mr. Abe Lincoln
If you don't resign we are going to put a spider in your dumpling and play the devil with you, you god almighty goddamn son-of-a-bitch,

*go to hell and kiss my ass, suck my prick and call my Bolics your uncle
Dick, goddamn a fool, and goddamn Abe Lincoln, and excuse me for
using such hard words with you but you need it—you are nothing but
a goddamn Black nigger.*

Yours,

A. G. Frick

*Tennessee, Missouri, Kentucky, Virginia, North Carolina and
Arkansas are going to secede—Glory be to God on high*

—⁓—

"Howard—!"

On February 16 Agent Harry Davies sat alone, having dinner at Guy's Restaurant, when the voice that would lead him into the belly of the beast came on a loud whisper, penetrating the din of the candlelit room.

No record exists of what Davies ate that night, but it's not improbable that he dined on rich seafood—most likely oysters—drowned in thick sauce. Davies, a man who, according to one historian, "made liberal use of his expense account," would have enjoyed the requisite cuisine of a Crescent City dandy. Oysters were hugely popular fare on the eastern seaboard at this time, sold on the streets and in saloons with drinks. Broiled, deviled, curried, fricasseed, fried, scalloped, or sautéed in heavy sauces, oysters were "the center attraction" of many fatty American meals.

"At dinner they have boiled pastes under the names of puddings," one British traveler wrote of Americans and their inimitable eating habits, "and the fattest are esteemed the most delicious; all their sauces, even for roast beef, are melted butter; their potatoes and turnips swim in hog's lard, butter or fat; under the name of pie or pumpkin, pastry is nothing but a greasy paste, never sufficiently baked."

Davies looked up from his meal and saw the jittery Lieutenant Hill approaching his table. Motioning for the man to join him, Davies pulled a chair back. Hill sat down and spoke urgently.

"Your nomination has been approved!" The excitable young man was referring to Davies's request that he be allowed to join the Palmetto Guards.

For the last forty-eight hours, Agent Davies had been lobbying diligently for entrance into the secret society. Writes historian Arthur Orrmont: "Davies' diatribes against 'that Black Republican Lincoln,' and his loud and oft repeated opinion that the South would be better off with Vice President Andrew Johnson at the helm, had their desired effect." Now, with Marshal Kane and others vouching for him, Davies would soon be sworn in.

"Tonight, you'll take the oath," Hill informed Davies. "But there's something else."

Davies looked at the man. "Yes?"

Hill eagerly explained in hushed tones that the secret league would decide, that very night, through secret ballot, who among them "would have the distinction of destroying the leader of the North." Davies listened very carefully, keeping his exhilaration to himself.

At last Davies replied that he would be honored to be among the candidates for such a task.

"All right," Hill said with breathless anticipation, "if it can be arranged, we'll then go together." Hill's voice lowered even further to avoid prying ears. "Should I draw the ballot, I'll not fear to kill. Howard, I swear it! Caesar was stabbed by Brutus. And Brutus was an honorable man." Then Hill's tone softened. "Lincoln need expect no mercy from me, though I do not hate him as some do." He paused. "It is more love of country with me."

Davies hurriedly finished his meal and prepared to depart as Hill whispered one last development.

"And consider this," Hill uttered. "The captain and our other leaders don't feel certain of the courage of everyone who'll be permitted to draw a ballot tonight, Howard . . . and they intend to not place *one* red ballot in the box to be drawn but eight of them. *Eight* different men will leave the meeting, each positive that on him and him only rests the safety of the South and the whole course of our freedom. What do you say to that?"

"Splendid!" Davies exclaimed, rising from his seat. He looked at Hill with a smile. "It looks as if the plan could not possibly go wrong."

By this point, as the icy February sun set behind Baltimore's back alleys, and gaslights sputtered to life, the preinaugural train bearing Abraham Lincoln and his family closed the distance between the president-elect and Pinkerton's operation to less than four hundred miles.

That night the special locomotive rumbled into Buffalo, New York, to the obligatory fanfare. "For Mary and the boys," writes Goodwin, "the trip was a 'continuous carnival' with 'rounds of cheers, salvos of artillery, flags, banners, handkerchiefs, enthusiastic gatherings'—in short, all the accessories of a grand popular ovation."

In Westfield, New York, earlier that day, Lincoln had playfully gotten off the train at a scheduled stop and found Grace Bedell, the little girl who, according to Goodwin, "had encouraged him to grow a beard." To the fervent cheers and laughter of the crowd, Lincoln gave the child a kiss.

Blissfully unaware of the dark developments unfolding to the south, Lincoln would have been in no mood to entertain the grave news that Pinkerton's undercover operative was about to unearth.

— —

The private parlor at the Barnum, lit only by flickering ceremonial braziers, gave off an air of medieval ritual. A few dozen men—some of them adorned with strange harlequin masks—knelt by a makeshift altar. The hush that held the rapt gathering only added to the eerie quality of the moment, as the firelight danced off the high ceiling and the elegant framed artwork.

The flamboyant "Joe Howard" of Louisiana stepped up to the edge of the altar. Cypriano Fernandina, clad in stylish evening attire—a long morning coat and tails, a solemn black cravat—stood over the initiate as a priest would stand over a communicant. The Italian raised a sword and asked Harry Davies to please kneel at the foot of the platform.

Davies knelt.

Fernandina laid the sword on Davies's shoulder and asked him to raise his right hand.

Then the Italian proceeded to have Davies repeat the words of a "long and terrible oath," pledging on his word of honor as a Southern patriot to carry out any order, regardless of the dangers or murderous results. The swearing-in took only a few minutes, but the gravity of the occasion rippled through the room in different ways.

"A kind of awe pervaded the assembly," writes Richard Rowan, "which had now increased to more than thirty. Though beholding them, mindful of the secretive obligations he had just assumed, Davies felt tempted to smile. All of them must have taken the same oath! Yet here he was, sitting among many of the least discreet and loudest tinder-tongues of Baltimore."

At the completion of the swearing-in, the other men crowded around Davies, shaking his hand and congratulating him. Fernandina waited patiently before bringing the room back to order.

With his gray eyes burning, Fernandina proceeded to lay out the plans for the assassination.

Agent Harry Davies, now a certified Palmetto Guard, listened carefully to every word.

—◦—

The conspirators had learned—most likely from members of the compromised police force—that Abraham Lincoln would have to change trains at the Calvert Street depot in Baltimore on the morning of the February 23.

Upon arrival, the president-elect and his party would be loaded into carriages and taken to the Eutaw House for a brief reception. They would then proceed by horse cart to the Camden Street station, where they would board the Baltimore and Ohio train for Washington.

The most vulnerable moment in Lincoln's passage through Baltimore would occur shortly after disembarking from the incoming train. To reach his carriage, Lincoln would have to traverse a narrow vestibule between the station and its front lot.

At that point, a fake fistfight would be staged in front of the building. The few policemen at the depot would be forced to rush out to quell the row, leaving Lincoln and his party unprotected, and in the words of Pinkerton, "surrounded by a dense, excited, and hostile crowd." It would be at this vulnerable moment that the fatal shots would be fired.

A small steamer boat had been chartered and would be stationed at one of the bays or streams running into the Chesapeake. In the chaotic aftermath of the attack, the assassins would flee via steamer to Virginia and the glory of their high accomplishment.

—◦—

The time had come to draw the lots. Fernandina put away his knife and ordered the few remaining lights in the room extinguished so that the results of the lottery would be anonymous.

Darkness fell. The silhouettes of nervous conspirators huddled and waited. As Fernandina put a large jug filled with ballots on a nearby table, he asked every man to pledge secrecy regarding his lot. One by one, the men swore confidentiality.

Harry Davies anxiously awaited his turn. The small paper ballots would have one of two colors. No message other than white or crimson-red.

White signified no obligation. Red signified "the duty of assassination." Eight red ballots lay in the vessel.

The process began. One by one the solemn conspirators moved through the gloom to the jug, carefully pulling pieces of paper from the container. Each one glanced at their destiny with thinly veiled stoicism.

At this stage Davies would have been watching Hill closely. The young lieutenant's uneasiness would have clearly shown on his shadowed countenance as he neared the moment of truth. Hill approached the container. He drew a lot and looked at it.

Later Davies would remark to Pinkerton that a "palpable and rather dissembled relief" showed on the young braggart's face. In the words of Rowan, "Hill had met the test and survived its stain."

When it was Davies's turn to draw, he struggled to mask the tension building within him. What if he drew red? How would that affect the investigation? How would it alter the intervention? How far could he continue the charade?

He reached into the jug.

He pulled a ballot.

He looked at it.

Late that night, long after the conspirators had adjourned to their debaucheries and congratulatory wine, anonymous figures moved busily behind the shadows of Baltimore's alleys and inner passageways.

On South Street a well-dressed phantom slipped into the Relay House through one of the hidden entrances. On the second floor, in the parlor of a rented office, the lamp oil already burned.

Pinkerton greeted Harry Davies warmly, not at all disturbed about being roused from bed at such an inhospitable hour. Davies had case-breaking news, and as soon as he had been able to disengage himself from Hill without raising suspicion, he had summoned his boss to this emergency meeting. He now sat down with Pinkerton to relate the particulars of the plot to murder Abraham Lincoln.

"The plan is to kill Mr. Lincoln at the Calvert depot," Davies explained. "The president-elect will have only a few friends with him. They'll never think Mr. Lincoln is in danger, so they won't be on guard."

Then Davies related all the details. He told Pinkerton about the Calvert vestibule, the bogus fight, the distraction of the police, the ambush of assassins. At last Davies explained the drawing of the lots, and he told Pinkerton that he did not know the identity of the eight chosen ones.

At some point it is likely Davies showed Pinkerton the paper ballot that he had drawn from the jug. It was white.

Pinkerton asked Davies to attach the ballot to a full report.

"We have to keep close watch on these madmen," Pinkerton said at last, once Davies had finished his breathless summary. "But we must *not* let them know they are being watched. Do nothing to alarm them. As long as they believe their plans have not been detected, they'll have no reason to change them."

Davies understood. His "Joseph Howard" would continue to "mix with the conspirators at Guy's and at Barnum's," and continue to send reports to Pinkerton as the plot progressed.

"We can develop a plan of our own to get Lincoln safely through Baltimore," Pinkerton said. "He must be in Washington on the fourth of March . . . and it'll be up to us to see that he gets there."

Davies concurred.

Pinkerton told Davies he could go now and should write up the report as soon as possible, as Pinkerton was going to need it.

Years later, in his memoir, Pinkerton would write, "My time for action had now arrived."

⁓

The next day, February 17, a smartly dressed woman rode alone in a crowded passenger coach, northward, across the Maryland state line, into eastern Pennsylvania. The train wended through the cathedrals of pine and hemlock, past the snaking tributaries of the Delaware River, past Valley Forge, past the sacred wilderness where Washington's army starved and froze and lived out the darkest moments of the Revolutionary War. The woman had *other* dark matters on her mind—perhaps equally epochal to the country.

Did Kate Warne wear the brooch of the rebellion on this journey? Did she travel with the telltale stamp of secession, its sepulchral black blossom pinned to her hat? Probably not. She was now crossing ideological borders as well as geographical ones. Her carpetbag, safely stowed nearby, contained explosive documents, freshly prepared by Davies and Pinkerton.

Earlier that morning, George Bangs, Pinkerton's proficient operations manager, had given Mrs. Warne her current assignment, one of great consequence: To travel to New York—which was the next scheduled stop for the Lincoln party—and hand-deliver a message of vital importance to Norman Judd. Pinkerton had sent a wire to Judd that he should "expect a call from a Pinkerton emissary."

The boss had other matters to address. By daybreak he had already embarked for Philadelphia—Lincoln's penultimate Northern stop before venturing into secessionist territory—to meet with Samuel Felton. The president of the PW&B Railroad would need to know the gravity of the situation, need to know the turn of events that had involved his rail line.

Upon arriving in Philadelphia Pinkerton found the historic city in the throes of patriotic fervor. Flags and bunting festooned the buildings, and an air of "joyous expectancy" contrasted greatly with the brooding atmosphere in Maryland. "Philadelphia wanted both to see Abraham Lincoln and to reassure him," writes Richard Rowan. "[They] wanted—with but a little Fifth Ward dissent—his national authority to begin."

Pinkerton wasted no time.

The detective went directly to Felton's office, and there, among the gilded maps and lushly appointed furniture, told Felton everything. Felton listened closely to the whole narrative, all the details of the plot, and when Pinkerton was finished, the railroad executive responded very simply: "What can I do to help prevent this terrible thing?"

"Frankly, I don't know if anybody can do anything as of yet," Pinkerton surmised. "I can't get near Lincoln—and he probably wouldn't pay any attention to me if I could. The only member of his party that I know is Norman Judd from Chicago. He's our one hope."

And it was up to Kate Warne to fulfill that hope.

───

That evening, Kate Warne arrived in the great, bustling metropolis. She proceeded directly to the Astor House, a fine old establishment located in a fashionable residential district on New York's south side, near St. Paul's Cathedral. Home of such luminaries of the day as Mathew Brady and Henry Wadsworth Longfellow, the Astor House would be receiving Lincoln the very next day.

Mrs. Warne kept a low profile that night, preparing her notes and planning her strategy for the next day. The hours must have dragged for her, enclosed in that stately room on the upper floor. She would have keenly felt the pressure of being a courier in such a weighty matter.

Over the last two weeks in Baltimore, she had pleased her boss, "cultivating the acquaintance of the wives and daughters of the conspirators," providing Pinkerton with daily reports. "This information she received was invaluable," Pinkerton recalled many years later, "and many hints were dropped in her presence which found their way to my ears, and were of great benefit to me."

But this assignment was different. This was a crucial link in a delicate chain of events that must connect properly. The truth of the matter, however, was that Kate Warne was more than capable.

As Pinkerton writes: "Mrs. Warne was eminently fitted for this task. Of rather a commanding person ... with an ease of manner that was quite captivating at times, she was calculated to make a favorable impression at once."

The next day, shortly after 4:00, she made just such an impression on Norman Judd.

Judd had arrived at the hotel late—missing the presidential train in Albany—and was probably still a bit flustered when there came a knock on his door. He and Captain John Pope were in the middle of a casual chat, and when he opened his door to find a hotel servant standing there, he was confused. The servant said, "There's a lady here, sir, in another room, who wishes to see you."

Judd followed the servant to the upper floor and then knocked on the woman's door.

"Come in," said a voice.

Judd entered and found a sedately dressed woman seated at a desk with documents in front of her. She rose and smiled. "Mr. Judd, I presume."

"Yes, madam," Judd replied.

The woman handed over a brief letter from Allan Pinkerton. The letter introduced this woman as a Mrs. Warne, the superintendent of the female detective department of the Pinkerton Agency, and informed Judd that she was acting as an official courier.

"Mr. Pinkerton doesn't like to trust the mail in so important a manner," she explained and then handed over a sealed envelope. "I have been sent to give you this, which contains the facts relating to the conspiracy previously mentioned, and also to arrange for a personal interview between yourself and Mr. Pinkerton."

"A personal interview?"

"The purpose would be to submit all the proof relating to the conspiracy."

"Very well."

"Mr. Pinkerton will notify you, immediately after your arrival in Philadelphia, of where to meet."

Judd told her that he would probably be in a carriage immediately after arriving, with Mr. Lincoln, heading from the depot to the Continental Hotel. While he told her this, another knock came from across the room.

Warne went over to the door, opened it, and standing there was Colonel E. S. Sanford, president of the American Telegraph Company, who also wanted to give Judd a message. Warne made the introductions, and Sanford showed Judd another letter from Pinkerton "relating to this affair."

Sanford explained that he wanted to help in any way that he could—as Pinkerton recalls, "tendering Judd the use of his lines for any communication Judd might have to make, and also Sanford's personal service if needed."

Judd thanked them both and returned to his private room to read the sealed report.

"The contents alarmed Judd," writes James Mackay, "to the extent that he wanted to show the letter to Vice President-elect Hannibal Hamlin." But when he returned to Kate Warne's room to ask her if he might show the report to Hamlin, Warne emphasized that "no one could be trusted, and that the only man who should be told is Lincoln himself—and then only if [Judd] considered it absolutely necessary."

Judd decided to keep the matter to himself—at least until they arrived in Philadelphia.

What Judd did not know at that point—in fact what had eluded, amazingly, the eye that never sleeps—was that a wholly separate undercover operation had been working in Baltimore at this time.

Somewhere, deep under cover, in the back rooms, in the ranks of treasonous connivers, an anonymous detective unaffiliated with the Pinkerton organization moved unseen among the conspirators.

Chapter Seven

Counterplot

February 21, 1861, 7:01 A.M.

A bright and clear sky graced Philadelphia that morning. The crisp winter air reverberated with the brassy sounds of martial music from strategically positioned bands. Expectant voices chattered along Chestnut Street. Flags and handkerchiefs fluttered with giddy anticipation.

"The streets were alive with the eager populace," writes Pinkerton, "all anxious to do honor to the new president, and to witness the scenes attendant upon his reception. Vast crowds lined the sidewalks and the enthusiasm was unbounded."

It was a momentous occasion on many levels. The next day was George Washington's birthday, and Lincoln was scheduled to preside over a flag-raising at Philadelphia's historic Independence Hall.

At length, the presidential train, aglow with its bunting and nearly two thousand miles of celebratory travel, roared and hissed into the 30th Street Station. Carriages awaited the presidential party.

Norman Judd accompanied Lincoln to the lead carriage. Each man, bundled in his winter coat, settled into his seat as "files of policemen" kept the throngs at a safe distance. The reins snapped, and the carriages set out for the Continental Hotel, where the party would lodge that night, about twenty blocks away.

The procession rolled down Chestnut Street, past the hurly-burly of well-wishers and waving Republicans. They were heading toward Broad Street, where, right at this moment—unbeknownst to anyone in Lincoln's party—a sharp-eyed young man waited in the mob of onlookers.

This young man was biding his time until the presidential carriage drew close enough to reach before the police had a chance to intercede.

"I saw a young man walking on the outside of the line of policemen," Judd wrote years later, "who was evidently trying to attract my attention." When the buggy reached the intersection of Broad and Chestnut, the boy made his move.

"He darted forward," writes William Wise, "and thrust a piece of paper into Norman Judd's hand."

Before Judd even realized what had just happened, the mysterious boy wheeled back around and vanished into the crowd. The incident occurred so abruptly and unexpectedly that it is unlikely that Judd's famous carriage-mate even noticed.

Judd would find out later that the mysterious young man was an attaché of the American Telegraph Company and a confidential agent of E. S. Sanford, the company president, whom Judd had met a few nights ago in New York.

That day, the young messenger was also serving in the capacity of secret courier for Allan Pinkerton. The boy's name was George H. Burns, and as Pinkerton notes in his war time memoirs, the young man would go on to "distinguish himself for his courage and daring in the Rebellion."

Judd glanced down at the small slip of paper, unfolded it, and read the following:

ST. LOUIS HOTEL, ASK FOR J. H. HUTCHINSON

Soon after knocking on the guest-room door, Norman Judd—who had stolen away from the Lincoln party in search of the mysterious J. H. Hutchinson—realized the gravity of the situation.

Judd stood in the hallway of the St. Louis Hotel, staring at an old friend from Chicago, an old friend who had been on Judd's mind lately.

Writes Richard Rowan: "'Hutchinson' himself had opened the door . . . a heavily built, black-bearded man of forty-one, with keen eyes, broad forehead, and resolute mouth—a face not likely to be forgotten."

Judd stared at the man. "Pinkerton!"

"Come in, sir," Pinkerton urged his old friend. "You're as prompt as I had hoped you'd be."

Judd went into the modest room and saw another man, tall, well dressed, with hirsute sideburns, standing in one corner with a pleasant and yet somewhat solemn expression.

"Mr. Felton here is the president of the Philadelphia, Wilmington & Baltimore Railroad." Pinkerton closed the door behind Judd. "We have many things to decide," the detective informed Judd, "and not much time to decide them."

Pinkerton suggested that Judd have a seat. Several large manila envelopes sat on a table across the room. Pinkerton pulled one, and he began reading Harry Davies's report on the specifics of the Palmetto Guards' plot to kill Lincoln at Calvert Station on the morning of February 23.

Halfway through the report, Judd could no longer sit still. He stood and began pacing, as Pinkerton continued the narrative of the plot, describing the narrow vestibule, the crooked police chief, the waiting ferryboat, all of it. Every few minutes Judd would "fire a question" at Pinkerton, until finally the stocky detective concluded the report.

Judd insisted on seeing all the evidence. The threesome spent, according to Judd's account of the meeting, "an hour or more" examining the documentation.

At last Judd "slumped in a chair," shook his head, and sadly said, "I've known there was strong feeling against the man, but I had no idea that things were this bad. Your evidence is too powerful to ignore, Allan."

Felton had also provided Judd with strong corroborative evidence from several of his top supervisors.

Finally Judd admitted, "I'm convinced all that you say is true—but getting Lincoln to agree with us is another matter."

"My advice," Pinkerton said then, "is that Mr. Lincoln proceed to Washington this evening by the 11:00 train, and then once safe at the capital, General Scott and his soldiery will afford him ample protection."

Pinkerton was referring to Lieutenant General Winfield Scott, the acting head of the United States Army. Scott would soon come into play in these tense negotiations in a completely unexpected way.

"I fear very much that Mr. Lincoln will not accede to this," Judd said after giving it some thought. "But as the president is an old acquaintance and friend of yours, Allan, and has had occasion before this to test your reliability and prudence . . . there's only one thing to do." Judd looked at Pinkerton. "Let's go and see him."

A mob of Republican well-wishers greeted Pinkerton, Felton, and Judd when their carriage arrived at the front facade of the Continental Hotel.

Interrupting Abraham Lincoln that night, amid his hectic schedule of receptions and toasts at the Continental—for no less than a private meeting—was going to be no small feat. Writes Sigmund Lavine of the difficulty Pinkerton and his associates had gaining entrance that night: "The trio pushed, shoved, lost their hats, and had buttons torn off their coats, but they could not get through the throng. Finally Judd turned to his companions and gasped, 'Let's get out of here and see if there's a door in the rear!'"

They found a service entrance—also clogged with gapers and bystanders—and, linking arms, pushed their way through. In the lobby, clothes torn, they found a military escort to usher them up the stairs to the parlor level.

They finally reached Judd's room, which was on the same level as the Ladies Parlor—the room in which Lincoln was holding court. Judd summoned John Nicolay, Lincoln's omnipresent secretary, and told the officious little man to please, if possible, fetch the president at once for "a matter of urgent importance."

The Ladies Parlor brimmed with Philadelphia's elite, the expectant chatter buzzing and droning as scores of socialites and political luminaries engulfed Lincoln.

The president saw Nicolay approaching through the crush of formally dressed partygoers, and it is likely that the expression on the secretary's face tipped Lincoln off that something of consequence had arisen.

Nicolay whispered in Lincoln's ear, and with a nod, Lincoln excused himself with, in Richard Rowan's words, "great patience and tact."

He followed his secretary through the crowded corridors, no doubt having to nod greetings and thank admirers en route to Judd's room.

When Lincoln finally reached the correct door, Nicolay gave a knock.

"I went in," Lincoln wrote later in a statement from his journals, "and found there Mr. Pinkerton, a skillful police detective, also from Chicago, who had been employed for some days in Baltimore, watching or searching for suspicious persons there."

These two self-taught, industrious, single-minded men, each with relentless ambition—whose paths had been converging ever so gradually for the last week and a half—greeted each other cordially.

"What have you men been doing," Lincoln asked playfully, "fighting wildcats barehanded?"

The men tried to appreciate the president's trademark humor, but the occasion for their meeting was no laughing matter.

Norman Judd, after inviting everyone to take a seat and introducing Samuel Felton to the president-elect, broached the subject at hand. "Mr. President, I confess I've known of a danger to you ever since we passed through Cincinnati, where I received the first warning from our friend, Mr. Pinkerton. I said nothing then—as, indeed, he recommended—for I didn't care to darken your journey with any premature foreboding. But now I want him to tell you what he and Mr. Felton have been telling me."

Pinkerton took over. Measuring his words very carefully, he said in his Scottish burr, "We have come to know, Mr. Lincoln, and beyond a shadow of a doubt, that there exists a plot to assassinate you. The attempt will be made on your way through Baltimore, day after tomorrow. I am here to help in outwitting the assassins."

Lincoln crossed his legs "in characteristic fashion"—as though presented with a complex mathematical problem—and his customary "good-humored, kindly" expression suddenly changed. "A shade of sadness fell upon his face," Pinkerton recalled years later. "He seemed loathe to credit the statement, and could scarce believe it possible that such a conspiracy could exist."

After a tense pause Lincoln said, "I am listening, Mr. Pinkerton."

Pinkerton described the murderous conspiracy in detail, interrupted only by Lincoln's pointed questions, each of which reflected his innate bearing as a lawyer. Pinkerton summarized the findings of each independent investigation—Davies, Warne, Webster, and Pinkerton's own—in the manner of a closing argument in a trial.

"Then do I understand, sir," Lincoln finally said, after Pinkerton had completed the narrative, "that my life is chiefly threatened by this half-crazed foreigner?"

"He only talks like a maniac," Pinkerton said of Cypriano Fernandina. "His capacity to do you harm must not be minimized. This conspiracy is a going concern—the most timely measures alone will serve to frustrate their plotting."

"But why?" Lincoln wanted to know, turning to glance at Nicolay, who sat across the room, appalled at what he was hearing. "Why do they want to kill me?"

Norman Judd piped in: "The plotters believe that if you were killed it would be a great victory for the Southern cause. Your death would leave the Union without a leader. A compromise could be reached."

"The plotters also think," Samuel Felton added, "that if they succeed in killing you, each and every one of them will be a hero in Dixie. They are fanatics, madmen—and madmen are capable of thinking and doing anything."

Pinkerton also attempted to explain—to the best of his ability, drawing on his political experiences going all the way back to Glasgow—the dynamics present in the border states at the moment. He speculated on how impossible it was for most Northerners to "comprehend the mad, fanatical feeling" prevailing in Baltimore. He also put into perspective, from his street-level view, the manner in which Lincoln had become a lightning rod for the most "incendiary elements" of these secessionists.

"With all due allowance for the menacing plans of the fanatics," Lincoln interrupted, "how do you happen to be so sure of the carrying-through of the preparations against me?"

"Because, sir, at least one of my men has penetrated to the very core of the plot and learned how thoroughly the whole thing has been prepared."

"And you vouch for the integrity of this detective?"

"I do, Mr. President," Pinkerton said. "He took the required oath very regretfully, perjuring himself only in the performance of a solemn duty to you and the nation." Pinkerton went on to explain the drawing of the lots, the red and white ballots, and the fervor with which the results were met. In the grim lull that followed this sickening revelation, Norman Judd spoke up.

"Mr. Felton," Judd said, turning to the railroad man, "you can corroborate all this?"

"I can," Felton said. "And from an altogether different source." He looked at Lincoln. "Not many days ago, Mr. President, I was visited by a Miss Dix, a lifelong friend and a lady above reproach, noted in the South for her charities. She came to my office that Saturday afternoon, saying that she had a terribly important warning to convey to me. And for more than an hour I listened while she put in tangible shape what I've been hearing in detached fragments since before I ever sent for Allan Pinkerton in January."

The railroad executive proceeded to relate the details of Miss Dix's warning; and with each word the atmosphere of doom in that hotel room must have thickened and intensified.

———

What the Dix woman had revealed was essentially a far-reaching, secret plan among Southern sympathizers to stage a coup d'état, cutting off all rail lines and telegraph connections between Washington, D.C., and the North, taking over the capital, and preventing the inauguration of Lincoln by killing him—either in Baltimore, during the preinauguration journey, or in Washington at the actual inauguration. The conspirators would declare themselves the de facto government.

"Miss Dix has proven her loyalty to the people of the South," Felton added. "But she cannot condone insurrection and murder."

Lincoln spoke up. "Granting, gentlemen, that all of this is true, what do you propose to do about it?"

"We propose," Pinkerton said, "to take you on to Washington this very night, Mr. President . . . and steal a march on your enemies."

Lincoln turned to Judd. "Has this your approval?"

"It seems to me for the best," Judd replied; but the young lawyer tempered his counsel with a subtle caution.

He warned Lincoln that the reports that had been laid out before him tonight could not be made public—as the lives of undercover operatives in the field would be at stake. Therefore the populace would not be aware of the mountain of evidence impacting Lincoln's movements.

"You will therefore perceive," Judd advised, "that if you follow the course suggested, that of proceeding to Washington tonight, you will necessarily be subjected to the scoffs and sneers of your enemies, and the disapproval of your friends who cannot be made to believe in the existence of so desperate a plot."

Lincoln had already made up his mind. "I fully appreciate these suggestions, and I can stand anything that is necessary, but—" as he said this, he rose to his full imposing height "—I cannot go tonight."

The room remained silent.

"I have promised to raise the flag over Independence Hall tomorrow morning," Lincoln explained, "and to visit the legislature at Harrisburg in the afternoon—beyond that I have no engagements. Any plan that may be adopted that will enable me to fulfill these promises, I will accede to, and you can inform me what is concluded upon tomorrow."

Then he "gravely shook hands with Pinkerton and Felton" and left the room.

⸺

In his memoir *The Spy of the Rebellion*, Pinkerton reflected upon Abraham Lincoln's attitude that night, marveling at the man's steely spine:

> *During the entire interview he had not evinced the slightest evidence of agitation or fear. Calm and self-possessed, his only sentiments seemed to be those of profound regret, that the Southern sympathizers could be so far led away by the excitement of the hour, as to consider his death a necessity for the furtherance of their cause. From his manner, it was deemed useless to attempt to induce him to alter his mind.*

Perhaps inspired by the president-elect's backbone, Pinkerton had a flash of inspiration within moments of Lincoln's departure from the room.

As was often the case with the brawny cooper from Dundee, the idea came to him fully formed—a counterplot using all the resources at hand to foil the conspirators and to deliver Lincoln safely to his ultimate destination.

What Pinkerton did not know, however, was that Lincoln would stumble upon another unexpected revelation only moments after walking out of Judd's hotel room that night—a revelation that would not only change Lincoln's mind but would alter the course of the preinauguration journey.

Earlier that day, in Washington D.C., Frederick Seward, a thirty-one-year-old Senate staffer, was working in the Senate gallery, when a page approached him with an urgent message: Seward's father, the longtime senator from New York, was waiting, at that very moment, in the lobby and needed to see Frederick immediately.

Seward dropped what he was doing and hastened to the foyer.

Born in Auburn, New York, in 1830, Frederick Seward had worked hard throughout his life to make a name for himself in the shadow of his famous father, William H. Seward. Graduating from Union College in 1849 and passing the bar in 1851, Frederick would split his time for the next ten years between assisting his father in matters of the state and working as an outspoken editor at the *Albany Evening Journal.*

A wiry, almost emaciated-looking young man, Fred Seward had the large, dark eyes of a late-night thinker. In photographs of the period, with his sad, haunted gaze, he bore a striking resemblance to Edgar Allan Poe.

That day, in the Senate lobby, Frederick Seward found his father, William, in a lather of nervous tension. The elder Seward held a note from Lieutenant General Winfield Scott. Scott was renowned as a stern military taskmaster who had earned the nickname "Old Fuss and Feathers" in the Mexican-American War (for his insistence on spotless uniforms, even on the field of the battle).

The message, of paramount urgency, needed to be delivered at once to Abraham Lincoln. Handing the dispatch—which was wrapped inside a brief note from William himself—over to his son, the elder man said, "Whether this story is well founded or not, Mr. Lincoln ought to know of it at once."

Fred Seward took the documents, as his father explained the troubling contents within.

"I know of no reason to doubt it," William gravely added as an afterthought. He explained that the note had been independently verified by Colonel Charles P. Stone, the man in charge of U.S. troops in Washington assigned to inauguration security. "Colonel Stone has facilities for knowing and is not apt to exaggerate."

Frederick understood and gave a terse nod.

"I want you to go by the first train," William Seward told his son. "Find Mr. Lincoln, wherever he is. Let no one else know your errand."

Frederick left the capital immediately, taking the next train bound for Philadelphia.

He rode the hundred and forty miles between the two great cities with the note safely tucked into an attaché. He had been told that Lincoln was staying at the Continental that night and would be "serenaded" in the evening. Seward arrived in Philadelphia just before 10:00 that night.

Proceeding without delay to the Continental Hotel, Frederick Seward encountered the same folderol swarming the front of the lodge that had so plagued Pinkerton and his party earlier that evening.

"The street was crowded with people," Seward would later recall, "the hotel brilliant with lights. Music and cheering made the scene a festive one."

The young courier fought his way inside the hotel and found the corridors practically impassable. "The halls and stairways were full of people," Seward writes. "In the parlors were throngs of ladies and gentlemen who had called to pay their respects to the new president. Presentations seemed to be going on. Certainly this was no time for the delivery of my secret message."

Seward asked to speak to the person in charge of Lincoln's schedule. He was shown to a room "at the head of the stairs," in which a group of young men were standing around "chatting and laughing." There, Seward met Robert Lincoln, the president-elect's seventeen-year-old son. Robert introduced Seward to Ward H. Lamon.

Seward told Lamon of the urgent need to meet with Lincoln.

Lamon took Seward's arm. "I'll take you down to the parlor, and present you at once."

Seward balked. "Sir, my interview must be a private one, and attract as little attention as possible."

Lamon laughed. "Then I think I better take you to his bedroom. If you don't mind waiting there, you'll be sure to meet him, for he's got to go there sometime tonight, and it's the only place I know of where he'll likely be alone."

Seward followed Lamon to the private suite and waited there for at least an hour.

Alone in that lavish chamber, the young courier would have been unaware that Abraham Lincoln was, at that very moment, meeting with Allan Pinkerton.

At length, a noise outside the suite door caught Seward's ear.

Lamon and Lincoln were walking toward the room. The door opened, and Lincoln came inside.

Many years later, in an address to Union College, Frederick Seward described his first impression of the president-elect:

I had never before seen him, but his portraits in the newspapers and on the campaign banners had made his face seem familiar. I could not help but notice how correctly they had given his features and how entirely they had failed to give his careworn look and his pleasant, kindly smile. After exchange of a few words of greeting, I told him of my errand and gave him the letter I had brought. He sat down by the table under the gaslight to read it. Naturally one might have expected that its contents would startle him. But he made no exclamation and I saw no sign of surprise on his face.

The message from Lieutenant General Scott verified in shocking detail much of what Allan Pinkerton had divulged only minutes earlier. According to Scott, an investigation—completely independent from Pinkerton's—had been under way in Baltimore for weeks now.

Apparently the superintendent of the New York City Police Department, John A. Kennedy, had taken rumors of foul play in Baltimore seriously and had sent one of his most experienced detectives, David Bookstaver, to Maryland to ferret out potential conspiracies. Working deep undercover in the guise of a music agent, Bookstaver penetrated Baltimore's high society and may have actually attended meetings of the Palmetto Guards under the very nose of the unsuspecting Harry Davies. Bookstaver's report advised Scott, as well as Scott's right-hand man, Colonel Charles P. Stone, that a very serious threat to Lincoln's life would present itself in or around Calvert Station on the afternoon of February 23.

"Did you hear anything about the way that this information was obtained?" Lincoln finally asked Fred Seward after carefully reading Scott's warning a second time. "Do you know anything as to how they got it?"

Seward explained that he had heard nothing in regard to it until that morning.

"Did you, for instance, ever hear anything said about such a name as Pinkerton?"

In fact, this was the first time Frederick Seward had ever heard the name.

Lincoln seemed to be turning over something important in his mind. "I may as well tell you why I ask," he said at last. "There were stories or rumors some time ago, before I left home, about people who were intending to do me mischief. I never attached much importance to them—never wanted to believe any such thing. So I never would do anything about them in the way of taking precautions and the like. Some of my friends, though, thought differently—Judd and others—and without my knowledge they employed a detective to look into the matter."

Then the president-elect described to Seward the meeting he had just attended with Pinkerton.

"Surely, Mr. Lincoln," Seward said after hearing of the plot uncovered by Pinkerton and his agents, "that is a strong corroboration of the news I bring you."

Lincoln smiled and nodded. "That is exactly why I was asking you about names. If different persons, not knowing of each other's work, have been pursuing separate clues that led to the same result, why then it shows there may be something in it. But if this is only the same story, filtered through two channels, and reaching me in two ways, then that don't make it any stronger. Don't you see?"

The logic here—the cold, open-eyed analysis—speaks to Abraham Lincoln's strength as an attorney and a leader. But it is not improbable that a deeper vein of consideration was at work here. Lincoln, a lifelong fatalist, would have wrestled internally with the somewhat futile quality of a Pinkerton-style intervention.

William Herndon, the man who was arguably closest to Lincoln, recalled many conversations with the future president in which Lincoln asserted that "all things were fixed, doomed in one way or another, from which there was no appeal" and that "no efforts or prayers of ours can change, alter, modify, or reverse the decree."

Writes historian Richard Carwardine:

> Lincoln often told his law partner that he had a foreboding of "some terrible end," but when Joseph Gillespie [an Illinois legislator] and others urged him to take precautions against assassinations, he took a fatalistic view. "I will be cautious," he told an anxious acquaintance

shortly before his final departure from Springfield, "but God's will be done. I am in his hands . . . and what he does I must bow to—God rules, and we should submit."

At some point in their tense meeting, however, Lincoln must have seen the concern—even disappointment—in the haunted eyes of Frederick Seward. The young man worried that Lincoln would not take the warnings seriously.

"Well, we haven't got to decide it tonight, anyway, and I see it's getting late," Lincoln said at last. "You need not think I will not consider it well. I shall think it over carefully, and try to decide it right; and I will let you know in the morning."

—~—

Lincoln "slept badly" that night, according to biographer Arthur Orrmont. Allan Pinkerton, as it turned out, did not sleep at all.

Around 11:00 p.m., Pinkerton stood in the crisp, wintry night outside the Continental with Judd and Felton.

The detective told his companions to meet him in his room at the St. Louis Hotel at midnight, at which time Pinkerton would propose a counterplot. "I'm going to ask G. C. Franciscus of the Pennsylvania Railroad Company, and Sanford, to join us," the detective added.

"Why?" Norman Judd wanted to know. "Are you going to ship Lincoln in a crate by Adams Express?"

Smiling grimly, Pinkerton replied, "That might not be such a bad idea."

His smile would have faded quickly, for what he had in mind would probably be just as difficult.

CHAPTER EIGHT

Cutting the Wires

FEBRUARY 22, 1861, 6:01 A.M.

Cannons boomed. The report shattered the frosty predawn air over the venerable marble columns of Independence Hall. A sea of top hats waved joyously as the long-limbed man of the hour, the crest of his stovepipe hat nearly seven feet high, squared himself on the rostrum, decisively grasped the rigging, then gave it a yank.

The symbolism here would not be lost on the ecstatic multitudes that morning, as they watched their beloved Honest Abe raising the Stars and Stripes himself. The new flag, with its thirty-fourth star representing Kansas, was emblematic of the whole of the Union—a precedent that Abraham Lincoln would stubbornly uphold from this point on, refusing to allow, even amid secession and war, any stars to be removed from the flag.

After the flag-raising, Lincoln went inside the great hall with his boisterous adherents for a much anticipated speech. The overflow audience, "crowding every corner," cheered wildly as Lincoln stepped up to the speaker's stand. Perhaps weary from his sleepless night, his dark mood showing on his face, Lincoln proceeded to honor the birthday of the country's first president by remembering the "dangers incurred" by the men who assembled in this room to frame the Declaration of Independence almost a hundred years earlier.

The *New York Times* later remarked on Lincoln's "worn, nervous, and bewildered look." As one reporter observed somewhat callously, "What struck us most in his appearance here, was his feeble and sensitive nature, and his lack of sturdiness and solidity of character."

But no one present that day could have conceived the doom coursing through the man's thoughts. As he concluded his speech, he referred once again to the Founding Fathers: "It was their hope that in due time the weights should be lifted from the shoulders of all men, and that *all* men should have an equal chance."

Pinkerton biographer William Wise writes of this tenuous moment: "He bowed his head for a moment, as though in thought. Then he asked if the Union could be saved on the basis of freedom for *all* men. If so, he would consider himself one of the happiest men in the world."

Lincoln, adding an ominous postscript, told the crowd: "But if this country cannot be saved without giving up that principle . . . I would rather be assassinated on this spot than surrender it."

— —

According to numerous accounts of the hours immediately following Lincoln's Independence Hall appearance, the president-elect kept to himself his thoughts on the matter of averting disaster in Baltimore.

A carriage awaited outside the hall to convey Lincoln's party to the train station, where the special car would take him to Harrisburg.

The Pennsylvania capital city had planned a gala reception and dinner for Lincoln at 5:00 that night. Governor A. G. Curtin—the recently elected Republican and great admirer of Lincoln—would attend the event, as would luminaries from the state legislature.

After boarding the train, Lincoln respectfully requested that everyone leave the car except Judd.

Once they were alone, Lincoln reached into his attaché and pulled out the documents submitted the night before by Frederick Seward. He handed the papers to Judd and commented dryly, "Seems as if Pinkerton knew what he was talking about."

Judd looked over the report from General Scott. If Judd was surprised, it is likely he kept the emotion to himself. Exhausted from a night without sleep—a night spent devising the counterplot in Pinkerton's room at the St. Louis—Judd played his cards carefully at this point.

Lincoln looked at his friend and said, "What are Pinkerton's plans?"

Judd groped for the words. Pinkerton had told him in no uncertain terms to refrain from discussing the plans with anyone until "the last possible moment." Finally Judd stammered, "Plans? Oh . . . yes . . . our detective friend is tending to them right now."

Lincoln's gaze did not waver. "What plans, Judd?"

"Well . . . you'll have to know sooner or later." Judd sighed. "So I'll tell you. According to your schedule, after speaking to the legislature, you're to be guest of honor at a dinner given by Governor Curtin. Then, after a public reception, you're supposed to spend the night at the executive mansion."

Lincoln listened carefully as Judd explained what would actually transpire.

Kate Warne—the unassuming, brilliant, strong-willed matron of the Pinkerton Female Detective Bureau—arrived in Philadelphia on the afternoon train. She had shed her role of a Southern belle as a snake sheds a skin, and by the time she disembarked at the 30th Street depot, she had assumed a new guise—a plain-Jane Northerner bound for Washington—per her chief's instructions.

She proceeded directly to the ticket counter, where she explained her special needs to the clerk. She asked for several tickets on that evening's express train to Washington—and she explained that she preferred the last two sleeping cars for her family, as they were bringing her "invalid brother" to a special hospital for treatment.

The clerk, oblivious to the ruse, began preparing the tickets.

"One other thing," she said. "I would ask that the door on the end of the last car be unlocked and stay that way so that my brother could use this entrance."

The ninety-mile journey to Harrisburg may have seemed endless to Norman Judd, but the jubilant atmosphere that greeted Lincoln's party at the Harrisburg station around noon that day belied the gloomy undercurrent of the trip. The president-elect's party disembarked to hurrahs and applause, and then traveled via carriage across town to the Jones House, where the group was expected to freshen up before moving on to a reception at the state Capitol.

Lincoln graciously chatted with well-wishers in the square outside the hotel before leaving for the State House. As Norman Judd recalls in a letter to Pinkerton, several members of Lincoln's entourage, by this point, suspected "something was afoot," so Lincoln took Judd aside before departing for the Capitol.

"I reckon they will laugh at us, Judd," Lincoln confided to his friend, referring to the reactions of his cronies when informed of the counterplot, "but you had better get them together."

Judd arranged for an emergency conference among Lincoln's inner circle immediately after the meeting with the Pennsylvania legislature.

Shortly after 4:00 that afternoon, they met in a parlor at the Jones House—Judge David Davis, Colonel Charles Sumner, Major David Hunter, Captain John Pope, John G. Nicolay, and Lincoln's old law partner from Danville, Illinois, the stocky, broad-shouldered, dashing Ward Lamon. Over the last two weeks, Lamon had taken on the mantle of unofficial bodyguard for Lincoln, and this prerogative would lead to interesting conflicts with Pinkerton.

Judd, who conducted the meeting and wrote about it later, found himself the subject of "very rigid cross-examination" from his skeptical colleagues. In the style of a courtroom examination, Judge Davis, the rotund engineer of Lincoln's political ascension, expressed no opinions "but contented himself with asking rather pointed questions."

At one point, Davis turned to Lincoln and said, "Well, Mr. Lincoln, what is your judgment upon the matter?"

"I have thought over this matter considerably," Lincoln replied, "since I went over the ground with Pinkerton last night. The appearance of Mr. Frederick Seward, with warning from another source, confirms my belief in Mr. Pinkerton's statement. Unless there are some other reasons, besides fear of ridicule, I am disposed to carry out Judd's plan."

Judge Davis knew the subject was closed. "That settles the matter, gentlemen."

Colonel Sumner, an old Army chum of Lincoln's from the Blackhawk War, could not be so easily convinced. Sumner, a tough-as-nails officer of sixty-four, with flowing white hair and an almost biblical-looking beard, had earned the nickname "Bull Head"—due to both his booming voice and a legend that a musket ball once bounced off his cranium. He now spoke up: "So be it, gentlemen. It is against my judgment, but I have undertaken to go to Washington with Mr. Lincoln and *I shall do it!*"

Momentarily taken aback, Judd explained to the old warhorse that the counterplot did not accommodate additional participants or passengers. Years later, Judd would write, "I tried to convince him that every additional person added to the risk, but the spirit of the gallant old soldier was up, and debate was useless."

Other things began to go wrong at dinner that night. Sitting beside Andrew Curtin, the handsome young governor of Pennsylvania, at the head of a sumptuous table in the crowded banquet hall of the Jones House, Lincoln politely excused himself at the appointed time of 5:45. The plan was for the president-elect to discreetly slip out of the dinner hall, per Pinkerton's instructions, and then "pass quickly and unnoticed from the hotel."

But no one had taken into account the one element consistently dogging the progress of the presidential party since it had departed Springfield: the omnivorous crowds.

Writes Richard Rowan: "The banqueting Pennsylvanians were not allowing their elective leader to slip down even an oyster unnoticed." Hordes of well-wishers clogged the corridors, blocking Lincoln's passage to his room (where he had planned to change into traveling clothes). Even larger and more unruly crowds mobbed the front of the inn, craning their necks "to get a glimpse of the next president." Many were demanding a speech from the nearest balcony, stomping their feet and clamoring "in the light of huge, blazing bonfires."

Lincoln made a snap decision, returning to the banquet room.

To the uninitiated observer present in the hall that evening, what transpired next would have appeared fairly innocent. Abraham Lincoln whispered something to Governor Curtin, and the governor nodded, pushing himself away from his meal and rising.

"Ladies and gentlemen," Curtin said calmly to those sitting nearby. "I am deeply sorry to announce that Mr. Lincoln is suffering from a severe headache. And though he would like to stay and meet everyone here, he regrets that he must retire to rest."

Curtin, who proved to be a skillful prevaricator, also made it clear to the guests that the president would be sleeping that night at the executive mansion just down the street.

Earlier in the day, Lincoln had confided in the governor of the assassination plot and the particulars of the counterplot. Curtin recalled years later, "He seemed pained and surprised that a design to take his life existed, and although much concerned for his personal safety as well as for the peace of the country, he was very calm, and neither in his conversation or manner exhibited alarm or fear."

That night, after begging the pardon of the guests, Curtin gave Lincoln his arm. And the twosome attempted to slip away with a minimum of fuss. But the crowd pressed forward and blocked their path. Writes Rowan: "Everywhere, the dining rooms and corridors of the hotel were thronged. . . ."

At last Curtin was able to extricate the President-elect by telling the crowd that Lincoln was suffering from exhaustion and needed a spot of rest.

Historians and biographers dispute the exact details of what happened next.

—— ——

Most accounts—including Pinkerton's—claim that Governor Curtin led Lincoln back through the crowded hotel to the room that had been designated for the presidential party. Most concur that approximately fifteen minutes passed as Lincoln changed out of his formal attire and into innocuous traveling garb.

When he reappeared, he wore, in the words of James Mackay, "a long, threadbare military coat." His hatless head—which was rare for the president-elect when in public—rose stork-like out of his upturned collar.

In Lincoln's pocket, a felt hat poked out. Over the years this hat has gained a sort of infamy, being variably called a "Kossuth hat" (Dunn), a "Tam o' Shanter" (Mackay), and "a Scotch Plaid bonnet" (*New York Times*). Much has been made over the years of Lincoln's disguise. Political cartoons of the day—long after the incident had come to light—lampooned the indignant quality of the sixteenth president of the United States masquerading as a derelict drifter.

What is well documented, however, is that, once Abraham Lincoln emerged from his room, prepared for departure, the gears of Pinkerton's complex counterplot quickly began to turn. Governor Curtin led the president down a back staircase, followed closely, stealthily, by Norman Judd and Ward Lamon.

As Lincoln approached the side exit, Judd whispered, "Lamon, you go ahead. As soon as Mr. Lincoln is in the carriage, drive off. The crowd must not be allowed to identify him."

The burly Lamon pushed his way forward, past the president, and shoved open the exit doors.

— ⁓

Outside, in the frigid dusk, C. G. Franciscus, general agent of the Pennsylvania Railroad, heard the creaking of the opening doors.

A woolen shawl draped over his arm, Franciscus stood by a nondescript, waiting "closed carriage," for which he had arranged earlier that day at a local livery. The night was cold enough for the vapor of the horses' breaths to puff intermittently, accentuating the tension in the air. Lamon was the first to appear in the mist.

Lincoln followed, reaching into his pocket and putting on the unassuming hat. Franciscus proffered the shawl, and Lincoln draped it over his shoulders.

Thankfully, most of the celebrants that night were concentrated around the corner of the building, under the balconies of the ballroom, and across the front facade of the hotel. This brief respite from the crowds gave the team valuable seconds in which to privately spirit away the president.

Others emerged from the side entrance: Judd, Governor Curtin, and the indomitable, old, gray warrior Charles Sumner, still hell-bent on ushering his leader to Washington. Lincoln followed Lamon through the hatchway and into the vehicle's cabin.

"Drive to the executive mansion!" Curtin ordered the carriage driver, loud enough—per Pinkerton's orders—for any nefarious ears to hear.

Curtin started to close the carriage door when Sumner started toward the enclosure. Suddenly Judd reached out and put a hand on the old man's shoulder.

"Colonel—" Judd said, with enough gravity in his voice to distract the officer.

Sumner whirled around and stared wide-eyed into Judd's face.

But before Judd could even say anything, the snap of the reins pierced the cold air . . . and the carriage was off.

Colonel Sumner was aghast that his beloved leader had left without him. For a moment, it seemed as though the old man might actually take a swing at this upstart Judd. Years later, Judd recalled, "The situation was a little awkward, to use no stronger terms, for a few moments."

Then Judd quietly said to the colonel: "When we get to Washington, Mr. Lincoln shall determine what apology is due to you."

— ❦ —

The carriage lit out at a fast clip and then slowed as it neared the governor's mansion. The horses reared and turned into the drive.

No one exited the carriage. Satisfied that the brief jaunt of a few blocks had gone undetected, Franciscus pulled out his pocket watch, glanced at it, then ordered the driver to pull back, turn south, and move with haste.

The reins cracked, plumes of vapor snorting from the team. The carriage sped off at a gallop toward the "lower end of the city."

— ❦ —

The last light of day faded like dying embers in the crags of the Appalachians to the west. The temperature plummeted. The cloudless sky became a needlepoint of stars—a cold, crystalline winter's night.

The darkness gathered around the lonely rail-crossing south of Harrisburg.

A pair of men paced nervously across the deserted platform, moving like ghosts in the great billowing gouts of steam that came from the "special" idling next to them, a small train—just an engine, a tender, and a coach car—hissing like a slumbering beast.

The men on the siding knew all about Pinkerton's counterplot.

John Pitcairn Jr., the younger of the two, worked for the Philadelphia and Erie Railroad as a telegraph specialist. He had ridden along on the presidential train that morning, charged with watching over the telegraphic instrument in case an emergency message needed to be sent.

The other man, Enoch Lewis, the general superintendent of the Pennsylvania Railroad, had arranged for the special train to be ready at sunset. Lewis had told neither the engineer nor the fireman nor the baggage agent the purpose of the trip to West Philadelphia.

Nor had he told them the identity of their illustrious passenger.

At length, the rhythmic sound of hooves thrumming on hardpack rose in the distance, approaching from the north. Then a covered carriage materialized like an apparition on the adjacent road.

The driver pulled alongside the platform, and the doors of the carriage swung open. Lewis and Pitcairn recognized the first man to disembark from the coach—G. C. Franciscus—who, without a word, turned and helped two other men descend the foot-rail. One of them was a large, bearded man of robust bearing.

The last man to emerge—a gentleman of substantial height—wore a long coat draped in a plaid, woolen shawl and a hat of soft felt.

Without delay the three men were hurried on board the special coach.

Lewis and Pitcairn followed them up the step rail and signaled the engineer to embark. The engine hissed—the great steel wheels beginning to turn.

And thusly the train began its eastward trek, the work of flesh-and-blood horses now being assumed by an equine of the iron variety.

As the special train rolled out of Harrisburg—all its running lights off, its headlamp dark, its hatches and windows blacked out—a wire sparked through the lines, connecting through the American Telegraph Company office in Harrisburg, then zapping its way to Norman Judd at the Jones House.

Judd, who had remained at the hotel with Governor Curtin, assuring the dignitaries and guests that Lincoln was "resting comfortably" and that his "headache was due only to fatigue," now sprang into action. He sent a special wire to Philadelphia for one J. H. Hutchinson: It said "Plums" (Pinkerton's code name) should be advised that "Nuts" (Lincoln) had departed Harrisburg safely.

Meanwhile, back in the Harrisburg telegraph office, a young lineman named Andrew Wynne, and two other men, waited anxiously for confirmation that "Plums" had received the message.

Wynne—handpicked by his superiors to perform a very special procedure on this night—was considered by his peers to have "the eye of an expert" as well as the "adventurous delight of youth." Wynne happily accepted the challenge of helping Pinkerton protect the president-elect.

When word came that the message had been received, the three men gathered up a supply of tools and rolls of copper wire. With gear clanging on their belts, they exited the office and headed south-by-southeast on foot through the darkness.

They marched over two miles, following the high-wire poles lining the train tracks to avoid observation, through the bitter cold and darkness, out beyond the city limits, until they found the main wires of the Northern Central Railroad. Richard Rowan describes the scene:

> *Here, in an unfrequented spot, Wynne put on his climbing irons, went up a tall pole, cut the Baltimore wires, and attached fine copper ground wires to the severed ends, rendering impossible all communication between a spy in Pennsylvania's capital and the simmering insurrectos on the Chesapeake.*

After the job was done, Wynne decided to be doubly sure he had fulfilled Pinkerton's relentless refusal to contend with, in his own words, "a single element of uncertainty" and allow "even one dispatch to get through to its destination." Wynne walked all the way back to a telegraph office in the heart of Harrisburg—one operated by the Northern Central—and boldly asked the operator to send a message for him to an address in Baltimore.

"Seems to be something wrong with the line," the operator said after repeated attempts to send the wire.

"Too bad," Wynne commented dryly. "Guess I'll have to wait, then, till morning."

Back at the Jones House, as Lincoln's absence began to dampen the volume of the celebration, a group of newspaper reporters—many of them from "prominent New York journals" such as the *Times* and the *Herald*—huddled in a side room designated for the press. They had followed the Lincoln party for nearly two thousand miles, and now they were restless—hungry to grab an interview with the president as the inauguration neared.

They must have begun to make a racket because an unidentified member of Lincoln's entourage barged into the room and told them it was too late to speak to Lincoln or glean any further perspectives.

The identity of this "visitor" is unknown. In his memoir, Pinkerton coyly refers to the man as a "gentlemanly individual, well-known to me." It is possible that the man was Norman Judd, but that seems unlikely. It might have been Colonel Sumner. But, again, this is mere guesswork.

The visitor proceeded to tell the reporters, in confidence, off the record, that Lincoln had left the city and was speeding over the railroad in the direction of Washington, which he would reach in the morning. What the visitor did *not* tell them was that Pinkerton had suggested, much to the chagrin and disapproval of Mary Lincoln, that the family and the rest of the party go on to Baltimore as planned. Judd had reluctantly agreed to this.

Hearing this news, the reporters "hastily rose," grabbed their hats, and headed for the door.

The visitor blocked their path. Pulling a revolver, holding it menacingly, the visitor calmly said, "You cannot leave this room, gentlemen, without my permission."

"What does this mean?" demanded one of the journalists.

"It means," the visitor softly replied, "that you cannot leave this room until the safety of Mr. Lincoln justifies it."

"I want to telegraph the *Herald*," insisted a second correspondent. "What's the use of obtaining this kind of news if we can't utilize it?"

"You cannot utilize anything at present, gentlemen. The telegraph will not be of any service to you, for the wires are all down, and Harrisburg will be separated from the world for some hours yet."

After a tense pause, one reporter humbly asked, "When do you propose to let us out?"

"Well, I'll tell you, gentlemen. If you will sit down calmly and bide your time and mine, I will make matters interesting for you."

The reporters settled back into their seats, and the mysterious visitor sent for drinks.

Then the visitor told them what was going on.

CHAPTER NINE

On the Night Train

FEBRUARY 22, 1861, 9:31 P.M.

The dark, renegade Harrisburg Special rumbled at breakneck speed toward Philadelphia. Knowing he had a clear track, the engineer kept the throttle wide open, zooming past tiny hamlets with unlikely names such as Salunga, Bird in Hand, Ronks, and Paradise.

As the clock approached half past 9:00, the train slowed near Downingtown, about thirty miles outside of Philadelphia, for the locomotive to take on water. The engine hissed to a halt under the water tower.

"Here," writes Rowan, "all save Lincoln alighted to get something to eat, the president-elect staying alone in the shadows until the others returned, bringing him the best supper they could surreptitiously manage—a cup of tea and a roll." The crew and passengers returned to their posts, and within minutes the train huffed back into motion.

The remaining few miles to Philadelphia passed uneventfully.

The firelight of West Philadelphia twinkled on the dark horizon, as the train closed in. Abraham Lincoln prepared to detrain.

"His long, bearded face, so easily recognized," writes Wise, "was completely hidden in shadows." He removed the shawl, and he wrapped a woolen muffler around his neck until it practically covered the lower half of his face. Then the soft felt Kossuth hat went on.

The air brakes sang out, the keening roar rising up into the starry sky.

The slight jerk of gravity would have nudged the president-elect slightly—a wake-up call perhaps. The most delicate of all the ploys prescribed by the counterplot was about to take place.

The train came to a stop shortly after 10:00 in the Quaker City.

Ward Lamon filled the doorway with his brawn, checking the platform.

Lincoln waited for the signal, and then, when the all-clear sign had been given, followed his former law partner and ersatz bodyguard out the exit-hatch, down the step-rail, and into the bracing chill.

A squat, muscular man greeted them on the platform. His chest as fulsome as the barrels he once fashioned from timbers along the Fox River, the man wore his trademark bowler hat and thick beard.

Lincoln, ever the dry Kentucky wit, laid eyes on the man and said, "Mr. Pinkerton, you look rather fatigued. I understand you have been waiting all day for a message from a certain elusive gentleman named Hutchinson."

The detective grinned. He had indeed stewarded a good many messages that evening revolving around the fictitious Hutchinson, including a coded message only an hour earlier that informed him the "Sumac" (telegraph) had been successfully cut down. "Now why should I do that, sir?" Pinkerton retorted wryly. "I never even met the man, though he does seem worth knowing."

With businesslike haste Pinkerton led Lincoln and Lamon across the platform to a waiting covered-carriage.

On top of the brougham, on the box seat, two gentlemen sat in the cold night air, awaiting further orders. One was the carriage driver, who grasped the reins nervously. Next to him sat the superintendent of the Philadelphia, Wilmington & Baltimore Railroad Company, H. F. Kenney, the man who had helped Pinkerton gather intelligence the previous week.

Pinkerton hurriedly introduced Kenney to the president before ushering Lincoln and Lamon into the buggy's enclosed coach.

The door clicked. The reins snapped, and the coach jerked into motion.

"We're to meet the 10:50 train, on the PW&B line," Pinkerton explained as they lit out. "The train has orders from Samuel Felton to wait for us. It won't leave until we're on board."

The PW&B station was across town. Following Pinkerton's orders, the driver steered the team into a side road, taking a roundabout route, moving slowly to avoid suspicion.

Around 10:45 that night, about twenty blocks away, a crusty old train conductor named John Litzenberg paced the siding of the PW&B switch-yard, trundling angrily back and forth beside his hissing locomotive, compulsively checking his pocket watch. He was due to pull out in five minutes, but there was a problem.

Litzenberg's boss, H. F. Kenney, had told the conductor, in no uncertain terms, that he had better not leave before he was in the possession of an extremely important package. The mysterious parcel—from Samuel Felton, the president of the railroad—needed to be hand-delivered to one J. E. Allen (a favorite alias of Pinkerton's) at the Willard Hotel in Washington, D.C.

To make matters worse, Litzenberg had found out from the station-master that a very sick man would be traveling that night in the sleeping car. Apparently the invalid's sister had purchased the last two sections of the train for their family—none of whom had arrived yet.

The conductor fumed and again yanked his watch fob. Where the hellfire *were* these people?

The covered buggy, its windows shaded, clopped and rattled down the fire-lit streets of nighttime Philadelphia.

Seated in the coach, across from Lincoln and Lamon, Pinkerton nervously puffed his cigar. Every few moments he would turn and raise the rear shade, checking for any suspicious followers.

"It was hard to imagine anyone following them at this point in the journey," writes Richard Rowan, "yet Mr. Pinkerton, with characteristic perfection of detail, left as little to chance as humanly possible."

Pinkerton saw nothing out of the ordinary as they clattered down Market Street to 19th, then up 19th to Vine, then over to 17th Street.

As they approached the PW&B depot, Kenney instructed the driver to slow down "as if on the lookout for someone." A block from the depot, Kenney told the driver to turn down Carpenter—a narrow cross-street lined with a tall, boarded fence—which ran adjacent to the station.

Shadows engulfed the carriage as Kenney signaled for the driver to pull the reins and stop. Inside the coach's cabin, Pinkerton gave a nod and pushed open the door. In tense silence, Abraham Lincoln followed the detective and Lamon out into the cold, opaque darkness.

Pinkerton cautiously led the party around the far corner of the fence.

To avoid the prying eyes of bystanders, Pinkerton ushered the president-elect—his chiseled faced obscured by his scarf, his carpetbag in tow—across the scabrous ground of the switchyard, over petrified rails and frozen, wagon-rutted earth. To a casual observer it would have been a strange sight—that long-legged man in the military coat, sidestepping icy puddles and frozen horse apples, as he followed his burly escort.

They reached the platform. They found a shed unoccupied and slipped inside it.

The time had come for Lamon, the self-styled bodyguard, to part company with his friend and former partner. In the "cold, drafty shed, with its acrid reek of smoke," Lamon reached into his pocket and pulled out a large-caliber, single-shot pocket pistol. He proffered the weapon—grip out—to his mentor.

Lincoln smiled sadly and declined the offer. Pinkerton was not amused. He clenched his fists—an involuntary tic—his way of tamping down emotion.

The detective would comment years later, "I would not for the world have it said that Mr. Lincoln had to enter the national capital armed. If fighting had to be done, it must be done by others than Mr. Lincoln."

Kate Warne was one of those "others"—now standing on the platform outside the rear sleeper car, bundled against the cold, waiting for her sick brother.

Underneath her cloak she carried her own small, single-shot pistol, along with extra charges. An African-American man named Knox stood next to her. Knox was the porter in charge of helping the "family" with their special arrangements.

In the distant cloud of steam, among the scattering of travelers, two figures emerged, slowly coming toward her. A tall, cloaked man in a muffler—hunched with apparent "infirmity"—walked gingerly along on the arm of a compact, barrel-chested man in a bowler hat.

Warne's heart most assuredly began to beat faster. This would be her greatest performance.

"Brother William!" she said, stepping forward to greet the man in the muffler, "you're indeed a sight for a loving sister's eyes!"

Lincoln gave the woman his hand, and Warne helped him up the step-rail of the rear sleeper car. George Bangs, already inside the car—also armed—greeted the twosome in the fashion of a doting older brother. The last passenger to board was the stocky, bearded man in the bowler hat.

Pinkerton paused on the foot-rail, asking Warne for the tickets.

Then he turned and called for the conductor. When Litzenberg appeared at the base of the steps, Pinkerton handed over the tickets, explaining that his sick family member was now onboard.

"The poor chap mustn't be disturbed," Pinkerton cautioned the conductor.

The conductor said he understood and waddled away, and Pinkerton vanished inside the sleeper.

Across the platform, H. F. Kenney, huddling in the shadows, proceeded with one last order of business. As Sigmund Lavine writes:

> *When Kenney saw Allan enter the car, he ran up the platform as if he had just arrived and handed Conductor Litzenberg a package. Litzenberg grabbed it with one hand and signaled to the engineer with the other. Grumbling, the trainman then stowed the package in a locker under one of the seats—he was taking no chance of losing his excuse for leaving five minutes behind schedule. Moreover, he was sure the thing was valuable, otherwise, why would Mr. Felton delay the train's departure for it? Fortunately he was an honest man and made no attempt to peer inside the bundle. If he had he would have been shocked. All it contained was old newspapers!*

In the moments before the train departed the station, Abraham Lincoln settled into a sleeping berth—most likely exhausted from the day's chaos and also relieved that his "performance" was complete, at least for the moment—as the three agents checked their weapons.

Although no official record exists of the specific firearms they carried, it's not implausible that Pinkerton was packing a revolver, probably a Colt model 1860, which would become the workhorse handgun for Union officers and men of Pinkerton's standing. A multiple-shot weapon, the Colt propelled its .44-caliber loads with black-powder caps.

It is likely that Warne and Bangs carried breech-loading Deringers of the single-shot variety—easily concealed in handbags and inner pockets. The .40-caliber balls were cumbersome to reload, but the pivoting barrel allowed seasoned shooters—such as Warne and Bangs—to recover quickly.

On that night, in the moments before the train rolled, cylinders spun, and breeches clicked. All was locked and loaded. It was now only a couple of minutes before 11:00.

Outside, in the darkness, the keen of the whistle pierced the cold.

The train jerked, and the last leg of Lincoln's journey to Washington—the most treacherous portion—began in a thundercloud of vapor.

———

Pinkerton moved through the rear hatch of the sleeper to the parapet.

His revolver, tucked and holstered inside his clerical-black coat, would have felt reassuring at this point. And so it was, there, on that windy precipice, that the husky detective lit another cigar.

As the train gathered speed, Pinkerton peered around the rear edge of the coach. Dead-ahead, in the dense, February darkness, the string of cars approached the first rail crossing along the winding, black Delaware River.

In the distance—like a twinkling star—the light of a lantern flashed. Two short blinks, then a pause, then two additional blinks. The signal told Pinkerton: "All's well! All's well!"

He puffed his stogie.

The train clattered onward, moving south, toward Wilmington.

———

Pinkerton had stationed his operatives at every switchyard, every crossing, and every bridge along the route. The agents used bull's-eye lanterns to send their signals. An oil-lit wick encased in a tin box, the bull's-eye utilized a refractive piece of glass behind a glowing centerpiece (hence the name). The yellow light would have flickered in the wind.

Still, as the first checkpoint passed uneventfully, Pinkerton could not relax.

A "late report" from Timothy Webster had warned Pinkerton of foul play that night among the local military regiments, ostensibly assigned to guard the railroad's property. Many of these regiments were corrupt with secessionists and were actually out to destroy tracks and bridges. Upon hearing the news, Pinkerton had immediately asked Felton to assign trustworthy workmen to go out and pretend to paint and repair all the bridges along the line that night.

These men would be secretly armed, so that they could put up a defense in case of trouble.

"The bitter cold wind stung Pinkerton's eyes," writes Lavine, "as he peered anxiously down the track, looking for the twinkling lights that blinked and vanished as quickly as a firefly's glow."

Unbeknownst to Pinkerton, one other passenger on board that 10:50 express train was armed.

John A. Kennedy, the renowned and capable superintendent of the New York Police Department, rode alone in the swaying shadows of the forward passenger coach. Bound for Washington, oblivious to the machinations of Pinkerton's counterplot, Kennedy had heard no further intelligence from his undercover agent David Bookstaver, nor from the two other operatives he had sent to Baltimore for follow-up.

Now Kennedy had decided to proceed to the capital to "take what steps he could in the safeguarding of Abraham Lincoln in his trip across Maryland." As it would turn out, Kennedy would remain blissfully ignorant of the tense drama unfolding a few mere feet from his seat. His pistol would remain in its holster throughout the night.

As Richard Rowan writes, "Like the detectives put on the case by him, he was unaware of the protection afforded by the railroad operating staff and the Pinkertons."

Inside the swaying, thumping darkness of the sleeping car, in the warmth of a small wood-burning stove, Kate Warne marveled at the proximity of the great man. "She was thrilled," writes Warne biographer Margaret Bzovy, "that she had the opportunity to assist such a marvelous man." But according to Bzovy, Warne also wondered: "Could she actually use the gun in her pocket if she had to?"

These thoughts surely passed through Warne's mind as the president-elect, only inches away from her, made futile attempts to sleep in the cold, drafty berth.

"Lincoln was pushed up into a sleeping berth far too short for him," writes one historian, "so that his huge legs had to be doubled up."

At length, Lincoln emerged from the berth and sat with Warne and Bangs.

Huddling by the stove, the tall man chatted genially with his protectors. In a soft, low voice, Lincoln told stories of his childhood; he told jokes; he listened to Warne and Bangs tell their own stories; and before long the miles began to melt away behind them.

Meanwhile, at regular intervals, Pinkerton would appear in the rear hatchway, wind-blown and anxious, a silhouette in the moonlight, checking on his precious human cargo.

Pinkerton once again marveled at Lincoln's calm, his indomitable spirit, his good humor in the face of such a disquieting passage. "I could not then nor have I since been able to understand," Pinkerton would later observe, "how anyone, under like circumstances, could have manifested such complete mental composure and cheerful spirits."

Pinkerton, on the other hand, was not nearly as sanguine. Later in the journey, in fact, Lincoln and Pinkerton would joke about Pinkerton's almost preternatural ability to foresee dangers.

At this very moment, in fact, as Pinkerton stepped back out onto the wind-lashed perch, he felt with every fiber of his instinct that something was wrong.

━ ⁀ ━

The train made excellent time traversing the upper corner of Delaware and was about to cross the Maryland state line. Within minutes it would be approaching the muddy, black snake of the Susquehanna River and the treacherous territory of rebel spies and Southern sympathizers.

Pinkerton squinted against the wind to see across the dark wetlands.

As the miles clocked by, the pinpricks of firelight in the far distance, dotting a small river town, came into view: Perryman, that wasp nest of secessionism, the place where Timothy Webster had first learned of the diabolical schemes being formulated in Baltimore.

Lighting another cigar—one of the many, many Cubans he would burn down to the nub that night—Pinkerton felt certain something was amiss. He hoped his feeling of unease was merely due to his imagination, his nerves, or perhaps his lack of rest.

"He had almost no sleep for the past three nights," writes William Wise. "Maybe his gloomy feelings were the result of being so very, very weary."

The train approached Perryman. The jerk of the air brakes signaled an imminent stop.

To cross the river, the locomotive would be forced to pull onto a ferryboat—one of the first extremely dangerous and tenuous stages of the journey. Pinkerton craned his thick neck to see around the rear edge of the sleeper.

In the distant night, only blackness stared back at the burly detective. The village of Havre de Grace—now visible on the far side of the Susquehanna—was Timothy Webster's checkpoint. Somewhere along the shadowy banks of the waterway, Webster's lantern would be the all-clear, easing Pinkerton's mind and pointing the way into Baltimore.

But no signal came: only the ominous fabric of darkness along the south bank.

Allan and Joan Pinkerton (Circa mid-1840s). COURTESY OF THE CHICAGO
HISTORY MUSEUM

William and Robert Pinkerton, age
nine and seven respectively. LIBRARY
OF CONGRESS

Joan Pinkerton (Circa mid-1830s).
COURTESY OF THE CHICAGO
HISTORY MUSEUM

Allan Pinkerton at age 41, around the time of Lincoln's ascendancy. COURTESY OF THE CHICAGO HISTORY MUSEUM

A portrait of Timothy Webster (Circa mid-1850s). This picture ran in *Harper's Magazine* around 1910. WIKIMEDIA COMMONS

The original "eye" logo of the Pinkerton National Detective Agency.
WIKIMEDIA COMMONS

(1.) THE ALARM.

"On Thursday night, after he had retired, Mr. LINCOLN was aroused, and informed that a stranger desired to see him on a matter of life and death. * * * A conversation elicited the fact that an organized body of men had determined that Mr. LINCOLN should never leave the City of Baltimore alive. * * * Statesmen laid the plan, Bankers indorsed it, and Adventurers were to carry it into effect."

"The Alarm," a political cartoon created sometime around 1861. COURTESY OF THE ABRAHAM LINCOLN PRESIDENTIAL LIBRARY AND MUSEUM, SPRINGFIELD, ILLINOIS

(3.) THE SPECIAL TRAIN.

"He wore a Scotch plaid Cap and a very long Military Cloak, so that he was entirely unrecognizable."

"The Special Train," another jab at Lincoln's integrity, artist unknown (Circa 1861). COURTESY OF THE ABRAHAM LINCOLN PRESIDENTIAL LIBRARY AND MUSEUM, SPRINGFIELD, ILLINOIS

Portrait of Lincoln disembarking after his Baltimore passage. Illinois congressman Elihu Washburn is on Lincoln's left, the ever vigilant Allan Pinkerton a step behind. COURTESY OF THE ABRAHAM LINCOLN PRESIDENTIAL LIBRARY AND MUSEUM, SPRINGFIELD, ILLINOIS

Portrait of Pinkerton operative Pryce Lewis (date unknown). COURTESY OF THE ST. LAWRENCE UNIVERSITY LIBRARY

General George B. "Little Mac" McClellan (Circa 1862). COURTESY OF THE ABRAHAM LINCOLN PRESIDENTIAL LIBRARY AND MUSEUM, SPRINGFIELD, ILLINOIS

Allan Pinkerton in a late 1861 albumen photograph by Mathew Brady. LIBRARY OF CONGRESS

Allan Pinkerton (seated on right) with operatives; (left to right) George Bangs, William Moore, unknown person next to pole, and Augustus Littlefield. For many years, it has been thought that the person holding the tent pole could be Kate Warne, dressed as a man, and this her only surviving photograph. (It is more likely that this is Hattie Lawton in male disguise; see other descriptions on pages 165 and 184.) LIBRARY OF CONGRESS

Allan Pinkerton (center, leaning against pole) with Secret Service at Antietam, October 1862. LIBRARY OF CONGRESS

Allan Pinkerton (hands in pockets) with operatives at Cumberland, May 1862. Note the unknown African-American agent in the lower right. LIBRARY OF CONGRESS

Allan Pinkerton (front) entertaining visitors from Washington at McClellan's behest. LIBRARY OF CONGRESS

Pinkerton on his trusty Sorrel at Antietam (the horse would perish days later).
LIBRARY OF CONGRESS

Rose O'Neal Greenhow, Secessionist
(Circa mid-1850s). WIKIMEDIA COMMONS

Greenhow with daughter at the Old Capital
Prison (1862). WIKIMEDIA COMMONS

Allan Pinkerton, President Abraham Lincoln, and
General John A. McClernand at Antietam (1862).
LIBRARY OF CONGRESS

"The Late Allan Pinkerton," a portrait from *Harper's
Weekly,* 1884. COURTESY OF THE CHICAGO HISTORY
MUSEUM

CHAPTER TEN

Nocturne on a Lonely Platform

FEBRUARY 23, 1861, 2:11 A.M.

Allan Pinkerton's heart raced as the train began to grind to a halt at the dock. Still no signal from the far bank. Pinkerton faced his first hard decision: He would have to hold the train, and he would have to rethink the entire route. He would also risk alarming not only his illustrious passenger but also the other travelers, potentially jeopardizing the success of the entire counterplot.

Starting toward the hatch, on his way to finding the conductor, he suddenly froze. In his peripheral vision, a faint wink of a light—just over his shoulder—flicked across the dark reaches of the Susquehanna River.

In the distance, Webster's bull's-eye twinkled faintly: One flash . . . another flash . . . pause . . . a third and fourth flash. All's well! All's well!

Meanwhile the train pulled onto the ferry.

As the boat churned and chugged noisily forward, the black surface of the water reflected the cloudless sky. Pinkerton moved his arms and legs to keep warm—and probably also to relieve the incredible tension in his bullish neck and shoulders.

The boat steamed across the river, then deposited the express on the south bank. The last leg of the journey stretched in front of the train, the beauty of the land giving lie to the menacing climate of the border state. The train clamored on.

The cathedrals of rolling hills to the west, the distant moon-gilded currents of the Chesapeake to the east, the hushed roar of Gunpowder Falls—all of it seemed to freeze and solidify in the aspic of a February chill.

They passed Havre de Grace—that hotbed of insurrection into which Webster had ridden like a vengeful ghost two weeks earlier. Pinkerton saw two flashes in the pitch . . . pause . . . then two more. They passed Magnolia—lamplight flickering in the dark. They passed over Gunpowder Bay. They passed Bowleys Quarters and Perry Hall.

Over bridges and through channels of thick forests they rumbled, as the winking of lanterns urged them toward the belly of the beast.

They crossed the outskirts of Baltimore shortly after 3:00 a.m., and soon the land flattened, and the trees cleared, and they were crossing the cinder-strewn switchyard of Calvert Station. Craning his neck, Pinkerton was relieved to see that the opulent depot—its Gothic Italian garrets rising up against the night sky, the stonework luminous in gaslight—was almost completely deserted.

"The city itself," writes Wise, "seemed to be asleep."

The train huffed into the station at exactly 3:30—precisely on time—the sparks spitting off the grinding iron wheels. The whistle shrilled. Chill winds bullwhipped across the empty platform.

Not a soul stirred.

Now Pinkerton would execute the trickiest, most dangerous maneuver of the entire journey to Washington.

—◆—

Before slipping back into the sleeper car, Pinkerton saw, in the near distance, a railroad man in filthy dungarees amble out of the shadows. The man approached the car with an expectant expression.

Pinkerton—tense, hyperalert, ready for anything—leaned down to exchange a greeting, and the man simply whispered, "All's well."

Pinkerton gave a nod.

And now came the uncoupling.

Writes William Wise: "Their sleeping car was disconnected from the train. A team of horses came up, snorting and whinnying, and began to pull the car along the streets. Up one street and down the other, through the dangerous sleeping city."

This was the part of the journey that Pinkerton dreaded the most. He grasped the rear railing of the sleeper as the conveyance rattled along, keeping close watch on the blind alleys and dark corners of the town. Years later, in his memoir, Pinkerton would recall the ruminations crossing his mind at this point:

The city was in profound repose as we passed through. Darkness and silence reigned over all. Perhaps at this moment, however, the reckless conspirators were astir perfecting their plans for a tragedy as infamous as any which has ever disgraced a free country—perhaps even now the holders of the red ballots were nearing themselves for their part in the dreadful work, or were tossing restlessly upon sleepless couches.

The distance between the PW&B depot and the connecting train at the Camden Street Station amounted to a few city blocks, but for Allan Pinkerton that brief horse-drawn interval would have seemed endless. His fists clenched the whole way, he prepared himself for a quick transfer.

At last, the Camden Street Station came into view in the moonlight.

Even at this hour, scattered travelers could be seen pacing across the entrance, awaiting southbound trains. Pinkerton remained on the sleeper's parapet, as the team dragged the car around the switchyard to the tracks.

Pinkerton hopped off the step-rail and turned toward the yard.

His heart practically stopped.

The track was empty. Not a single engine or car occupied the rails. No train waited to shuttle the president to his inauguration. This was not acceptable. In fact—for a man of Pinkerton's fastidious, controlling nature—this was downright catastrophic.

The detective remained stoic. He turned and climbed back up into the sleeper. He quickly told Warne and Bangs to stay alert and to stand guard while he investigated.

The burly Scot went back outside the car and found the stationmaster in his office. Careful not to appear anxious or inordinately alarmed, Pinkerton nodded a greeting and calmly asked, "Where's the train from the west?"

"Delayed," the stationmaster told him. "Maybe an hour—maybe more."

Abraham Lincoln—contorting his long limbs in the cramped berth—finally gave up trying to sleep. Or perhaps he sensed trouble.

Regardless of the reasons, as the muffled voices and footsteps of anonymous denizens rose outside the sleeper, Lincoln climbed out of the compartment and joined Warne and Bangs at the stove.

A moment later, Pinkerton returned to the sleeper car. Did Lincoln read the stiff expression on the detective's face? The man in the bowler hat explained that the Chicago train, which would convey the president to Washington, was late—already more than an hour behind schedule.

Lincoln offered a reassuring smile. "Did you anticipate this delay, too, Mr. Pinkerton?" The gentle, good-natured rib revealed something poignant developing between the two men. "If you say no, I'll be disappointed."

"Sorry to disappoint you, sir," Pinkerton retorted, "but I cannot predict the future—at least not that well."

"Are you sure, Boss?" Warne interjected. "I've been telling Mr. Lincoln about your precautions along the route, and he thinks you're capable of miracles."

"If I were capable of miracles," Pinkerton mused, "we'd already be in Washington."

The noise outside the sleeper grew. Liquor-fueled voices chortled. Scuffling footsteps approached. Perhaps the taverns had closed—or perhaps something worse was going on. Perhaps word had somehow leaked and spread of the important passenger waiting in the sleeper.

At some point—as more than one historian has suggested—Pinkerton would have likely extinguished the lights. He would have made sure that Lincoln stayed in the shadows. It would have been as dark as a tomb in that sleeper car. The minutes would have crawled.

They lowered their voices. And waited. And still the minutes dragged.

"Does this waiting make you nervous, Mr. Pinkerton?" The president-elect's Kentucky rasp broke the tense silence of the shadowy cabin. Another hour had passed. The voices outside the sleeping car had grown more feral, intoxicated, rambunctious.

Pinkerton looked down at his clenched fists. "I'm afraid that it does, Mr. Lincoln."

"In your profession," Lincoln went on, "I should think the unexpected must occur very often."

Indeed it did.

And it was about to occur again.

Inside the sleeper cabin, the sound of low, secretive voices reached a momentary lull. They had been waiting for nearly two hours now—an eternity, considering the situation—and Lincoln was temporarily out of stories. Pinkerton had just finished telling how he had become a detective, and now the muffled voices outside the car dwindled as well.

The silence ratcheted the tension with the pressure of a vise. The gloomy darkness inside the sleeper must have seemed even darker at that point. It was a sticky darkness, full of faint, unidentified noises.

Outside the shaded window closest to where Lincoln sat came the shuffling sound of drunken footsteps. The footsteps paused.

The unidentified figure—only inches away from Lincoln—began to sing.

The slurred, inarticulate, phlegmy crooning could not have sounded more sinister.

The singing seemed to go on forever. Was it a signal? Was it a taunt? Was it an overture to violence? Or was it merely the inebriated drone of a reprobate?

The song being butchered outside Lincoln's window—composed by a Northerner only two years earlier—originated in the blackface minstrel shows in New York. It was used as a "walk-around" number (in which performers preened and waved their lampblack-painted hands).

Written in high-comic style by Daniel Emmett of Bryant's Minstrels, it was sung in an exaggerated version of African-American vernacular. The song told the story of a freed black slave pining for the beautiful plantation of his youth:

Well I wish I was in de land of cotton
Old times dar am not forgotten
Look away! Look away! Look away! Dixie Land.

In Dixie Land whar I was born in,
Early on one frosty mornin',
Look away! Look away! Look away! Dixie Land.

For the young nation the song had been an instant success and even became a favorite of Lincoln's—it was played often during his 1860 campaign—but by 1861 the song had taken on a new context. Secessionists appropriated the sentimental tribute as an anthem of rebellion—especially the stanza that climaxes with the line, "In Dixie Land I'll take my stand / To live and die in Dixie."

The *Natchez Courier* would eventually crown it as "The War Song of Dixie."

But on that cold, crystalline February night, coming through the walls of a stranded sleeper car, the dissonant serenade must have put gooseflesh on the arms of the four souls waiting in the dark.

It is not unlikely that Pinkerton, Warne, and Bangs all reached for the hand-grips of their pistols.

Perhaps recognizing the volatile situation, Lincoln glanced sadly at the detective. Very softly, under his breath, the president-elect said, "No doubt there will be a great time in Dixie by and by."

Pinkerton tried to smile.

The singing continued.

"Such impressive songs," Lincoln whispered, "and sung with such moving fervor."

Warne smiled. "Oh, there are many patriots in Baltimore."

This elicited soft laughter from all the gentlemen in the sleeper.

But the laughter, alas, was short-lived.

CHAPTER ELEVEN

In the Kiln of Prophecy

FEBRUARY 23, 1861, 5:32 A.M.
Did Kate Warne jump when she finally heard the steam whistle of the connecting train shatter the predawn stillness? Perhaps she and her traveling companions all started slightly—their nerves wound as tight as armature wires.

The Chicago train rolled into the station, and the whetstone keen of iron wheels must have sent sighs of relief throughout the sleeper car. Perhaps the hammers of breech-loaded pistols were slowly, discreetly eased back into their safety positions.

Allan Pinkerton rose and exited through the rear hatch, taking his place on the parapet, as the couplers slammed and latched onto the sleeper coach.

Within minutes, the Chicago train completed its loading and transfer rituals, then slowly started out of the depot. The sleeper lurched as the engine pulled it clear.

At long last Abraham Lincoln was moving again, traveling south under the dawning light of the eastern sky.

———

It took only half an hour for the train to complete the last portion of its journey. Shortly after 6:00 in the morning, on February 23, 1861, the express bellowed into Washington Station in a thunderhead of vapor and noise.

When the sleeper coach finally jolted to a stop, it must have felt to Lincoln as though he had landed on a foreign shore. "Thank God this prayer meeting's over," Lincoln muttered, more to himself than anyone else.

Pinkerton exited the coach first, checking the crowded platform.

The drawn, sleepless faces of Timothy Webster and other operatives greeted "the Boss" at the foot of the step-rail. The depot swarmed with travelers arriving and departing, and Pinkerton made sure it was safe.

At last, the famous passenger appeared in the rear doorway of the sleeper with a sheepish expression. He descended the steps slowly, heavily. Writes Arthur Orrmont:

> *Surrounded by Pinkerton men, the president, exhausted from sleep-lessness and the strain of his journey, moved slowly toward the exit. A corner of his traveling shawl dragged along the ground, and Allan Pinkerton bent forward and picked it up.*

Some of the faces in the crowd turned and recognized the tall, lanky individual towering over his companions, being escorted like an anonymous king. As Lincoln approached the exit, an old friend of his, Illinois congressman Elihu Washburne, hurried up and excitedly shook the man's hand.

Accounts vary as to whether Washburne knew of the counterplot. But what is certain is this: Pinkerton worried that danger still existed, especially if the president-elect were surrounded by a crush of admirers.

"No talking here!" the detective interrupted the effusive congressman.

Washburne turned to Pinkerton and said with great indignation, "And who might *you* be, sir? Your face is unfamiliar to me."

"That's Allan Pinkerton," Lincoln told the man. "And his face won't be unfamiliar to you very long."

———⁓

William Seward greeted the president-elect outside the front of the depot with a waiting carriage. Pinkerton remained at Lincoln's side until he was safely ensconced in the covered buggy.

Seward told the driver to proceed to the Willard Hotel at Fourteenth and Pennsylvania—a celebrated establishment within view of the White House.

The Pinkerton team rode in a second carriage behind Seward's.

When Lincoln finally arrived at the place he would be lodging for the next two weeks, Pinkerton watched him vanish inside the entrance of the lavish hotel. Pinkerton later recalled:

On his arrival at the hotel, Mr. Lincoln was warmly greeted by his friends, who were rejoiced at his safe arrival, and leaving him in the hands of those whose fealty was undoubted, I withdrew.

—————

Webster took the next train back to Baltimore, and Pinkerton and Warne checked into a local hotel of more modest means than the Willard.

It was at this meager inn that Pinkerton sent a coded telegram to Norman Judd in Harrisburg:

PLUMS ARRIVED WITH NUTS THIS MORNING

Identical telegrams dashed over the wires to Samuel Felton and E. S. Sanford in Philadelphia. In Harrisburg locked doors flew open and reporters scurried for the nearest telegraph office to file their stories of the Secret Nocturnal Passage of Abraham Lincoln to Washington.

Upon hearing the news, Ward Lamon wanted to telegraph the entire story of the counterplot to the *Chicago Journal*, but Pinkerton dissuaded him. Tensions between Lamon and Pinkerton kindled into a feud. Some believe the animosity between the two men had begun the night before, when Pinkerton scorned Lamon's offering of a pistol to the president-elect.

Years later, Lamon would write a biography of Lincoln that dismissed Pinkerton's counterplot as nonsense, and worse, a political faux pas. "Afterwards, Lincoln was convinced," Lamon wrote, "that he had committed a grave mistake in listening to solicitations of a professional spy and of friends too easily alarmed."

Over the next few days, the world press would have a grand time mocking Lincoln's surreptitious passage to Washington. Political cartoonists would caricature the Scotch plaid cap and the cattle-car hideaway. The prominent Southern newspaper, the *Charleston Mercury*, opined, "Everybody here is disgusted at this cowardly and undignified entry." Even Pinkerton noted how Lincoln later came to regret "stealing into the capital life a thief in the night." But, as Pinkerton is quick to add, Lincoln also stubbornly insisted to one of his visitors, "It ain't best to run a risk of any consequence for look's sake."

But for proof of the dangers averted, one need look no further than the crowds that lined the streets outside Calvert Station in Baltimore that day.

The special train from Harrisburg, originally scheduled to convey the president-elect through Baltimore, arrived at Calvert Station in all its requisite pomp and circumstance around 11:00 that morning.

Even though scurrilous rumors had circulated throughout Baltimore that Lincoln had availed himself of an earlier train and was already in Washington, thousands lined the streets outside the depot and along the route to the Eutaw House, where the presidential party was scheduled to lunch that day before departing for the capital.

Minutes later, Mary Lincoln and the boys, and the rest of the party—including Judd, Lamon, Sumner, Davis, Pope, Nicolay, and the rest—walked down that narrow passageway between the station and the street. Norman Judd must have had his hackles up as he crossed this menacing threshold. This was the lion's den. Hungry eyes were every-where. Were the conspirators eagerly scanning the party for the tall man who would never appear?

Exiting the station without incident, the party traveled in carriages down Calvert Street to the noisy jeers of the mixed crowd. Huge luggage wagons, piled high with trunks—the telltale initials, "A.L.," scrawled on many of the tags—followed the carriages.

By this point, the absence of Lincoln had become known to many, and it was almost as though the crowd had resorted to shouting at the trunks, taking out their frustration on the luggage.

"There was a very large trunk or two in the collection," it was later reported in the *Baltimore Sun*, a vehemently anti-Lincoln newspaper. "And it was suggested that the lost president-elect might have been stowed away in one of them, to be smuggled through, but his great reputed length at once dissipated that idea. The crowd, however, having nothing better to escort, escorted the baggage."

By the time the procession reached the Eutaw House, the unruly mob had grown to ten thousand—including a large contingent of Southern sympathizers. The mood had gone sour. As the carriages came to a halt, the crowd gave, in the words of Mackay, "three terrific cheers" for the Confederacy, three more for Jefferson Davis, and finally, with much venom and malice, three loud and prolonged groans for Abraham Lincoln.

"Had the president-elect been present," writes James Mackay, "there is no doubt that his life would have been in jeopardy, plot or no plot."

———

In Baltimore that morning, not long after the first rays of sun drove the shadows from the back alleys and secret lairs of secessionists, Cypriano Fernandina and his fellow conspirators stewed in the anticlimax of their foiled assassination. One by one they shifted their plans from aggression to evasion.

———

Meanwhile, in Washington, Lincoln had breakfast at the Willard with William Seward—"choosing from an elaborate menu," writes Goodwin, "of fried oysters, steak and onions, blancmange, and pâté de foie gras."

Afterward, Seward escorted the president-elect to the White House for a meeting with outgoing chief executive James Buchanan, described by Goodwin as "tall, stately, [and] stiffly formal in the high stock he wore around his jowls." Buchanan, the only U.S. president who never married, had his niece, Harriet Lane, serve as hostess for the surprise visitor.

After meeting with the cabinet, as well as with General Winfield Scott, Lincoln rode for an hour through the streets of Washington, discussing the pressing issues of the day with Seward. It began to rain. The dismal, chill weather reflected the grim, uphill battle facing Lincoln in the coming months. Seward suggested they return to the hotel. Mary was due soon, and Lincoln had many meetings to attend that evening.

But he had one piece of unfinished business that would not be on any formal schedule.

———

After enjoying a bath and a late breakfast, Allan Pinkerton received word that the president-elect desired to see him at the Willard for a brief meeting. Kate Warne should come along as well.

Pinkerton and Warne took a carriage to the Willard, and there, in one of the lavish parlors they found Lincoln in a gracious, appreciative state of mind. After what biographer Richard Rowan calls a "firm hand clasp" for each benefactor, Lincoln offered, in the words of Pinkerton, "warm expressions of thankfulness" to the detectives for their exemplary duty.

To Kate Warne, Lincoln softly said, "I am sensible, ma'am, of having put you to some inconvenience—not to speak of placing you in danger." Warne's response, the exact words of which are not recorded in any account, were probably humble. As the head of the Female Detective Bureau, she had simply done her job.

Lincoln turned to Pinkerton and commented dryly, "I believe it has not hitherto been one of the prerequisites of the presidency to acquire in full bloom so charming and accomplished a female relation."

"That she is, sir," Pinkerton said with a smile.

"Mr. Pinkerton," Lincoln said then, as if turning a page to a new chapter. "Such talents as yours should be used. You will be hearing from me."

"I am delighted, sir." Pinkerton then chose his words carefully. "About the plotters . . . do you wish their arrest?"

The president shook his head. "I have no desire to make martyrs out of madmen and cowards."

Pinkerton returned to Baltimore that evening, after having completed, in the words of Richard Rowan, "the first experiment in official secret service."

Arriving at the Baltimore station at dusk, Pinkerton ran into J. H. Luckett, the secessionist broker from whom Pinkerton had probed information. The man was on his way out of town and "was very excited and swore against those damned spies who had betrayed him."

Proceeding immediately to the South Street office, Pinkerton repressed his desperate need for sleep. Completely spent and bone-tired, he still could not resist meeting with Webster and Davies for one last postmortem on the counterplot (and also, perhaps, a well deserved bit of schadenfreude at the expense of the foiled conspirators).

The rendezvous between the three detectives was a low-key yet jovial affair. Cigars came out, along with a finger or two of whiskey for the younger men, as the private parlor at the Relay House droned with the fraternal buzz of battlefield tales. Writes Rowan: "[At] South Street that night . . . a trace of a grin or even a derisive chuckle would not provoke indignation."

According to Davies, the conspirators learned of the dodge as early as 9:00 that morning. Many of them, indignant and frustrated, whined of "Yankee slickness" and vowed revenge. Like vermin exposed to the light, the ringleaders fled the city. Guy's Restaurant sat practically deserted that night. Fernandina was gone. The Barnum suffered a mass exodus. Even Marshal Kane, the head of the corrupt police force, had packed up his family and lit out for Richmond.

It seemed that the plotters had not only been foiled, but they had also been spooked. To Fernandina and his minions, one historian writes, "an underground swarm of Yankee police were imagined to infest the rebellious town; when all there was or ever *had* been was wholly extemporized and ninety-five percent Pinkerton."

It is not unlikely, however, that Timothy Webster sat in his comfortable chair that night, savoring his Cuban, but focusing his thoughts on darker portents swirling around Perrymansville. Webster wanted to stay in Baltimore for the time being—still under deep cover in the militias—to help the government stanch the tide of war.

But Pinkerton had been away from Chicago too long. He needed to return at once—to address unfinished business at the agency. Many open cases required his attention. Pinkerton needed to tend to security on various railroads circumnavigating the South. He needed Webster—his most valued and dependable operative—back at headquarters.

The obligations of the Pinkerton National Detective Agency would not wait.

The pressure exerting itself on "the Boss" that night—even amid his celebratory chat with his men—would prove so exhausting that the cheerful postmortem would come to an abrupt, unexpected close.

As Harry Davies continued his breathless report, happily detailing the furtive activities of fleeing conspirators, Timothy Webster suddenly nudged the Frenchman in the ribs. "Stop, Harry," Webster said.

"What?" Davies looked at Webster.

"Can't you see?" Webster nodded toward the boss. "The chief's not with you anymore."

Davies glanced over at Pinkerton and saw that he had fallen fast asleep in his chair, his cigar still smoldering.

Chapter Twelve

That Which Is Most Dangerous

MARCH 1861

The landslide of events leading to war tumbled and fell, one after another, over the next sixty days.

On March 4, Abraham Lincoln marked his inauguration with a carefully drafted speech that groped for peaceful purchase on the slippery slope of secessionism. "We are not enemies, but friends," he opined to a vast crowd stretched out below the east portico of the Capitol building, the dome still under scaffolds, in the throes of remodeling.

Washington, D.C.—ostensibly a border city surrounded by hostile elements—would become a porous war zone in the coming months. On inauguration day, General Winfield Scott had stationed sharpshooters on the roofs of buildings along Pennsylvania Avenue, as well as a battery of light artillery on Capitol Hill. All passageways to the Capitol had been boarded to avoid assassination attempts.

"We must not be enemies," Lincoln went on. "The mystic chords of memory, stretching from every battlefield, and patriot grave, to every living heart and hearthstone, all over this broad land, will yet swell the chorus of the Union, when again touched, as surely they will be, by the better angels of our nature."

Reaction to the address, in the words of historian David Herbert Donald, was "predictable": "In the Confederacy it was generally taken to mean that war was inevitable." Prominent Southern newspapers such as the *Charleston Mercury* viewed the pronouncement from "the Ourang-Outang at the White House" as "the tocsin of battle."

The *Columbus Daily Capital City Fact* went further. It predicted that Lincoln's policies would ensure that "blood will stain the soil and color the waters of the entire continent—brother will be arrayed in hostile front against brother."

In the meantime, Pinkerton, back in Chicago, struggled to focus his restless ambition on the routine work of his agency. Pinkerton writes of this period in *The Spy of the Rebellion*: "I was engaged in the energetic practice of my profession as a detective, which, large as it was, and constantly increasing, required a personal supervision, which absorbed my undivided attention."

Micromanagement notwithstanding, Pinkerton somehow found time to court the press during these weeks. Captivated by the bold, ingenious counterplot in Baltimore, newspaper reporters clamored for interviews. "A great believer in the value of publicity *after* a case was solved, Allan answered all their questions," writes Sigmund Lavine, "characteristically stressing the fact that he could have accomplished nothing without the aid of his loyal operatives." Singling out Timothy Webster, Pinkerton told one interviewer, "He among all the force who went with me deserves the credit for saving the life of Mr. Lincoln, even more than I do."

Pinkerton had no idea, however, of how large Webster would soon loom in the destiny of the nation.

On March 9, Lincoln's cabinet met to debate what to do about a South Carolina federal garrison called Fort Sumter. Considered one of the strongest fortresses ever built, the brick ramparts, with eighty-five soldiers under the command of U.S. Army Major Robert Anderson, stood on a small craggy island at the mouth of Charleston Bay—deep in the heart of Confederate territory—a sort of symbolic blemish on the defiant face of Southern independence.

Rebel forces, led by General P. G. T. Beauregard, had surrounded the stronghold, starving it of supplies, and the standoff had become a sort of ticking time bomb in the showdown between North and South. Beauregard, a highly skilled military tactician, had dazzled his gunnery teacher at West Point years earlier, serving for a time as the instructor's assistant.

That very instructor, Major Robert Anderson, now huddled in the sights of Beauregard's cannons.

Lincoln felt that the crisis would likely blow over and diplomacy would keep things from deteriorating further. But dissenting voices favored immediate evacuation. Emissaries—including Ward Lamon—traveled to South Carolina hoping to find a solution.

Anderson reported that the situation was hopeless, and his forces could not hold out past April.

Throughout March, Pinkerton barely saw Joan and the children. The distractions of the agency, as well as a vague sense of unfinished business with the U.S. government, became all consuming.

Pinkerton's eldest son, William, now fourteen, would begin to gravitate toward the family business. The pull of detective work on an imaginative, strong-willed boy would have been irresistible, and William would soon insinuate himself into the operation.

But most importantly, Pinkerton found himself obsessed at this time by a notion brewing in the back of his mind, an idea born out of his improvised "protective service" on the preinaugural journey.

The coming weeks would put the concept to the test.

On March 28 Lincoln ordered the evacuation of Fort Sumter—but for some reason changed his mind. Perhaps out of his innate optimism, Lincoln decided a week later to send additional troops to relieve Anderson, perhaps to buy time. By April 11, the Confederate Congress lost its patience and gave Beauregard the orders to fire on the garrison.

At 3:20 a.m., on April 12, Confederates sent word to Anderson that they would open fire in one hour. At 4:30, a single mortar round bloomed in the darkness—exploding in the black sky over the island garrison. A tremendous, roaring volley of mortar fire from forty-three separate guns at Fort Moultrie followed.

Sumter—designed to hold out against a naval assault but vulnerable to land-based cannons—became a fountain of deadly light. Anderson attempted to return fire with his meager resources, but after constant bombardment for thirty-three and a half hours, resulting in the deaths of two soldiers, Anderson gave up. At 2:00 p.m. April 13, Anderson called for a truce and officially surrendered.

The American Civil War had begun.

On April 15 President Lincoln issued a call for seventy-five thousand volunteers. Over the next few nights, fires erupted in the darkness along the Philadelphia, Wilmington & Baltimore rail lines. Shadowy figures climbed telegraph poles and slashed wires connecting the Northern cities to Washington. Explosions rocked the Maryland countryside, as bridge trestles collapsed and switchyards smoldered.

On April 19, the Sixth Massachusetts Infantry Regiment, attempting to cross Baltimore to get to Washington Station, found itself ambushed by angry mobs screaming, "Death to the Union!"

Pinkerton's prophecy was coming true night after night, as the insurgents and hostile militia unleashed their reprisals and sabotaged the communication arteries of the North. Washington was effectively amputated from the rest of the Union, and soon the only way to get critical messages to the capital was via the stealth and cunning of undercover couriers.

A lone traveler moved through the Pennsylvania dusk with silent, dispassionate haste.

At Philadelphia he hailed a carriage and rode to the Baltimore depot. Another train sped him through the night to the Perryville station. Due to ruined rail lines and collapsed bridges, the train could go no farther, so the traveler, a handsome Englishman in a long greatcoat, took a small boat across the Susquehanna.

At Havre de Grace the Brit talked his way into a covered coach and then rode to the outskirts of Baltimore, where hostile secessionist militia stopped the wagon. The traveler recognized one of the militiamen, a fellow conspirator from Perrymansville.

The traveler—after explaining to the soldier that he was an emissary of the Confederacy carrying dispatches to Southern sympathizers in Washington—received a "talismanic pass" in the form of a small document. The permit, to be shown to Confederate guards and rebel forces along the way, enabled the traveler to proceed uninterrupted across the skirmish-torn roads leading into the capital.

Outside Washington the traveler was arrested and detained in a temporary jail. But once the federal guards realized the courier's true identity, they released him and escorted him to the White House.

Less than an hour later, Timothy Webster was being ushered into the office of John Nicolay. Webster had carried, all the way from Chicago, important documents that Kate Warne had sewn inside the collar lining of Webster's waistcoat. The courier now "took off his coat, tore off the collar, slit the lining of his vest and removed the messages."

Minutes later, Webster was alone with the president in his private office.

"I hear you are hard on clothes," Abraham Lincoln quipped from across the room. The president sat at his desk, examining the dispatches. "You have brought quite a bit of mail with you, Mr. Webster—more, perhaps, than it would be safe to attempt to carry another time."

"Yes, sir," Webster agreed. "I don't think I'd like to carry so much through Baltimore again."

"Mr. Webster, you have rendered the country an invaluable service."

The president, at this embryonic stage of the war, would have put a high premium on timely communication. Over the last several days, in the wake of all the sabotage, prominent Chicagoans had come to the Pinkerton Agency in order to get vital information through to Washington. The expediency and quiet competency with which Webster completed his task was one of the factors that was about to change the way military intelligence would be gathered.

"I'm glad to be of any service," Webster told the president, "and I've done nothing more than my duty. If you have any further commands for me, Mr. President, I'm ready to obey them."

Lincoln assured Webster that he would avail himself of these vital services soon enough.

＊＊＊

Over the waning days of April, the wheels of fate began turning swiftly for Pinkerton.

On April 23, Pinkerton's old friend from the Illinois Central Railroad, George McClellan—the aristocratic West Point prodigy—accepted the command of the Ohio militia. Writes historian James Mackay:

This was an immense task, for the state arsenal at Columbus had little equipment, and much of that dated from the War of

*Independence. He had no money, few officers and men, no orders
and no supplies. To make matters worse, Ohio was cut off from
Washington by the riots in Baltimore, and the neighboring state
of Kentucky was unstable, with Confederate sentiment growing
stronger by the day.*

In his herculean effort to organize the haphazard resources of Ohio,
Major General McClellan began to ponder—almost simultaneously
with his former business associate Pinkerton—the need for a formal
intelligence-gathering unit.

"Military intelligence," writes Mackay, "was another matter which
was then barely understood and certainly undervalued." But McClellan—who would soon be promoted at the youthful age of thirty-four to
major-general of the Union army, the second highest-ranking officer after
General Scott himself—saw the answer to the intelligence question in the
form of a stocky Scottish detective from Chicago.

Pinkerton, at this same time, sent Timothy Webster back to Washington with two important letters for the president on the subject of
intelligence.

The passage back to the capital became increasingly precarious and unstable. Webster was nearly lynched in Pennsylvania. His guise as a Southern
dandy began to draw suspicion from all quarters, and he was threatened
with arrest at every turn.

When he finally arrived in Washington, the materials in the secret
compartments sewn into the lining of his stylish waistcoat were retrieved.

Ushered by military guards into the beleaguered chambers of the
White House, Webster met with Lincoln in a private office, handing the
president a pair of messages.

The first letter, from Norman Judd, recommended that Lincoln consider the Pinkerton Agency for wartime intelligence. "His men can live
in Richmond and elsewhere with perfect safety," Judd enthused. "I have
no doubt the importance of this, surrounded as you are by traitors." Judd
closed the message with the following admonition: "Aggression is the only
policy now."

Lincoln turned his attention to the second letter, addressed to "His
Excellency A. Lincoln, Prest. of the U.S.," from A. Pinkerton:

When I saw you last I said that if time should ever come that I could be of service to you I was ready. If that time has come I am on hand.

I have in my Force from Sixteen to Eighteen persons on whose Courage, Skill, and Devotion to their country I can rely. If they with myself at the head can be of service in any way of obtaining information of the movements of Traitors, or Safely conveying your letters or dispatches, on that class of Secret Service, which is the most dangerous, I am at your command.

In the present disturbed state of affairs I dare not trust this to the mail. . . .

Secrecy is the great lever I propose to operate with. Hence the necessity of this movement (if you contemplate it) being kept Strictly Private, and that should you desire another interview with the Bearer that you should so arrange it as that he will not be noticed.

The bearer will hand you a copy of a Telegraph Cipher, which you may use if you desire to telegraph me.

My Force comprises both Sexes—all of good character and well skilled in their business.

After carefully considering both messages, Lincoln prepared a response.

Finishing the note, he sealed the document and handed it over, the ink still wet, to Webster.

In light of the exceedingly treacherous territory to be crossed, Lincoln asked the courier how he planned to carry the message.

Webster showed the president a beautiful, lacquered walking stick. The cane "unscrewed into two hollow cylinders," which fascinated Lincoln. "If you would like one of these for yourself, Mr. President," Webster said then, "I can have it sent from Philadelphia."

Lincoln laughed. "I'm just a country boy, Mr. Webster. On the day I can swing so elegant a cane without looking foolish, New York will secede from the Union."

The United States Secret Service—as it exists today—traces its origins back to July 5, 1865, not long after the Great War Between the States had etched its bloody story on the annals of history. On that date, William P. Wood—former superintendent of the infamous Old Capitol Prison, a volatile man whom Mackay calls a "rather sinister figure"—was named its first chief officer.

The reference in Pinkerton's letter, however, to a "Secret Service" may arguably be the first time in history such an agency was proposed. It certainly signaled the beginning of a complex, maddening, dangerous game of cat and mouse with the convolutions of insurrection.

Lincoln's reply to Pinkerton's proposal, which Webster spirited back to Chicago, said very simply: "Come to Washington as soon as possible for your services are greatly required for the government."

Part III
The Thorn of the Rose

O Virgin daughter of Babylon; sit on the ground without a throne, / O daughter of Chaldeans! / For you shall no more be called tender and delicate. . . . / Your nakedness shall be uncovered, and your shame shall be seen. / I will take vengeance, and I will spare no man.

—Isaiah 47

CHAPTER THIRTEEN

A Nest of Lovely Snakes

SUMMER 1861

In the early months of war, few Washingtonians—at least those who called themselves Union loyalists—would have ever imagined that a woman of such estimable status and elegance as Rose O'Neal Greenhow could be a Confederate spy.

Mrs. Greenhow moved in the rarified air of the capital's high society—hobnobbing with the wives of senators, attending lavish functions in the ballrooms and banquet halls of the city. Like an exotic bird of prey, she changed her colors according to the needs of each social occasion. She wore the gowns and the gild of the upper crust, and she spoke well the small talk of the privileged Northern class.

"From her first appearance in Washington," writes biographer Ishbel Ross, "Rose's fresh looks, her knack for repartee, the swing of her agile body, the sparkle of her vivid face between the slats of her bonnet, tended to ruffle the emotions of political warriors who found cold comfort in the boardinghouse atmosphere of the capital while Congress was in session."

In many ways the socialite Rose Greenhow represented the strange dichotomy gripping Washington in the mid-nineteenth century—a place of solemn ceremony and governance on top of a crumbling foundation of mud and rot. Greenhow embodied the paradox of high ideals mingling with baser instincts.

The essence of Washington, D.C., Greenhow's natural habitat, could be found in the lovely "whalebone" crinoline hems of ladies' skirts—whalebone, made from the delicate horn-like teeth of Baleen whales, gave dresses that patented grandiose fullness and stiffness—dragging, as they did on a regular basis, in the ubiquitous filth.

By the time war had broken out, Washington's population had exceeded seventy thousand.

Nestled in the bosom of two branching tributaries of the Potomac—the cross-hatch of roads stretching to the north and east from the Capitol dome like a spider web—the town soon became a vast, overcrowded army camp, practically under siege by an enemy whose own capital was less than a hundred miles away.

Drunken bluecoats wandered the back streets of the capital at night. Taverns, saloons, and gambling dens—open until midnight—lined practically every major road, and the Canterburies (music halls) were hotbeds of vice where customers were routinely drugged, robbed, or sometimes even murdered.

Washington also attracted prostitutes by the trainloads. They came from New York, Boston, Philadelphia, and Chicago—originally to serve the "seasonal business" during congressional sessions—now to exploit the anything-goes atmosphere of the militarized zone. High-class brothels along Pennsylvania Avenue hosted senators, congressmen, and government executives.

In this chaotic, amoral environment, Confederate agents blended in with the greatest of ease. Women with rebel sympathies regularly traded intimacies for the secrets of patrons of bordellos and gambling halls. Tongues loosened by drink divulged all manner of government business. It would prove to be a herculean task for the Northern authorities to stanch this hemorrhage of information.

The pandemonium in the capital that summer mortified the methodical, punctilious Allan Pinkerton. Answering Lincoln's April 28 summons to Washington, the detective presented his notions of a secret intelligence service to the president's new cabinet, expecting to be embraced by the besieged heads of government.

"Gentlemen, Southern spies are invading the north like locusts," Pinkerton told the cabinet members in a private meeting on May 3rd, "They have a big head start already." The detective went on to warn the cabinet that traitors were in their midst and that Washington was especially vulnerable. But his proposal to put hundreds of operatives in the field was met with skepticism and derision.

Salmon P. Chase, the secretary of the treasury, was especially dubious. "Sir, I wish you could prove your allegations," he fired back at the detective. "The fact remains that as yet we have not caught a single important Southern agent."

"And why?!" Pinkerton demanded. "Because we have no one to catch them with!"

The meeting ended with nothing accomplished. "Lincoln seemed preoccupied with weightier matters," writes Arthur Orrmont. "He thanked the detective for coming to the capital at his own expense," adding that it was "probably too soon to put a secret service into operation; the new administration was in too great a state of confusion."

One member of the Union cause who was not confused was Major General George McClellan. Struggling to whip the Ohio regiments into a lean fighting force, the intellectual gentleman-soldier shared Pinkerton's pioneering vision for clandestine intelligence gathering. McClellan—a master strategist, often misunderstood by his superiors; a man who would one day employ such innovative wartime reconnaissance methods as giant weather balloons—decided to draft a letter to Pinkerton.

On May 6, stopping at Philadelphia to pick up forwarded mail from Chicago, Pinkerton received the following message from his old friend:

Have heard of your achievement in protecting the President and would appreciate your coming to see me in Cincinnati. Observe caution. If you telegraph me, be sure to use only your first name. Let no one know your plans.

One week later, "E. J. Allen" was born. Using the alias suggested by McClellan, Pinkerton gladly accepted the post of major with McClellan's Department of Ohio (which combined the armed forces of three states—Ohio, Illinois, and Indiana). Assuming the role of a gentleman from Augusta, Georgia—traveling the backwaters on horseback, infiltrating troubled border areas—Pinkerton became head of "McClellan's

Secret Service," overseeing all the intelligence gathering throughout the western theater.

Pinkerton practically idolized the brilliant, cultured McClellan and was galvanized by the opportunity to serve the major general's cause. McClellan told the detective: "If Washington leaves me alone to equip and train a real Union army, I can win the war within twenty-four months."

"How long do you think the war will last otherwise?" Pinkerton asked the general.

"Four or five years, definitely," McClellan answered.

McClellan also agreed to use Timothy Webster, who had gone deeper into the ranks of Southern insurgency, and was now routinely moving freely behind rebel lines. Additionally Pinkerton brought in a half dozen more men and bought a new horse for the rigors of wartime fieldwork.

The chestnut gelding, in its own way, would become one of the detective's key assets throughout the Great Conflict. Sturdy, muscular, built low to the ground, the horse was a sorrel with a rich, rust-colored coat and a long flaxen tail. The animal was built like his master—and just as stalwart in temperament.

Pinkerton spent May and June logging many miles on the back of this staunch animal, collecting meticulous intelligence behind enemy lines. His reports to McClellan during this period, written in his own neat, precise handwriting, reflect the detective's obsessive attention to detail:

> The Rebels have sunk two boats loaded with stone at the mouth of the Kanawha River near the Red House Shoals twenty or thirty miles from Charleston [West Virginia], and they are now erecting a battery of two six-pounders concealed by bushes. There are fifteen hundred troops in the Kanawha Valley, about one thousand near Charleston, say about one mile below on the level ground by the river and about five hundred at the mouth of the Cold near Charleston. . . . There are only fifty soldiers at the Red House. . . . They had little ammunition at either of the above places. . . . The soldiers are equipped with muskets and poor rifles and with the exception of the Kanawha Rangers (100 strong) were very poor specimens of mortality, many not exceeding fifteen years of age.

Pinkerton's destiny, however, now closely aligned with McClellan's, would take a dramatic turn in July.

Virginia, with its alarming proximity to the capital and countless rebel strongholds, became a worrisome territory for the Union. The state had officially seceded in April, and now General Scott sent his top commander, Brigadier General Irvin McDowell, to Bull Run—near the city known today as Manassas, Virginia—with a force of thirty-five thousand troops to suppress Confederate movement.

The chaotic battle with General Beauregard's army—a bloody mêlée, which became known as "Black Monday"—ensued on July 21 around the town of Manassas Junction, only twenty-eight miles from Washington. It was the first great catastrophe for the unseasoned Union army.

General Beauregard knew the Yankees were coming. He had a panoply of spies in Washington, the most gregarious of whom was the irrepressible, charming, refined Rose O'Neal Greenhow. Five days earlier, Greenhow had sent one of her girls—"a brunette with sparkling black eyes"—to the Fairfax County Courthouse with a coded message for General Beauregard. "She took out her tucking comb and let fall the longest and most beautiful roll of hair I have ever seen," one Confederate general later recalled. "She took then from the back of her head, where it had been safely tied, a small package, not larger than a silver dollar, sewed up in silk."

Greenhow had sewn the ciphered warning of the Union's troop strength into the silk, a bit of intelligence she had learned in the boudoir of a high-ranking government official. Learning of McDowell's plans, Beauregard immediately sent for reinforcements, and the subsequent battle went far better for the South than it would have otherwise.

The North suffered great losses at Bull Run: Nearly three thousand men killed, wounded, or missing. An eye-opener for Lincoln and General Scott, the battle signaled to both sides that the war would be greater and bloodier than anyone had imagined—far longer than the ninety-day affair many had predicted. It was also a dark revelation to the jaded, cynical Washingtonians who ventured to Manassas Junction that day with picnic baskets and bottles of wine.

They had come for a pleasant afternoon lounging along the banks of Bull Run Creek, watching the battle as though they were spectators at a game of cricket. What they saw was a gruesome, appalling portent of miseries to come.

The rout at Bull Run was providential for McClellan.

A few weeks earlier, with McDowell still in the planning stages on Manassas, McClellan initiated his own attack in the Kanawha Valley in West Virginia. Using a small attachment of half-trained soldiers, McClellan surrounded and overwhelmed the occupying forces of Colonel G. A. Porterfield, who had been sabotaging railroads and cutting off communication lines into Washington.

The Confederates sent reinforcements, but McClellan's Army of the Ohio prevailed—thanks, in no small measure, to Pinkerton's excellent field intelligence. It was a timely victory. The North needed good news, and it needed professional help for its military, and McClellan delivered on both counts.

"The West Virginia campaign may have been nothing more than a side show, and its battles comparatively insignificant," writes Mackay, "but the newspapers of the North and West eagerly seized on them and magnified McClellan's victories. (He was hyped as a great conqueror and the epithet 'Young Napoleon' was freely used.")

On Monday, July 22, 1861, McClellan received two telegrams.

One was from Washington: "Circumstances make your presence here necessary. Charge [William] Rosecrans or some other general with your present department and come hither without delay." The promise of a promotion seemed implicit.

The other message was from Allan Pinkerton: "The hopes of the nation now are upon you," the detective exclaimed in his note. "All say McClellan is the man. He can and will carry our flag to victory."

McClellan replied to Pinkerton: "Keep me fully posted and be prepared to hear from me that I need your services elsewhere."

Early Tuesday morning, July 23, McClellan left Wheeling, West Virginia, on horseback, with his chief of staff Seth Williams. They caught a train forty-eight miles to the east and arrived in Washington on Friday afternoon.

The next morning President Lincoln met with McClellan and promoted the young strategist to commander of the Army of the

Potomac, comprising McDowell's forces as well as the defenses of the nation's capital.

"I find myself in a new and strange position here," McClellan wrote giddily to his wife, Ellen, that evening. "By some strange operation of magic I seem to have become *the* power of the land."

———

Within days McClellan sent for Pinkerton. The detective writes in his memoir: "It was about this time that the city of Washington was placed under martial law—a measure deemed necessary to correct the serious evils which existed, and to restore order to the city."

Colonel Andrew Porter of the Sixteenth United States Infantry, a spit-shine-stern taskmaster, became the new provost-marshal, taking command of all the available infantry, as well as his own squadron of cavalry.

McClellan declared the city out of bounds to all officers and men except those on public duty. The midnight closing time for taverns was officially moved up to 4:00 in the afternoon. Congress swiftly passed an act prohibiting the sale of liquor to any soldier.

But, in the words of James Mackay, this desperate attempt to buckle down was "a dead letter from the beginning." The capital city—in which Pinkerton arrived on July 30—still thrummed with the feverish pulse of degradation. In a survey of saloons and drinking dens that the detective would soon conduct for McClellan, Pinkerton found no fewer than thirty-seven hundred "fountains of ruin," and "the lowest places of intoxication" occupying all sides of Market Square.

The day after his arrival, Pinkerton found himself in conference with the president and the cabinet. At McClellan's urging, Lincoln and his top men agreed to establish a new agency to be known as The Secret Service of the Army of the Potomac—under the management and control of one Allan Pinkerton.

In *The Spy of the Rebellion*, Pinkerton recalls:

> *I was to have such strength of force as I might require; my headquar-*
> *ters for the time located in Washington. It was arranged that when-*
> *ever the army moved I was to go forward with the General, so that*

I might always be in communication with him. My corps was to be continually occupied in procuring, from all possible sources, information regarding the strength, positions and movements of the enemy. All spies, "contrabands," deserters, refugees, and prisoners of war, coming into our lines from the front, were to be carefully examined by me, and their statements taken in writing.

—

Under the name Major E. J. Allen—officially assigned to the provost-marshal under orders from the War Department—Pinkerton moved into a comfortable house on I Street, which would serve as both office and living quarters.

Pinkerton immediately sent a wire back home to Joan in Chicago, urging her to bring the family to Washington. The house would accommodate the Pinkertons nicely, and the detective needed the stability of his family to gird him in the coming months.

It is not unlikely that Pinkerton felt as though his children were growing up without him. Little Belle was already six years old, and the boys, William and Robert—currently in boarding school in Indiana—were in their teens. In his letter to his wife, Pinkerton must have waxed poetically about "casting their lot with McClellan," because the ever-cautious, ever-perceptive Mrs. Pinkerton wrote back an encouraging yet ambivalent reply.

"I would rather you worshipped President Lincoln," she wrote, "since I suspect that a general is a hero only so long as he wins battles, and no general wins them all." Writes Arthur Orrmont: "In McClellan's case, it was to be a more accurate prophecy than she knew."

Joan agreed to close up the house in Chicago and bring Joanie to the capital within a week. Pinkerton—now with the promise of his wife and daughter soon to arrive, secure in his new post—immersed himself in the business of intelligence gathering.

He began by writing elaborate mission statements and requisitions to McClellan. Insisting that the very existence of his new agency be known to as few people as possible, Pinkerton explained that his operatives would gain access to every walk of life in and around the capital—from the highest to the most menial.

His agents would "have the entrée to the gilded salon of the suspected aristocratic traitors, and be their honored guests, while others will act in the capacity of valets, or domestics of various kinds . . . and all strangers arriving in the city, whose associations or acts may lay them open to suspicion, will be subjected to a strict surveillance."

Pinkerton also informed McClellan of his plans to penetrate enemy lines. Men such as Timothy Webster would focus their energies on obtaining accurate information on enemy positions, the nature of their defenses, the number of troops under their command at various points, and the activities of spies and counterspies.

This massive undertaking would require hundreds of operatives of both genders, uniforms, disguises, firearms, petty cash, identification documents, teams of horses, rolling stock, and much more. McClellan agreed to it all—giving Pinkerton "almost unlimited funds." Disgusted by the state of affairs in Washington, McClellan privately scorned General Scott's strategy for protecting the capital.

What could prevent the enemy from shelling the city from nearby heights? And why in God's name were the streets still, as Arthur Orrmont writes, "filled with straggling officers and men," many of them absent without leave?

"I mean to make a modern army out of all this chaos, and I will!" McClellan declared one day to Pinkerton in a private meeting.

"In order to do that," Pinkerton calmly replied, "you'll have to get rid of the political appointees who hold important military offices. Can you survive the enemies that will make for you?"

The general, taken aback by the detective's stoic Scottish logic, commented humorlessly: "Better watch out major, if you keep on being so good a strategist, I'll make you my chief of staff."

In retrospect, it is not clear whether the comment was a joke or a threat.

～

Working sixteen-hour days, inundating the War Department with detailed reports, Allan Pinkerton focused his attentions on the three main concerns of the Secret Service: military espionage, counterespionage, and a department called "general intelligence."

The counterespionage category devoured most of Pinkerton's time, due to the fact that it targeted rebel spies in the capital: no small order, since the city crawled with all manner of questionable characters.

Pinkerton had his hands full, and his life would acquire an extra degree of complication one day after Joan arrived in Washington with little Joanie, when a visitor was shown into his office.

"Hello, Dad," young William Pinkerton said jauntily upon seeing his father. "You've gained a little weight."

"Bill!" The detective rose and came around his desk. The five-foot-eight fireplug of a man had indeed put on some pounds from all the rich food shared with suspected traitors at ceremonial dinners. "What on earth are you doing in Washington?" the detective asked, rigorously shaking the boy's hand. "You're supposed to be at school."

"There's a war on, Dad," Bill said, glancing around the cluttered office. "No pictures up yet, I see. How's mother?"

Speechless, bemused by this sturdily built, self-possessed boy—the spitting image of Pinkerton himself—the detective merely stared at the wily teen.

"I want to work with you, Dad. I hope you won't argue about it, because I'm here to stay."

Pinkerton narrowed his eyes. "Is that so?"

The boy nodded, displaying the same obstinate, upturned jaw that his father had shown over the years to friend and foe alike. "Think what great experience the Secret Service would be for my work later on at the agency."

"There's one difficulty," the detective told his son. Pinkerton had expected this—William was destined to join the family business—but not so soon. "You're not yet sixteen, Bill. I'd have to get special permission from the president, and of course your mother. Chances are one or both would refuse."

"Oh, Mother's no problem." The boy stared at his father. "Let's go see the president now."

"Hold on there, lad. Lincoln isn't as easy to see as all that. I'll have to write him a letter."

Bill reached for a pencil and paper and sat down as though he were Pinkerton's personal secretary. "Go ahead, Dad, I'm ready for your dictation. How do you address him? 'Dear Mr. President' or 'Dear Abe'?"

Arthur Orrmont writes:

Pinkerton didn't write President Lincoln that day, but shortly after-
ward a note went to the President from I Street regarding William.
Joan had already agreed to let Bill join the Secret Service provided he
took no part in espionage activities that could conceivably end with a
rebel rope around his neck. Nevertheless, and without his father's per-
mission, Bill would go on scouting parties and once narrowly avoided
capture while in civilian dress. Hearing of this, his mother insisted
her adventurous son be given a desk job at the I Street house. Here Bill
acquitted himself reluctantly, but well.

Others in Pinkerton's extended family of intelligence agents would
not be so lucky.

"Webster! You're *here*, are ya?!"

In a crowded, smoky saloon, the bark of a gruff voice startled Timothy Webster.

It came from behind the dapper spy as he sat at a table, trading stories and wine with his fellow rebel sympathizers. For three weeks now
Webster had been living in Baltimore at Miller's Hotel—a haunt for
secessionist ruffians—cavorting with the Southern element (but secretly
following Pinkerton's directives to "gather as much information as possible as to the intentions and movements of disloyal citizens").

In the execution of his duties, Webster had stepped up his convivial,
debauched persona—romancing the town's Southern ingénues and being
the hail-fellow-well-met to all the Copperheads. With his rebel hat now
jauntily tilted on his handsome, long-haired head, he had become the
"returning prodigal son" to the insurrectionists, and he had played the
role to the hilt, telling the funniest jokes, buying the most rounds, and
proclaiming the strongest anti-Union screeds. Webster was also delivering—often in person—a steady influx of intelligence to Allan Pinkerton
in Washington.

But sooner or later—as is the case with all high-wire acts—the tight-rope walker slips and falls: And with this unexpected peal of a booming voice, Timothy Webster's long streak of good luck would begin to change.

Webster turned and saw the owner of the bellowing voice—a town bully named Bill Zigler—one of the ringleaders of the April 19 riots in Baltimore, which ended in bloodshed for many Union soldiers. A big, swaggering lump of a man, Zigler was a venomous rebel with a taste for knife play. More than a few Union soldiers had felt the man's steel.

Giving the thug a blank stare, Webster said, very softly, "Did you speak to me, sir?"

"Yes I 'spoke to you, sir,'" Zigler taunted, mimicking Webster's smooth diction. "I been lookin' for ya, and when I'm finished speakin' my piece, I reckon this town will be too hot to hold you many hours longer."

Webster kept staring. "I don't understand you."

Zigler chortled with laughter. "You been playin' it fine on the boys here for the last three weeks, but damn you I'll spoil your little game!"

"I would appreciate it if you would stop speaking in riddles," Webster said sharply, his honest anger—born out of a fear of exposure—beginning to rise.

"I'll tell ya what I mean!" the bully blustered. "Gentlemen!" Zigler turned to the rest of the party at the table, each of whom sat horror-struck. "This man is in league with the Yankees, and he comes among ya as a spy!"

A dumbfounded silence spread across the room, the men at the table gaping at Zigler.

"Oh nonsense, Zigler." One of Webster's companions spoke up. "You must be drunk. There isn't a better Southern man in Baltimore than Tim Webster."

"I am as sober as the soberest man here," Zigler declared with violence in his eyes. "And I reckon I know what I'm talking about. I saw that fellow in Washington yesterday!"

Webster retorted: "I can well believe you saw me in Washington yesterday for I certainly was there! I was just telling these gentlemen what I saw and heard there."

"Maybe you *were*, but I'll bet you ten dollars you didn't tell them that you had a conversation with *the chief of the detective force* while you were there!"

Years later Pinkerton would write of this incident with pained hindsight. Considering the whirlwind of events that engulfed Timothy Webster over the next four months, the burly Scot most likely saw a turning point here in Webster's fortunes. The detective writes: "Webster, it must be admitted, was wholly unprepared for this. But he realized in an instant that the bully's insinuation must be denied and overcome."

In a split second, in the darkness of that crowded tavern, Webster took decisive action. With feigned rage he howled at Zigler: "You are a liar and a scoundrel!"

"I am, eh?" The ruffian said this through clenched teeth, and before anyone could stop him, Zigler lunged toward Webster.

What happened next happened very quickly. Without missing a beat Webster delivered a tremendous right jab to the bully's face, hitting him square on, right above the bridge of the nose.

Zigler reeled halfway across the room and fell prostrate between two tables.

With an inarticulate roar, Zigler gathered himself up and brandished a knife. He lurched back across the room—directly at Webster—with the blade raised and ready.

Webster calmly drew his pistol—"as if by magic," writes Pinkerton—from the inner lining of his elegant waistcoat and stopped the man cold with the muzzle pressed against Zigler's heart. Zigler balked.

"Stop," Webster commanded in a steady, calm voice. "Hold your distance, you miserable cur, or your blood will be on your *own* head."

Zigler recoiled.

Writes Pinkerton: "The frowning muzzle of the pistol, the unmistakable meaning of those words, and the deadly purpose expressed in the cold, calm face before him were too much even for his boasted bravery." Going pale and stiff, Zigler backed away, muttering to himself.

"Coward," Webster commented softly. "If I served you right, I would shoot you down like a dog; and I'm afraid I can't resist the temptation to do so anyway, if you don't immediately leave the room. Go! And in the future be careful of who you accuse of being in league with accursed Yankees!"

Zigler slunk out of the pub.

Webster holstered his gun, returned to his party, and worked hard to play the indignant reb whose intentions had been besmirched to his friends. His cronies believed him. His cover remained intact.

"I'd as soon suspect Jeff Davis of being a Yankee spy," joked one reveler.

Boisterous laughter rang out across the tavern, but the seams in Webster's guise had begun to show. Soon Baltimore would become too tenuous, too dangerous for Timothy Webster, and he would turn his attentions to other territories in the conflict, territories behind enemy lines, in which he would soon encounter even greater misfortune.

CHAPTER FOURTEEN

Darkening Skies

AUGUST 21, 1861

The sky boiled and threatened throughout the morning, churning with low, dark thunderheads rolling in off the Atlantic. A nor'easter brewed somewhere up in the stratosphere, and residents throughout the Washington, D.C., area shuttered their windows and stabled their horses.

The dismal weather that day reflected the tribulations of those early weeks of the war. Still stinging from its humiliation at Manassas, the Union struggled to find traction—despite the "perfect pandemonium," as McClellan called it, gripping the capital. Meanwhile the great West Point scholar and military mind, Robert E. Lee, was marshaling his forces of over ten thousand Virginians to fortify the Confederacy's eastern army.

To a large extent, this early Southern momentum was due to the hemorrhaging of military intelligence, slipping through the battle lines like water through a sieve. "In our part of the world, there were no secrets," recalls one Southern historian, Harry Thompson, curator of the Port O' Plymouth Museum. "Everybody working on the Confederate side . . . went over to the Union side at some point or another. . . . Everybody knew everybody else's plans."

Even the press seemed complicit. As the war progressed, Lee would actually have Northern newspapers and periodicals smuggled across the Mason-Dixon Line, reading of future strategies and adjusting his battle plans accordingly. Something had to be done. One remedy for this troubling transparency seemed to lie in the apprehension of Southern spies.

And so it was, by late afternoon, on that stormy day in August, that four members of the Secret Service force, led by its burly chief, left the headquarters on I Street and then walked, in the gathering rain, several blocks, to an area of tree-lined streets just northeast of the White House ("Quite a fashionable quarter," writes Pinkerton).

"I was then quite a stranger in Washington," Pinkerton recalls, "and localities were not as familiar to me as they afterward became; I therefore preferred to reconnoiter by daylight."

On this day, however, the sky was so dark it might as well have been night.

By the time Pinkerton and his three operatives reached the mansion at Thirteenth Street, the rain had begun to fall. It was a miserable, steady deluge, sluicing down the wagon-rutted streets and dripping off the walnut trees across from the offending residence. A promise of more violent weather to come crackled behind the rain, comet tails of lightning slashing the dark sky.

Pinkerton relieved the pair of agents who had been stationed behind the trees in the wooded square at the corner. The Thirteenth Street house had been under surveillance for almost a week, with no breaks yet in the case, but tonight would be different—despite the weather—which worsened with each passing moment.

"Umbrellas were a useless commodity," Pinkerton writes of that night, "and, unprotected, we were compelled to breast the elements, which now were warring with terrible violence."

The arduous wait, as Pinkerton would soon learn, would be worth the trouble.

Washington swarmed with female Confederate moles—many of whom fraternized with the highest levels of society or government. Working under his Major Allen pseudonym, Pinkerton had encountered more than a few of these lovely and cunning adversaries at receptions and soirees around town. "Many of these ladies were extremely fascinating in their manners," Pinkerton writes, "and being gifted with great personal beauty and with rare conversational qualities, they had gathered around them a brilliant circle of acquaintances, to whom they dispensed regal hospitalities and most delicate courtesies."

Rumors had circulated that some of these ladies had already snared government officials with these delicate courtesies. Torrid affairs were allegedly going on between the Southern belles and high-level army officials. Some liaisons involved cabinet members.

The names of these grandes dames of the Old Regime went into innumerable reports to army brass. Writes Richard Rowan: "McClellan, in truth, had a voracious appetite for intelligence reports; and the private detective in Mr. Pinkerton made him an indulgent caterer."

One particular name kept appearing in reports and in conversations: Rose O'Neal Greenhow. A society belle with ties to the highest levels of government, she was turning out to be one of the Confederacy's most valued assets.

While in Baltimore, Timothy Webster had learned about Greenhow from an arms dealer named Merrill, who claimed this woman was a secret weapon for the South. Webster had sent many wires to his boss about this individual, and Pinkerton had gotten to know the lady's background in detail long before the assistant secretary of war, Thomas A. Scott, had come to Pinkerton's office on I Street to request a full report on "the baneful activities" of this dangerous jezebel.

Historians have alluded to Pinkerton's fascination with Greenhow—perhaps even *inordinate* fascination—and it does appear as though she became a sort of bête noire for the detective, a sort of dark obsession over those seven days of surveillance.

One thing is certain: The woman became a thorn in the side of General McClellan, who had stepped into Irvin McDowell's shoes after the defeat at Bull Run. "She knows my plans better than Lincoln or the cabinet," McClellan complained of the mysterious widow, "and has four times compelled me to change them."

The woman's name was Rose O'Neal Greenhow, and she was about to become one of Pinkerton's most celebrated and controversial cases.

The brick house—"while not at all imposing in appearance"—encompassed a large lot and rose a full two stories above the landscaped parkway. Inside its shuttered windows were roomy parlors, elevated several feet above the ground, and furnished, in Pinkerton's words, "with every consideration for wealth and tasteful refinement." The main entrance sat at the top of a long flight of stone steps.

On that miserable night, Pinkerton stationed his three other operatives in the rainy, wind-tossed shadows around the property's periphery.

On one flank huddled Pryce Lewis, the young, dapper Brit whom Pinkerton had recruited early in his agency's history, around the same time as Webster. Lewis had put his witty charisma to good use earlier that summer in the Kanawha Valley, where he roamed the countryside disguised as an "Englishman traveling for pleasure"—gathering intelligence that aided McClellan in his early victory in West Virginia.

In Pinkerton's words, "Lewis wore a full beard, and this was trimmed in the most approved English fashion . . . presenting the appearance of a thorough well-to-do Englishman, who might even be suspected of having 'blue blood' in his veins."

On the other flank lurked another English-born operative: John Scully. A man of "coarser nature" than the urbane Lewis, Scully gave off an air of the Cockney workman. He struggled with the high-pressure assignments coming his way now that war had broken out, and he secretly fortified himself with regular nips of alcohol.

In fact, Scully's taste for drink would soon be his (and to some extent, the agency's) undoing. But on that rain-swept night, Scully—like the others—managed to keep his eyes glued to the entrance of the Greenhow house.

The third operative, Samuel Bridgeman, took up a position on the far side of the property. Bridgeman had accompanied Lewis as a groom and man-servant on their reconnaissance trips across West Virginia. Pinkerton later would call Bridgeman a "jolly, good-natured, and fearless Yankee" who had proven himself on several occasions "worthy of trust and confidence in matters that required tact as well as boldness, and good sense as well as keen wit."

The darkness of dusk that night, as well as the violence of the storm, proved beneficial to Pinkerton's team. Most passersby had retired to their shelters, and those stragglers who did brave the elements paid no attention to any matter other than simply getting home.

Pinkerton crept across the street and huddled in the shadows beneath the front windows of the house.

He saw lights burning behind the parlor windows but could not get a good enough angle to see inside the partially drawn shades. For the past week Pinkerton had silently cursed the height of those windows, which lay just beyond the reach of his sight line on the ground. Now, with the torrential winds buffeting him, he got angry enough to take immediate and decisive action. A workman must occasionally shore up an uneven seam with brute force; the instincts of the barrel cooper, bending the wooden stave with bare hands, flowed through the detective.

Pinkerton called out—under his breath—just loud enough for Lewis and Scully to hear him. The two agents came over. Pinkerton kicked off his boots. In his memoir, the detective writes: "I made use of their strong, broad shoulders in a manner quite novel to me, and quite ludicrous, no doubt, to a passerby who did not understand the situation."

Positioning the two men side by side, facing the front windows of the house, Pinkerton climbed on their shoulders and got his first decent view of another world. In the pale light of candles and shaded lamps, the detective saw a world of wealth and refinement, of expensive art on the walls, of velveteen furniture and marble statuary.

He saw a world alien to that of a self-made, immigrant entrepreneur—the genteel air of Southern aristocracy—a culture that was anathema to Pinkerton's left-wing Chartist origins. Chances are it motivated the detective on an even deeper level to catch this woman.

Pinkerton started to whisper something when Pryce Lewis said, "Boss, ssssshhhh!" Then a tense whisper: "Look! Somebody's coming!"

———

Did Rose Greenhow expect a visitor that night? It is probable that she put on her most seductive gown earlier that evening and made sure her décolletage showed abundant flesh. The knock on the door that followed—most certainly a gentleman caller—would have put her in a manipulative mood.

At this point in her career as a spy, Greenhow was getting more and more brazen, even careless.

A week earlier she had visited the Old Capitol Prison to deliver baskets of food to Confederate prisoners-of-war and had yelled an insolent warning at the stern warden: "The South has prisoners a hundred to one if the North wants to retaliate!" Days later Pinkerton's operatives tailed Greenhow and her lady friends on a picnic near the Union's Fort Ellsworth, which was still under construction. The next day Rose sent blueprints of Ellsworth to Confederate Colonel Thomas Jordan, along with a memorandum detailing her master plan to kidnap McClellan, cut telegraph wires, and cause mayhem in the capital. Marvels James Mackay:

"Her report, preserved to this day in the National Archives, is a master-piece of detail."

In many ways, Rose Greenhow was bred to be a secret emissary of the South.

Born in 1817 in Port Tobacco, Maryland, Maria Rosatta O'Neale (the "e" was later dropped) was orphaned as a baby when her father was killed by a slave and her mother was left destitute with a failing farm. In her teens Rose was invited—along with her sister Ellen—to live in the stylish Washington, D.C., boardinghouse run by her aunt, Maria Ann Hill. It was there that the attractive young girl with the olive skin and flawless complexion earned the nickname "Wild Rose." It was also there that young Rose made lifelong connections to the upper crust of Washington's social scene.

"Mrs. Hill kept her nieces busy but on display," writes Ishbel Ross. "They attended classes. They were schooled in the social graces. They went to parties carefully chaperoned. Mrs. Hill steered them adroitly through all the mud and excitement of the [President Andrew] Jackson era."

In 1833 Greenhow's sister married James Madison Cutts, Dolley Madison's nephew, and a year later, Rose fell hard for Virginia lawyer and linguist Robert Greenhow. A pillar of the Jacksonian South, Robert Greenhow was related—as an uncle—to the famous senator Stephen A. Douglas of Illinois. Rose and Robert exchanged vows in 1835, and Rose Greenhow began to cultivate the skills and social ties that would later become her arsenal in her secret campaign to destroy the Union from the inside.

Through her husband's work for the State Department, Greenhow got to know central figures in the proslavery movement, such as Vice President John C. Calhoun. She bore four daughters with Robert and learned linguistics and history from the man. By the time her husband passed away in 1854, dying in a street accident, Rose Greenhow was a fixture in Washington society circles, on close terms with such luminaries as President Franklin Pierce, James Buchanan, and even William Seward. Her Southern loyalty—expressed in frequent diatribes at lavish dinner parties—never wavered.

But it was her manner rather than her politics—her exquisite seductiveness—that ultimately would lead to her recruitment as a Southern spy. Notwithstanding her stunning, patrician good looks, her long swan-like neck, and her dark, piercing eyes, she had a certain brazenness about her—seen in the way she nurtured flirtatious relationships with cadres of politicians, and recruited innocent, promising young girls into her web of deceit.

Her unrepentant nature even showed in the way she scoffed at being caught, referring to Pinkerton—whom she knew, by August 1861, was tailing her—as "that German-Jew detective." She had a wry, defiant sense of humor, which would have been in full bloom that rainy night when she heard the knock on her door.

Sweeping across the front parlor in her elegant flounce, she answered the door with a flourish, her face a gorgeous blank mask, prepared to transform, chameleon-like, at a moment's notice.

On the other side of the door stood a "tall, handsome man of commanding figure of about forty years of age." He was a Union officer, drenched to the bone, trembling with restless anticipation.

The man's name was Ellison, and he was an infantry captain in command of a very important station with the provost-marshal of Washington. The moment he laid eyes on the lady of the house, his face, in Pinkerton's words, "lighted up with pleasure." With great dramatic effect Ellison gave Greenhow a "courtly little bow."

Greenhow returned the man's bow with a smile that could have seduced a Sphinx.

"Boss!"

Pinkerton, out in the rain and wind, balancing precariously on the shoulders of his agents, heard Lewis's voice hissing a warning.

An innocent passerby was approaching in the mist. Pinkerton splashed to the ground in his stocking feet, and all three men hid themselves under the Greenhow stoop until the pedestrian had safely passed out of sight.

When the detective climbed back onto the men's shoulders, he saw through rain-dappled window glass and partially open shades that the captain and Mrs. Greenhow had moved to a table in the rear part of the room.

Pinkerton could hear fragments of their conversation in muffled tones, under the roar of the rain, but he could not make out much of what was being said. In *The Spy of the Rebellion* Pinkerton recalls: "I heard enough to convince me that this trusted officer was then and there engaged in betraying his country, and furnishing to his treasonably inclined companion such information regarding the disposition of our troops as he possessed."

Inside the lavish parlor, in the warm light of the hearth, Captain Ellison reached into his coat and pulled out a roll of documents. Mrs. Greenhow watched intently as he produced a map of the eastern seaboard, unrolling it across the tabletop. He carefully began pointing out positions—most likely fortifications—in and around Washington.

Remembers Pinkerton: "My blood boiled with indignation as I witnessed this scene, and I longed to rush into the room and strangle the miscreant where he sat, but I dared not utter a word, and was compelled to stand by, with the rain pouring down on me, and silently witness the traitorous proceeding."

Ellison and Greenhow spent a few more minutes discussing specific points on the map.

Another pedestrian passed, interrupting the vigil. And when Pinkerton climbed back up onto his human perch, he saw that the room was empty. Had the captain retired to an inner chamber with the widow? Could this be the "reward" phase of the treasonous transaction?

An hour passed.

At length, the sound of furtive footsteps inside the parlor drew their attention back to the house.

At the sound of the front door opening, the three agents crouched down behind the porch. Pinkerton heard Ellison emerging. With a whispered goodnight and something that sounded very much like a kiss, he descended the steps.

At this point, ignoring the fact that he was shoeless, Pinkerton followed the officer.

Moving through what Pinkerton describes as a "blinding mist and pelting storms," Ellison strode rapidly across central Washington, and Pinkerton had to struggle to keep up and yet maintain a discreet distance.

Recalls Pinkerton: "I was compelled to keep pretty close to him, owing to the darkness of night, and several times I was afraid he would hear the footsteps of the men who accompanied me—mine I was confident would not be detected as, in my drenched stockings, I crept along as stealthily as a cat."

As Ellison reached the corner of Pennsylvania Avenue and Fifteenth Street, Pinkerton thought he saw the glistening flash of a revolver in the officer's hand but could not be sure. A guard suddenly appeared out of the shadows of a government building.

Ellison nodded a greeting to the man and then vanished inside the edifice.

This happened so quickly and unexpectedly that Pinkerton had no time to turn back or react in any way. He found himself standing in his soaked stocking feet in front of the building, momentarily flummoxed.

A noise rang out on one side of Pinkerton, then on the other, and before he knew what was happening, the shadowy forms of soldiers darted toward him. They had fixed bayonets raised, and they lunged toward the detective, the blades pointed menacingly at his chest.

"Halt, or I fire!" ordered one soldier—most likely the officer of the guard.

Pinkerton froze. He raised his hands. He realized almost instantly that resistance or escape would be foolish and useless. "I was out late," the detective tried to explain. "And I lost my way."

The guards were having none of this. They ordered Pinkerton inside the guardhouse, and they made him sit and wait in the outer chamber for what seemed an eternity, dripping rain and sweat on the floor. After a half hour, the guards ushered the detective upstairs to the office of the commanding officer.

There, in the lantern light of a spartan room, Pinkerton came "face-to-face with Captain Ellison."

———

For quite a while the captain paced angrily back and forth in front of Pinkerton, glaring fiercely at him without saying a word. Writes Pinkerton: "I was a sorry figure to look at, and as I surveyed my weather-soaked and mud-stained garments, and my bare feet, I could scarcely repress a laugh, although I was deeply angered at the sudden and unexpected turn affairs had taken."

Ellison finally took a seat in front of Pinkerton and spoke. "What is your name?" he demanded.

"Major E. J. Allen."

"What is your idea in following me?"

"I wasn't really following you, sir. You see, I'd lost my way in the rain and was hoping to catch up with you so that I could ask directions."

"Stop your lies!" thundered Ellison. "What is your business?"

"I have nothing further to say, and I decline to answer any further questions."

"Ah, so you're not going to speak. Very well, sir. We'll see what time will bring forth."

For a time, the captain sat behind his desk and "played restlessly with the handles of two revolvers," but the impervious Pinkerton, a keen student of human nature, saw that the man was actually riddled with nervousness, perhaps even guilt and shame. At length, Ellison called to his sergeant: "Take this man to the detention cells but allow no one whatever to converse with him; we will attend further to this case in the morning."

Time crawled for Pinkerton that night. Locked up in the moldering, filthy guardhouse, surrounded by drunken louts who were "laying about the floor like logs" or "laughing and singing," he worried about the Greenhow residence and all the other potential transactions occurring there on a regular basis. But for the moment he was helpless—a prisoner at the hands of the very man he would be charging with treason—and the damp chill of the cell only made matters worse.

Pinkerton recalls: "I shook like an aspen, and my teeth for a time chattered like castanets."

At long last Pinkerton managed to strike up a conversation with a guard, a "jovial, kind-hearted fellow," who brought Pinkerton a blanket and an overcoat. The detective and the guard chatted and told jokes to each other well into the wee hours, until Pinkerton finally asked the guard if he would consider delivering a note—perhaps when he got off his shift that morning, perhaps without arousing the suspicions of the captain of the guards—to the assistant secretary of war, Thomas A. Scott.

The guard agreed.

The shift change occurred at 6:00 a.m.—the hastily scrawled note departing with the guard. Pinkerton waited patiently. An hour later the guard returned, passing the bars of Pinkerton's cell.

"How's the weather out there?" Pinkerton asked the passing soldier.

"All right, sir," the guard said with a wink. Pinkerton knew his note had reached its destination and his release was simply a question of time. Sure enough, around half past 8:00 that morning, the sergeant of the guards appeared outside the cell with a document in his hand.

"E. J. Allen and William Ascot!" the sergeant called out.

Pryce Lewis had assumed the name "Ascot" over the last few weeks of undercover work. The previous night, Lewis had been captured shortly after Pinkerton and sequestered in another part of the guardhouse. The ever-resourceful Lewis had struck up a conversation with a fellow prisoner, initiating a relationship that would one day yield a good deal of intelligence.

Pinkerton followed the sergeant back up to Captain Ellison's office.

"The assistant secretary of war has been informed of your arrest," Ellison grumbled at the detective from behind the desk. "You will be conducted to him at once, and then we shall see if you remain silent any longer!"

Captain Ellison himself led the detail of four soldiers and Pinkerton down Pennsylvania Avenue. The rain had lifted, and the city bustled in the overcast light of morning. They reached the residence of Thomas Scott. A gray-haired, professorial-looking man, his face fringed with lush pork-chop sideburns, Scott had been the head of the Pennsylvania Railroad for years before joining Lincoln's administration. Pinkerton and Scott were old friends.

Pinkerton recalls of that morning: "He was awaiting our arrival, and as we entered the room, he ordered the guards to release me and directed me to accompany him to his room. I followed him immediately, and as the door closed behind us, he burst into a hearty laugh at my uncouth and unkempt appearance. I was a sorry spectacle indeed, and as I surveyed myself in the mirror, I joined in his merriment, for a more realistic picture of a 'drowned rat' I never beheld."

"Request Captain Ellison to come here!" The authoritative bark of Thomas Scott's voice echoed through the front parlor, where the guards and the captain awaited Pinkerton's fate.

Ellison sheepishly entered the private room, looking ill at ease, as though something was wrong. Pinkerton stood beside the assistant secretary's desk, still dripping, undoubtedly a righteous expression on his bearded face.

"Captain," Mr. Scott said, leveling his gaze at the officer while pointing at Pinkerton, "will you give me the particulars of the arrest of this man?"

"I had gone to visit some friends . . . residing on the outskirts of the city," Ellison dissembled. "And on returning at a late hour, I noticed I was being followed by this gentleman. Figuring him to be a foot-pad or a burglar, I ordered his immediate arrest."

Scott stared at the officer. "Did you see anyone last night who is inimical to the cause of the government?"

The captain flushed. He darted a quick glance at Pinkerton, hesitated for a moment, and then answered in a faltering voice, "No, sir! I have seen *no* person of that character!"

"Are you quite sure of that?"

"I am, sir."

"In that case, captain," Scott said, his gaze still fixed on the officer, "you will please consider yourself under arrest. And you will at once surrender your sword to Captain Mehaffy."

In his memoir, Pinkerton described Ellison's reaction: "The captain was completely unmanned as these words fell from the lips of the secretary, and sinking into a chair he buried his face in his hands, seemingly overcome by his emotions."

The captain was placed in close confinement at Fort McHenry.

The next day, before Pinkerton had a chance to interrogate the man, Ellison hanged himself in his cell.

The previous morning, before Pinkerton departed the residence of Mr. Scott—in search of dry clothes, a shower, and the recovery of his boots—the detective and the assistant secretary of war discussed what to do about the Wild Rose of the Confederacy. "Mrs. Greenhow must be attended to," Scott declared. "She is becoming a dangerous character."

Pinkerton agreed.

"You will therefore maintain your watch upon her," Scott instructed, "and should she be detected in attempting to convey any information outside of the lines, she must be arrested at once."

The detective gladly accepted the assignment, unaware of how soon he would be obliging Scott's request.

Chapter Fifteen

The Devil Is No Match for a Clever Woman

FRIDAY, AUGUST 23, 1861, 10:55 A.M.
Rays of morning sunlight bathed the stately homes north of Capitol Hill. The air, washed by recent rains, would have smelled clean and fresh. The afternoon heat had not yet tightened around the throat of the city. Washingtonians filled the streets in carriages and on foot, availing themselves of the pleasant weather despite the dark maladies of war afflicting the times.

Two figures, a man and woman, leisurely promenaded down Thirteenth toward I Street, oblivious to the tensions about to erupt at the corner. The man, a member of the diplomatic corps, had enjoyed many such morning walks with the woman and had no reason to believe anything was amiss.

The woman, a dark-eyed beauty in a hoop skirt and bonnet, decided to stop by a neighbor's house on her way home, ostensibly to check in on a sick child. She bade farewell to her gentleman friend in front of the child's home, which was across the street from the woman's own spacious two-story mansion.

She knocked on the neighbor's door, and the child's mother appeared in the doorway, alarmed and nervous. Evidently the mansion across the street had been under surveillance these past two days, notations being made on all the visitors. And now a guard lurked around its borders, looking purposeful and grim.

Rose O'Neal Greenhow knew immediately what was happening. She had sensed someone following her all morning, perhaps two men, but had ignored them, secure in the presence of her illustrious escort. Now she glanced over her shoulder and saw these same two figures walking past her house with an air of authority, pausing at the foot of her drive, then turning to stare back at her.

After politely inquiring about the sick child, Greenhow thanked her neighbor and calmly turned and walked to the edge of the neighbor's property. Another figure, an ally of Greenhow's, most likely one of her female "agents," materialized out of the shade of a nearby tree.

Greenhow whispered to her confidante: "Those men will probably arrest me. Wait at Corcoran's Corner, and see. If I raise my handkerchief to my face, give information of it." The agent whirled and vanished.

With a boldness born of Southern privilege and defiance, Greenhow strode directly toward the steps of her mansion, reaching into the sleeve of her gown as she walked and pulling out a small page of cipher (which she had intended to give to the agent).

She ate the coded message, swallowing it whole as she ascended her steps.

By this point the two men had converged on the mansion's porch, and before Greenhow had a chance to open the door and let herself in, a gruff voice, colored with a faint Scottish burr, called out: "Is this Mrs. Greenhow?"

Greenhow pivoted in her crinoline with the grace of a spirited belle and met the speaker's gaze. "Yes it is. And who are you and what do you want?"

Writes historian Ishbel Ross of this powerful moment: "She studied the men openly, appraising them in her shrewd way. This was her first direct encounter with the sturdy, bearded Mr. Pinkerton, a strong anti-slavery man. No doubt *he* studied Rose with equal interest as she stood silently challenging him."

"I've come to arrest you," the bearded detective informed Greenhow, "for conspiracy against the United States government."

"By what authority?"

"By sufficient authority!"

Greenhow stood her ground. "Then let me see your warrant."

The bearded man said something about the War and State Departments, a convoluted explanation that Greenhow didn't quite follow.

"I have no power to resist you," Greenhow said, while skillfully whisking her handkerchief to her face. "But had I been inside of my house, I would have killed one of you before I had submitted to this illegal process."

Without missing a beat, Pinkerton replied, "And that would have been wrong, madam, as we only obey orders, and both have families."

Pinkerton and his prodigious young protégé, Pryce Lewis, ushered the suspect inside the mansion. They ordered Greenhow to take a seat in the front parlor. Pinkerton noted the lavish decor—the rooms divided by portieres of crimson Indian silk, the rosewood pianoforte in the corner with the pearl keys, the candelabra in gold sconces, the gilded bric-a-brac woven around all the portraits of America's most important statesmen.

"And what are you going to do now?" Greenhow wanted to know.

"We're going to search," Pinkerton replied bluntly. He told Lewis to keep an eye on the woman, but before Pinkerton could turn over a single paper, Greenhow sprang to her feet.

"I will facilitate your labors," she said insolently, as she swept over to the fireplace mantle in her rustling skirts. She drew from a vase a torn slip of blue paper, turned, and flung it angrily at the detective.

Pinkerton picked up the torn paper and calmly read the handwritten note emblazoned at the top of the excised letter: *"Manassas, July 23. . . For Mrs. Rose Greenhow . . . with the compliments of Col. Thos. Jordan, who is well but hard worked."*

Greenhow burned her gaze into the detective's eyes. "You would like to finish this job, I suppose."

It is not improbable that Pinkerton, pocketing the note, smiled coldly at that point. He would have easily seen through her ruse of cool indifference. He asked the woman to please return to her seat and once again cautioned Lewis to keep a close eye on her.

As biographer Ishbel Ross writes, "A number of detective police now appeared from different quarters, and the hunt began." Among these detectives was Hattie Lawton, one of Kate Warne's trusted female operatives.

The olive-skinned Lawton particularly irritated Rose Greenhow, who in her memoir referred to Lawton as a woman with a face like "one of those India rubber dolls, whose expression is made by squeezing it, with weak grey eyes, which had a faculty of weeping."

With Greenhow safely pinned to her chair in the front parlor, the agents searched under beds, in drawers, behind dressers, inside wardrobes, and along every square inch of shelf space. They concentrated their efforts in the library—a well-stocked storehouse of rare editions and countless letters, journals, and correspondences—and they found enough examples of guilt-by-association to bring down half the administration.

"There is nothing yet that can come under the charge of treason," one police detective commented to Pinkerton early in the search, "but enough to make the government dread and hold her as a dangerous adversary."

Ishbel Ross writes of the correspondences found in the library: "To Calhoun, to Buchanan, to Breckinridge . . . and innumerable others . . . she was always 'My Dear Madam' or 'My Dear Mrs. Greenhow.' They were always most respectfully hers. [Her] papers quickly persuaded Pinkerton that the 'irresistibly seductive' Rose had been trading the sweets of love for the secrets of war."

The search went on for hours, with Pryce Lewis guarding the increasingly enraged Greenhow, her ire building as fast and intensely as the humid summer heat.

—~—

At 3:00 p.m., with the mercury rising, a knock on the door got Pinkerton's attention. The detective went over to the entrance and stood out of sight behind the door, as Lewis answered it. Standing on the porch were two lady friends of Greenhow's—a Miss Lilly Mackall and her sister—each red-eyed from crying.

Miss Mackall lurched into the parlor, gaping at the lawmen and then searching for Greenhow. Finding her in the rear of the room, simmering with anger on her chair, Mackall rushed over and burst into sobs, kneeling and putting her head on Greenhow's shoulder.

Word had spread quickly of Greenhow's arrest. In fact, many in the neighborhood had probably first caught wind of it when they heard the mournful cries of Greenhow's youngest daughter, Rosie, reverberating over the rooftops.

Writes Ross: "A high wall surrounded three sides [of the house] . . . so that the guard was not on view from the street. But the little 'rosebud' saw to it that her mother's couriers had ample warning not to approach. In the midst of all the confusion, she ran into the garden, climbed a tree, and started chanting: 'Mamma has been arrested! Mamma has been arrested! Mamma has been arrested!'"

Inside the house, Pinkerton watched Greenhow comfort her visitor.

"I did not know what they had done with you," murmured Lilly Mackall.

"Oh, be courageous," Rose Greenhow told her friend, "for we must outwit these fiends."

As Greenhow claimed in her memoir: "I was a keen observer of [the investigators'] clumsy activity, and resolved to test the truth of the old saying *The devil is no match for a clever woman.*'"

What Pinkerton did not know—nor did anyone present that day, other than Greenhow—was that she had papers in the pockets of her gown that she intended to destroy at all costs or die trying.

One of the things that drove Greenhow temporarily insensate with rage that day was the fact that the men were tossing Gertrude's room. Earlier that year, in March, Greenhow's second-oldest daughter had succumbed to an illness, and her room had been untouched since her death. All her toiletries and jewelry still lay spread across her dressing table.

When the detectives started in on Gertrude's room, manhandling the precious memories, Greenhow resolved to use all her feminine wiles to disrupt the search—and, most importantly, to destroy the second coded message hidden in her dress.

She also had incriminating letters from William Seward and Massachusetts Senator Henry Wilson, the powerful chairman of the Military Affairs Committee, hidden away in the nooks of her library.

The correspondences from Wilson—each one romantically signed, "Yours H"—would prove especially damning. The love letters had ignited rumors around Washington's Southern underground that Wilson was Greenhow's primary source for military secrets. Now Greenhow faced a moment of truth. She would burn down the house if she had to. In her memoir she writes: "I had already taken the resolution to fire the house from garret to cellar, if I did not succeed in destroying certain papers in the course of the approaching night, for I had no hope they would escape a second day's search."

At this point, she got very still, and with the guile of a predator, focused her charm on the young Brit keeping watch nearby.

Pryce Lewis would have seemed a likely target for Rose Greenhow's feminine allure. With his finely chiseled features, his aquiline nose, and his meticulously groomed sideburns, he had an air of the fop about him. But this impression of vanity, and of frivolous, sybaritic fecklessness, only served to aid Lewis in his undercover work. People underestimated the gregarious Englishman.

Greenhow pleaded with Lewis to allow her a moment alone in her boudoir.

She wanted to change. The oppressive heat had pressed down on the house by this point, and perspiration had broken out on all those present. Greenhow poured on the charm and pleaded and pleaded, until Lewis finally relented and agreed to accompany the woman upstairs—along with Hattie Lawton.

Once upstairs, alone, inside her chamber, Greenhow frantically undressed, removing her overskirt and flounce, and retrieving the documents hidden beneath her bodice. Too voluminous to swallow, the papers comprised her cipher system used in communications with General Beauregard. She madly destroyed the documents, tearing them into bits and spreading the pieces throughout the boudoir.

A knock at the door was followed by a muffled voice. "Madam! Madam!"

Greenhow finished her disposal of the cipher book, then continued shedding her gown. The door burst open, and Lewis gazed inside the chamber in time to see the Wild Rose partially clothed—in Greenhow's words "legitimately employed"—and Lewis withdrew immediately.

Now, seething with anger, Greenhow turned to the mantelpiece. She kept a pistol—most likely a single-action model—hidden there for emergencies. Apparently without thinking of the consequences of such a brazen act, and with the lack of an endgame, she grabbed the gun. A moment later, another knock signaled Lewis's return.

The Englishman entered.

Greenhow made her move. In the words of James Mackay, she moved "in a typical theatrical gesture, twirled around, and pointed the barrel at Lewis's head."

Lewis simply stared at the muzzle.

Greenhow snarled: "If I had known who you were when you came in, I would have shot you dead!"

Lewis seemed unimpressed. He smiled wryly at her and said, "Madam, you will first have to cock that pistol in order to fire it."

Pinkerton found an abundance of evidence in "Castle Greenhow" that day—more than enough to convict the Rebel Rose of treason. By nightfall, he had recovered a vast array of documents, each one more impressive and alarming than the last:

- Detailed reports of regimental movements.
- Greenhow's "pen portraits" of the prominent men she had seduced in the course of her intelligence gathering.
- Love letters from some of the most powerful figures in Washington.
- Greenhow's diary, which contained the names of her agents and couriers.

Writes James Mackay: "The little red-bound diary alone incriminated an astonishing array of politicians, lawyers, bankers, railroad officials, businessmen, civil servants, drunkards, drug addicts, psychopaths, and extremists, not to mention the ladies of Greenhow's inner circle."

Apparently Pinkerton made only one tactical error that night (in what was otherwise a well-run operation): He decided to leave the premises, permitting the spy-mistress to remain in the mansion under house arrest until matters could be sorted out the next day.

The detective left the Greenhow mansion around 9:00.

Still under constant guard—surrounded by no fewer than four local police detectives at any one time—Rose Greenhow bided her time and silently schemed. She still had documents, in Ross's words, "of immense value" hidden in the library—undiscovered by the initial search—and she would not rest until that evidence was destroyed.

She got an idea. Once again dialing up the charm, she ingratiated herself to her captors. She had the finest brandy and rum money could buy stored away in her cupboards, and she offered it around. The men, evidently, saw no reason to demur.

The liquor flowed freely as Greenhow played the dual role of hostess and innocent victim. The men became well lubricated and boisterous. Writes historian Ishbel Ross: "When they became quarrelsome among themselves, Greenhow whipped up further excitement by encouraging racial disputes—pitting English, German, Irish, and Yankee against one another." The drinking accelerated and soon the men became drowsy and lethargic, which was the exact effect Greenhow desired.

Late that night, with her friend Miss Mackall (who was also under house arrest) keeping watch, Greenhow slipped into the library. Not a single lamp was lit, and Greenhow worked quickly, "with only the moonlight to guide her," mounting a stool and reaching up to the topmost shelf. She found the documents.

She hid the papers in the folds of her skirt and made her way back to her bedroom.

Lilly Mackall waited in the darkness of the private chamber, whose only other inhabitant was a slumbering guard. Greenhow instructed the girl to hide the documents in her stockings and boots, and hopefully, if and when she was allowed to leave, Mackall could safely abscond with the evidence. If confronted with a bodily search, Greenhow explained, Mackall was to suddenly "express compunction about deserting her friend, and return to the house to 'share in the honors of the conflagration.'"

Writes Ross: "Rose had thought of everything."

⚊ ❧ ⚊

The guards did allow the Mackall sisters to leave—around 4:00 a.m. the following morning—and Rose Greenhow retired to her elegant, regal bed, falling fast asleep, secure in the knowledge that she had cleansed her residence of all smoking guns. She was unaware, however, of all the actionable materials already taken from her home, which at this very moment were being processed by Allan Pinkerton.

When she awoke the next morning, she learned that she would be under house arrest until further notice. Lilly Mackall returned around 11:00 a.m.—her mission accomplished—and the girl joined Greenhow for the duration of her captivity, however long that might be.

In her autobiography Greenhow describes the subsequent days of house arrest:

> For seven days my house remained in charge of the detective police, the search continuing throughout all that time, as also the examination of my papers and correspondence. The books in the library were all taken down and examined leaf by leaf. There would have been some wisdom in this the first day. Several large boxes, containing books, china, and

glass, which had been packed for several months, were subjected to the like ordeal. Finally, portions of the furniture were taken apart, and even the pictures on the walls received their share of attention also. My beds even were upturned many times, as some new idea would seize [the investigators]. I now watched the clumsy proceedings free from anxiety, as I had, under their own eyes, sent off or destroyed all my papers of value.

The scandalous findings at the Thirteenth Street mansion rocked the capital, embarrassing the Lincoln administration and putting further pressure on Union forces to stanch the flow of leaks to the Confederacy.

Wholesale arrests ensued over the next couple of weeks, reaching all the way to the highest levels of government. Pinkerton even found evidence that Rose Greenhow had developed a cozy relationship with the mayor of Washington, James G. Barret, who was subsequently arrested after having been "found to be implicated in a plot to detach Maryland from the Union." Barret spent several weeks in the stockade, before earning his release by taking an oath of loyalty and resigning from office.

Lincoln, overwhelmed by tremendous Union losses at battles such as Big Bethel, Manassas, and Wilson's Creek, was too busy grappling with problems at the War Department to worry about embarrassment. George McClellan and General Winfield Scott were constantly at odds, and Lincoln found himself in the middle, trying desperately to make peace between his commanders. Plus, Lincoln was starting to wonder about McClellan's abilities. Privately the president worried that McClellan might be too slow and reluctant to go into battle.

"While Lincoln and the cabinet are disputing who is to blame," complained Edwin Stanton, who would soon be secretary of war, "the enemy is at hand!"

Indicative of the chaos in Washington, the authorities treated Greenhow with incredible leniency—perhaps due to the intercession of powerful friends—allowing her to remain under house arrest, where she managed to continue communicating with the enemy. This exasperated Pinkerton. He sent report after report to Seward's State Department, claiming that "Fort Greenhow" was still serving as a "rendezvous for the most violent enemies of the government." But Seward had many other issues distracting him—one of them directly affecting Pinkerton's future as head of the Secret Service.

William Seward, according to one historian, "had an unquenchable zeal for dabbling in everybody else's business." And it is not unlikely that Seward felt threatened by Pinkerton's success, his broad jurisdiction, and his close relationships with Lincoln and General McClellan.

Toward the end of August, in a kind of paranoid power play, Seward established his own Secret Service to be officially called the Union Intelligence Service. The new agency would serve the State Department, as well as General Scott, and be run by a colorful, controversial character named Lafayette Baker.

Born in 1826 in Stafford, New York, the stocky, intense Baker grew up with the high expectations of a war-hero family. His grandfather, a man named Remember Baker, had fought as a captain under Ethan Allen in the Revolutionary War. His father, christened Green Mountain Boy Baker, also served in the military and carried on the tradition of stoic warrior. Young Lafayette, in the words of James Mackay, "had a swashbuckling career as one of California's leading vigilantes in the 1850s." Writes Mackay of Baker's almost mirror-image relationship to Pinkerton:

> In many respects [Baker] was remarkably like Pinkerton, both physically and mentally. Short, but heavily built, he was lithe and sinewy, his forehead was "of intelligent outline," he wore a beard, and his grey eyes, "cold in repose, were sharply piercing when he interviewed a victim of his vigilance."

Many, however, might have missed a subtler aspect to Baker's piercing stare: Although the man reportedly had few vices, he had a touch of corruption behind his gaze. One government official called Baker "rapacious," and whether or not this was true, Lafayette Baker would ultimately become Allan Pinkerton's nemesis.

Baker would, for the rest of his life, claim that it was he, and not Pinkerton, who first founded the U.S. Secret Service.

Pinkerton had neither the time nor the luxury in those early days of September to worry about political infighting and factionalism. During the weeks of Rose Greenhow's house arrest, the detective closely monitored the comings and goings of all visitors to "Fort Greenhow"—including a mysterious young gentleman named Michael Thompson (code-named by Greenhow "Colonel Empty"—a play on the man's initials).

The detective described Thompson as "a man of subtle intellect, finished education, particular energy, polished manners, and an attractive address." It was at this very address—Thompson's palatial home in Washington—that Pinkerton would ultimately arrest the man and find a cornucopia of incriminating materials, including a copy of a Confederate cipher book, which revealed the code used by Colonel Thomas Jordan in all his correspondences with Greenhow.

Now, armed with the codebook, Pinkerton secretly devised an ingenious new approach to infiltrating Southern forces. He would concoct bogus messages with false information and send them behind enemy lines. To create the messages, he would use Kate Warne, who could render a reasonable facsimile of Greenhow's flowery hand.

To get the messages to Jordan and Beauregard, Pinkerton would assign his best courier, his most trusted operative—the fearless, cunning, soft-spoken Englishman who had practically become Pinkerton's surrogate son.

Currently in Baltimore, Webster had gained a reputation among rebel sympathizers as the finest friend the South could have. He had spent the last three months picking up letters and notes from Copperheads in Washington and delivering them to relatives and friends up north (after Pinkerton had fully reviewed and vetted the messages). In mid-September Webster commenced delivering a series of false ciphers to Confederate commanders, serving the dual purpose of confounding Southern strategists and elevating Webster's almost mythical status in Baltimore. Writes Arthur Orrmont, "[Webster's] reputation as a courier for whom Northern pickets and provost-marshals were child's play was firmly established, and his status was close to a hero."

The trust Webster engendered among rebels in Baltimore paid large dividends.

Inducted into the shadowy, nefarious Knights of Liberty—a secret society far more dangerous and prolific than even the Palmetto Guards—Webster learned of a plot to organize a mass uprising against the vulnerable U.S. capital. As September rolled into October, Webster dutifully traveled back and forth from Baltimore to Washington, reporting to Pinkerton on the alarming activities of the Knights of Liberty and their imminent revolt.

By November, the war of words between General Winfield Scott and McClellan came to a messy conclusion with Scott's resignation and McClellan's promotion to Federal general-in-chief. This emboldened Pinkerton, who by this point had placed enough of his operatives inside the Knights, and had amassed enough evidence through Webster, to act.

On Thanksgiving 1861—while besieged Union troops tried to enjoy their camp dinners of turkey and mince pies after crushing defeats at Lexington, Missouri, and Ball's Bluff, Virginia—Pinkerton ordered a raid on the Knights of Liberty in Baltimore. At midnight, as the Knights assembled for a secret meeting, a "stream of blue-coated soldiers" broke down the door and arrested the conspirators at gunpoint. Only one of the plotters managed to escape.

In Orrmont's words:

Webster disappeared from Baltimore long enough to indicate he had a healthy respect for Yankee justice. He then turned up at the fashionable Miller Hotel with a span of fine horses and an elegant carriage. Before long he was the center and leading figure of a new group of serious, if not fanatical, secessionists. His handsome horses became well known at the races, and he was a special favorite with the ladies.

Webster's amazing streak of luck as a counterspy, however, would not last much longer.

Through a series of circuitous events, Timothy Webster was about to go back behind enemy lines, deep into the heart of Dixie, where he would meet a far different fate from the one he had enjoyed in the taverns of Baltimore.

PART IV
THE ENDLESS TIME OF
NEVER COMING BACK

Ye who read are still among the living; but I who write shall have long since gone my way into the region of shadows. For indeed strange things shall happen, and secret things be known, and many centuries shall pass away, ere these memorials be seen of men. And, when seen, there will be some to disbelieve, and some to doubt, and yet a few who will find much to ponder upon in the characters here graven with a stylus of iron.

—EDGAR ALLAN POE

CHAPTER SIXTEEN

Sealed in a Fever

CHRISTMAS 1861

The thousands of Union troops encamped around the capital, drilled relentlessly by McClellan's commanders, paused in their exercises to observe the solemn day. Morning sunlight gleamed off the frozen ledges of the Potomac. Icy winds drowned the cheerful harangue of church bells.

The soldiers' silent prayers and heads bowed in holiday meditation contrasted with the furtive, whispered plans being laid at this moment inside the I Street headquarters of the Secret Service of the Army of the Potomac.

"I'm ready now, major," Timothy Webster said, buttoning the collar of his winter frock. His slender chest, normally inconspicuous, now bulged with the artificial girth of correspondences. The coded letters, sewn into the lining of his coat, were bound for rebel authorities in Richmond, to whom Webster, by this point, had thoroughly ingratiated himself. Since mid-October, the handsome double agent had been engaged in a dangerous gambit—traveling back and forth from Baltimore to the Confederate capital. He had fully insinuated himself as a trusted courier among the upper echelons of Southern leadership, including the Confederate secretary of war, Judah Benjamin.

Over the previous two months Webster had become a fixture at the fashionable Monument Hotel near the center of Richmond, boldly using his own name in all his transactions. His reports to Pinkerton during this period, meticulously compiled in Webster's neat handwriting, told of troop placements, weaponry, and rebel hardships with the coming winter.

In one massive report, which took Pinkerton and two clerks an entire night to transcribe, Webster reported the incidences of sickness rising in the Confederate ranks due to the lack of overcoats and proper footwear.

Writes Mackay: "He even included the prices in Confederate currency of foodstuffs and fodder, adding, 'Hay very scarce, all sorts of prices.'" The only problem with this thirty-seven-page report was an inaccurate estimate of Confederate forces in and around Richmond. Webster estimated the number at 116,000, which, it turned out, was 40,000 too high.

This overestimation would ultimately delay George McClellan's campaign and stall Union operations. It would also exacerbate the growing rift between McClellan and Lincoln. The president was losing patience with the general's delaying tactics.

The error would also lead to one of the great controversies hounding Pinkerton scholars—a controversy that would come to full boil before the war had even ended.

"Have you any further commands?" Webster finally asked his boss on that cold Christmas morning in the I Street headquarters. George Bangs sat across the room, patiently waiting for the courier to depart. Both Bangs and Pinkerton had families waiting for them, the holiday festivities demanding their presence.

It is likely, however, that Pinkerton felt a pang of melancholy that morning, sizing up his loyal operative in the warm light of the office. Did Pinkerton sense something different about this mission?

In retrospect, considering the events that were about to unfold, it's easy to read more beneath the surface of these exchanges than what was originally inherent in them. It is easy to speculate that Pinkerton felt a premonition of doom for his star protégé. In his Civil War memoir Pinkerton fusses a great deal over these farewells.

"No, Webster," Pinkerton said at last, "I have no commands to give except for you to take good care of yourself."

"I'll try and do that," Webster replied with a smile, patting his coat where the letters lay snug against his chest. "I'll take good care of my mail as well."

Writes Pinkerton:

With a warm clasp of the hand, and a hearty goodbye, Webster went out into the bright sunlight and frosty air of a winter's morning, and was soon lost to view.

Procuring a coach and a driver from a local livery, Webster left Washington that afternoon, clattering eastward on Pennsylvania Avenue, bumping along through icy gales toward the outskirts of the capital.

The winding route took him across the east branch of the Potomac and past numerous checkpoints, at which Union guards scrutinized his papers. He was allowed to pass without incident.

Soon, dusk rolled in on the war-torn Christmas day, and Webster found himself chilled to the bone in the drafty compartment. For hours the coach banged over the frozen, rutted trails of southern Maryland.

The coach wound along the Patuxent River in the darkness, the ocean of black cedars stretching into the void. It passed tobacco plantations and sleepy little villages like Bryantown, Charlotte Hall, and Mechanicsville. By the time he reached the southern port of Leonardtown, Webster was shaking almost convulsively from the cold.

Established in 1708, situated on a prime inlet connecting the mouth of the Potomac with the Chesapeake Bay, Leonardtown suffered greatly during the War of 1812, when the British blockaded the bay and looted and plundered local ports. At the outset of the Civil War, the Union navy had occupied the town, and now the residents—most of them Southern sympathizers—were leery of all visitors.

All except the legendary Timothy Webster.

As his carriage pulled up in front of the local hotel, a gentleman stepped out of the entrance and into the frigid predawn air to greet Webster with enthusiastic hospitality. The man's named was John Moore.

As a village elder, and landlord of the hostelry, Moore openly professed to be a Union man, but in his heart he was a strong secessionist. He knew of Webster's reputation as an important Southern emissary and always gave the Englishman royal treatment.

Webster paid the coachman with numbed hands and then followed Moore inside the lodge.

With the coming of daybreak, a jug of steaming punch, and the warmth of a fire of crackling logs in the parlor's large open fireplace, Webster felt his joints loosen and his spirit strengthen.

The two men were alone, but still, they spoke discreetly, under their breaths.

"Well, John," Webster ventured softly, after a bit of chat, "what are my prospects of crossing the river tonight?"

"We can't cross here at all anymore, Tim," Moore informed him with a bitterness reserved for cuckolded husbands and unrepentant jailbirds. "Damned Yankees are too sharp for us."

"Is there no way of getting over?"

Moore looked at his guest with a sudden, subversive glint in his eye. "There's a way for some people … and I guess you're included in that number."

Webster gave a nod, hiding his vague uneasiness with the direction the conversation had taken.

Moore explained that there was a spot not far from there, where a small boat could slip the clutches of the Union pickets unnoticed.

Then Moore added, "I have a favor to ask of you, Tim. I've got two ladies here, who are wives of army officers now stationed in Richmond. These ladies have been living North for some time, and are anxious to get to their husbands; they have three children with them, and I want you to take charge of the party, and see them safely on their way."

Hiding his reticence, Webster said, "I'll do that with pleasure, John."

——⌁——

Cobb Neck, a point of land about fourteen miles southeast of Leonardtown, lay shrouded in darkness. On either side of the neck stretched a wide inlet where a boat could easily put out. A dense thicket of pine and underbrush covered the soft, marshy ground, preventing the placement of vigilant pickets. That night, by the time Moore's covered carriage reached the general vicinity, the weather had taken a turn. Brooding clouds veiled the moon and deepened shadows across the cape, and the wind kicked up, cold and raw. Moore directed the driver to the trail's end, whereupon the carriage stopped and its passengers disembarked.

Moore led the party—which included Webster, two grown women bundled in overcoats and scarves, and three small girls, tagging along in their winter apparel—to the end of the point. Moore then put his fingers to his lips and emitted a shrill whistle.

Another whistle answered.

A moment later, they heard the splashing of oars, and a small sailboat materialized in the darkness, approaching the bank. The sound of a man's voice: "Here I am, captain! On time, as ya see."

"All right, Tom," Moore said to the young boatman, who was silhouetted against the night sky, "I've got a party here that you must take good care of."

"Very well, captain, I'll do the best I can, but I'm afraid the wind ain't right for landin' on the other side."

Webster could see that the river was running swiftly, agitated by the winds. In the distance, the wide, black reaches of the Chesapeake churned and roiled. The gusts came more frequently now, creaking noisily in the trees—not the best conditions for a clandestine crossing.

Writes Pinkerton:

The wind through the low pines was sighing like a human being in distress, and the ladies gazed fearfully and shudderingly at the dark waters and the frail craft, which was to carry them to the opposite shore. Webster uttered words of courage and assurance to the shrinking ladies, and assisted in comfortably bestowing them in the boat, and then, with a parting salutation to John Moore, the boat pushed off from the shore.

After pushing clear of the land, the boatman hoisted sail. Almost instantly the wind lashed at the boat with unbridled ferocity. Webster and the others clutched their collars, shivering in the gales. The boatman struggled with the batten, wrestling the sail toward the stern.

Sailing against the wind is tricky, but not impossible. The experienced sailor swings the mainsail away from the wind—as opposed to the right-angle position, which is assumed when the craft is moving with the wind—and he takes frequent, short tacks. The backward sail acts as a foil, and the boat gradually makes progress.

On that tempestuous winter night, employing these same techniques, the young boatman nearly got his illicit cargo all the way across the mouth of the Potomac to the Virginia shore—with Webster helping tack the sails, and the women frantically clutching their children—when all at once the boatman called out, "The storm's comin'! The women better cover up!"

Almost on cue, the storm roared. Cold, diamond-hard rain slashed down upon the boat, and the winds tossed the waves over the bulwark. The little vessel rocked violently, at the mercy of the turbulent whitecaps. The sail buffeted and flagged, and the boat was pushed off course.

Within moments, a thunderous vibration shuddered through the decks and companionway. The boat lurched sideways into shallow water, and the keel scraped the rocky river bottom with an alarming wrenching noise. The boat nearly tipped over. Webster cried out for the boatman to lower the sail, and the boatman obliged.

The sailboat teetered in the wind, grounded, at least a hundred yards from the shore, and about a mile below their intended landing place.

If they stayed this way for long, they would perish. Webster did not hesitate, did not even say anything; he simply grabbed two of the little girls—one in each muscular arm—and hurtled off the bulwark into the water.

—

Waist-deep and as cold as liquid ice, the water threatened to drag Webster down.

Fixing his bleary gaze on the horizon, he trudged through the impossible currents toward the shoreline. It took an unbearable amount of time to cross the distance. Finally reaching the banks, Webster deposited the girls on the rocky shoreline, then immediately turned and waded back through the miserable currents toward the foundering boat.

The effects of the misadventure began to seize Webster's body. His lips turned blue. His joints tightened and cramped. By the time he reached the boat and began assisting the ladies, the third little girl, and the boatman, he was trembling convulsively.

At last, Webster managed to get the entire party safely to shore, only moments before the wind and the waves had their way with the pitiful remnants of the sailboat. The party looked on with horror as the boat vanished into the icy, black currents of the Potomac.

Webster, however, refused to allow the elements to get the better of him. He spoke words of encouragement to the ladies and asked the boatman to help carry the children through the storm-wracked woods. A cabin owned by one of the rebel wives lay in the darkness a mile away, north of Colonial Beach, and the party agonizingly followed Webster through the wilds and freezing rain toward the shelter.

—

The cabin at Monroe's Creek, a small village not far from George Washington's original birthplace, provided Webster's party an oasis of warmth and blessed relief from the miserable night.

The weary travelers replenished themselves and dried their clothes by the roaring fire. Pinkerton writes, "Thanks to a flask of good brandy, which Webster fortunately had with him, the ladies were strengthened and sustained sufficiently. . . [and] their words of gratitude to Webster were heartily and unstintingly uttered."

The boatman also profusely thanked the dashing Englishman before taking his leave.

Webster, overcome with fatigue, had no choice but to sleep in the outer room in his damp clothes, while the ladies and their children retired to private inner rooms. In front of the crackling hearth, Webster prepared to "take his much-needed rest." He spread a blanket, the chills still gripping him. His joints complained painfully as he settled down.

At this point, it is likely that he had developed a fever. His breathing came at a price, his chest throbbing painfully with each breath. But as he stretched his stiff, sore limbs upon the blanket, he noticed, lying upon the floor a short distance from him, a small packet.

The package, wrapped in oiled cloth and tied with red tape, belonged to one of the ladies. It had evidently slipped free in all the excitement, and Webster picked it up and examined it carefully in the flickering light of the fire. The packet contained a lengthy correspondence.

Addressed to "The Hon. Judah Benjamin," the message elucidated a plethora of critical intelligence culled from high-level Union strategists, apparently secreted out of the capital by one of the treasonous women slumbering in the next room. Forgetting his aching limbs, his chest pains, and his troubled breathing, Webster tucked the packet into his coat for safekeeping.

The discovery so galvanized Timothy Webster that he went fast asleep that night, oblivious to the fact that his life was now in danger from a very unexpected source.

In the middle of the nineteenth century, with the advent of bacteriology still decades off in the future, physicians often found themselves groping in the dark. Pasteur in France would not open the door to the study of microbiology until the late 1880s. In the early 1860s, however—as the Civil War ramped up, and field surgeons at such places as Fort Henry and Roanoke Island sawed off gangrenous limbs with filthy blades and dug mini-balls from gaping wounds with bare hands—little was known about bacteria. In fact, even less was known about the causes and potential treatments of such serious conditions as rheumatic fever.

Historians believe that as many as 160,000 soldiers in the Civil War suffered from acute rheumatic fever. The condition is often passed through cow's milk, which, when unpasteurized, can be crawling with the Streptococcus bacteria, which cause the illness. The flu-like symptoms—fever, sore throat, diarrhea, joint pain, heart palpitations, fatigue—are stubborn and recurring, and when untreated can lead to permanent heart damage and even death.

Timothy Webster harbored a chronic case of "rheumatism" (the early term for the condition), which Pinkerton calls, in his memoir, "an old and relentless enemy." The condition had plagued Webster intermittently throughout his adult life. The post-Christmas journey to Richmond had touched off the worst case yet, and he spent the next several weeks trying to work through it, trying to conceal the pain, trying to ignore the devouring fever.

He spent several days in Fredericksburg, attempting to recuperate. Then he made his way to Richmond.

Distracted by the sickness, the naturally cautious Webster may have let his guard down over the next few weeks of the new year. He met with Judah Benjamin, who congratulated him for making it through the ever-tightening battle lines. But then, proceeding to the Monument Hotel, Webster spent the next few days on his back, almost delirious from the fever and the arthritic vise-grip on his joints.

Fellow Pinkerton agent Hattie Lawton arrived at the hotel to nurse her colleague back to health. Often posing as Webster's wife, or sometimes even his male assistant, the androgynous Lawton took full advantage of her boyish features. The two agents had grown very close—so close, in fact, that some historians hint at a romantic tie between them. But regardless of the underpinnings of their relationship, Lawton now worried that her counterpart was in trouble.

Webster had planned to return to Washington as soon as possible, and he needed to secure passports from the "weasel-faced" Confederate war clerk, John P. Jones (Mackay's description). For months now Jones had voiced concerns to his superiors over the possibility of counterspies poisoning the ranks of Southern couriers, and Webster was turning out to be a lightning rod for Jones's mistrust.

Writes James Mackay:

Jones was a naturally suspicious individual whose gimlet eye missed nothing. On one occasion Webster turned up with a diminutive figure in a lieutenant's uniform, but the war clerk, sensing something not quite right about the lieutenant's "fullness of breast," refused to grant him a pass. Jones even had the lieutenant arrested but to his chagrin Judah Benjamin ordered the man's release and sent him on his way. The lieutenant was, in fact, Hattie Lawton in disguise.

Somehow, with torturous effort, marshaling his strength and masking all the pain, Webster managed to secure the requisite passports—despite all the suspicion—and laid plans for his trip back to the capital. He collected a large number of letters from Secretary Benjamin and Confederate General Charles Sidney Winder—a long-haired dandy from a rich Maryland family who six months later would be killed at the Battle of Cedar Mountain—and set out for Washington in the last week of January 1862.

Webster made it through the pickets and outposts of both Union and Confederate forces without incident.

It would have been a herculean effort, at this point, to hide his malady, but Webster did just that. The fever waxed and waned throughout the journey, and by the time he reached Washington, Webster had managed to completely conceal his condition.

Perhaps in an effort to convince his boss of his continued vigor—or maybe to convince himself of it—Webster immediately proposed a return trip to Richmond. Numerous contacts in and around Washington and Baltimore had fresh correspondences for the courier.

One bright winter's morning, toward the end of that month, Webster reported to Pinkerton for last-minute orders. The evidence of Webster's

determined effort to conceal his condition is apparent—albeit subtly so—
in the recollections of that day from Pinkerton's autobiography:

> *I often recall, and with an emotion that I cannot control, the appear-*
> *ance of Timothy Webster as I saw him that day. Brave, strong, and*
> *manly, he stood before me. The merry twinkle in his eyes seemed to belie*
> *the sternness of the set lips, which were even now curved with a smile of*
> *good humor. No trace of fear or hesitancy was apparent in his manner.*
> *He seemed to be animated solely by an earnest desire to serve his country*
> *to the best of his ability. He well knew—as did I—that his journey lay*
> *through a hostile country; that danger was lurking everywhere around*
> *him, and that if his true character was discovered, the consequences*
> *would, no doubt, prove fatal to him. Notwithstanding this, there was*
> *no quivering of the compact muscles, the hand that grasped mine was as*
> *firm as iron, and the brave heart that throbbed in his bosom was insen-*
> *sible alike to a thought of shrinking, or a desire to evade, the responsi-*
> *bility that devolved upon him. I did not know then that I had looked*
> *upon his face and manly form for the last time, and no hint of subse-*
> *quent fate came to me as I sat watching his retreating figure.*

CHAPTER SEVENTEEN

The Worm Turning

FEBRUARY 1, 1862

"Pickets!"

Timothy Webster hissed the word in a loud whisper as he huddled down in the shadowy bulkhead of an oyster boat.

Darkness had fallen upon the Potomac like a funeral pall, broken only by the cold radiance of the moon. Covered with a rime of frost, the woods and wetlands along the isthmus lay silent and still—as though held in suspended animation in the eye of a storm—the winds of war percolating in all directions.

From the outbreak of the Conflict, the Union navy had attempted to blockade the entire eastern seaboard, including much of the Chesapeake as well as the Gulf of Mexico, until small ports such as Leonardtown must have felt like claustrophobic archipelagos. Southerners stranded in such hamlets murmured constantly of insurrection and escape. After nearly a year of civil war, paranoia reigned. People did not readily know whom to trust.

"PICKETS!" Webster called again, vexed by the lack of response from the Confederate troops stationed along the southern banks of the river. His dinghy floated at a dead stop. The other passengers waited in the chill wind. In the moonlight, across the black mirror of the Potomac, Webster could see the lanterns and fortifications of the rebel guards, who knew his voice well but were not responding. Why? Why weren't they giving the all-clear?

The oyster boatman looked on nervously. Something was wrong.

Next to the boatman sat Hattie Lawton, the slender, olive-skinned, faithful companion, clad in her masculine garb, stoic if not quite sanguine.

Lawton trusted Webster implicitly, trusted him with her life, trusted him in any situation that might arise.

Trained by Kate Warne, and proving herself the bravest and most resourceful of all the operatives in Pinkerton's Female Detective Bureau, Hattie Lawton had spent months in Baltimore posing as Timothy Webster's wife. It is likely—regardless of whether Lawton and Webster had ever consummated their close working relationship—she had come to esteem Webster beyond simple professional admiration.

Webster called out for the pickets a few more times and got no reply. The lanterns winked out. In the ensuing darkness, Webster ordered the boatman to land downstream a few hundred yards.

The boatman complied, and moments later the dinghy struck ground.

They off-loaded their provisions, and Webster bade the boatman a farewell. With his oar the boatman pushed himself off the shore and vanished into the darkness. Webster and Lawton turned and crept through the dense shadows of the forest, carrying their packs, trying to get their bearings and figure out why the Confederate soldiers had behaved so strangely.

Around midnight they came to a farmhouse. A sudden eruption of dogs barking heralded their arrival. Webster would have been shivering, the cold and the stress touching off his rheumatism. A farmer, roused by the noise of the animals, came to the door and demanded to know the reason for such an intrusion at this ungodly hour.

Webster calmly explained the situation, and the farmer, a rebel sympathizer, became instantly accommodating and invited them inside. But they had no sooner shed their overcoats, and had started warming their numb fingers at the fire, when a loud knock rang out.

Webster and Lawton hid in the shadows, while the farmer answered the door and found a Confederate guard standing outside, demanding to know the identity of the newcomers. "I've been ordered to bring them immediately before the captain of the guard," the guard informed the farmer.

"Why didn't you tell them that when they called out to you before?" the farmer wanted to know.

"We didn't know who they were, and we didn't think it was safe."

"Ah ... so you were afraid of them, were you? So afraid you ran away?"

At this point, Webster came out of hiding and confronted the guard. In short temper Webster looked the guard in the eye and said, "Tell your commander that I will not stir from this house until morning! My name is Timothy Webster. I am in the employ of the Confederacy, and if you had answered my call, there would have been no difficulty."

After a tense moment, the guard decided not to press the issue and went away.

Webster breathed a sigh of relief. But the mood inside the genial warmth of the farmhouse had shifted. All present that night would have felt it. In the wake of the rising tide of bloodshed in the war, as well as the frantic efforts to catch traitors, trust was in short supply.

After a night of restless, feverish dozing, Webster awoke the next morning in a spasm of pain. Every joint in his body stabbed with the sharpness of broken glass.

He struggled through breakfast, and then, thanking the farmer, set out with Lawton for the rebel encampment two miles away.

He arrived at the picket line and asked to see a Major Beale, the officer in command. Webster was told that Beale was stationed twenty miles away. But upon telegraphing the man, a terse, succinct reply came back to the troops: "Let Webster go where he pleases."

Rheumatic fever lies in wait in a sufferer's body. Playing a cat and mouse game with the immune system, it can flare up at a moment's notice, or it can sneak up with the agonizing slowness of a low-grade fever inching up the thermometer.

En route to Richmond, Webster's condition deteriorated. Hattie Lawton would have known the situation without asking. Webster's complexion had become wan and ashen, and his movements lethargic and labored. The pain etched itself on his face.

By the time they reached the Monument Hotel in the heart of the Confederate capital—which thrummed with the beat of troops on the move—Webster had a hard time standing in place without falling over. It could not have been a worse time to be in a compromised condition in the rebel stronghold.

On the western front, Nashville was under siege by Union forces, and a former dry-goods clerk named Ulysses Grant was leading a Federal force up the Tennessee River and establishing camp at Shiloh Church. Robert E. Lee's main army was about to fall back from Manassas to the Rappahannock River, and security in Richmond had tightened to unprecedented levels. General Winder was starting to listen to his paranoid war clerk, refusing to grant passports for regular couriers.

The scene at the Monument Hotel had grown solemn and tense, and upon his arrival, the normally jovial Webster immediately retired to his room.

By dawn the next morning, he could barely move.

—◦—

Three weeks passed.

In Washington, the pressure to act weighed down on George McClellan. For months he had been planning and drilling for a mammoth operation to be known as the Peninsular Campaign—which would culminate in the capture of Richmond—but his careful, solicitous style ate at Lincoln and his cabinet. Pinkerton watched all this discord with outrage and defensiveness. In his memoir, he writes:

> *The delay, which General McClellan wisely deemed necessary for the perfect equipment and education of his army, was being used as a pretext by those who envied the young commander, to detract from his reputation, and to impair the confidence, which a united people had reposed in his loyalty and ability. The President was besieged by inopportune cavilers, the burden of whose refrain was the defamation of the hero of West Virginia, and it is not surprising, however much to be regretted, that Mr. Lincoln gradually permitted their clamors to disturb him, and eventually partook of some of the distrust with which they endeavored to impress him.*

More immediate problems plagued and distracted Pinkerton at this point. Timothy Webster had dropped off the edge of the earth. Pinkerton had heard nothing from the man in weeks, which was highly irregular. Normally Webster would check in with his boss once a week, or at minimum every two weeks, but it was now late February and no word had come from Richmond.

On February 23, 1862, Allan Pinkerton called an emergency meeting with every agent available who wasn't in the throes of an active intelligence operation. Of the six operatives who arrived at Pinkerton's headquarters that day—all friends or admirers of Webster's—Pinkerton favored two men to go on the dangerous mission into enemy territory to "make inquiries about the missing operative, and come to his rescue, if necessary."

With the benefit of hindsight, Pryce Lewis seemed a likely candidate. The dapper Brit knew the South intimately and—with the exception of Webster—was probably Pinkerton's best man. John Scully, the fiery young Irishman with a taste for wine and spirits, would turn out to be a disastrous choice. Pinkerton reasoned that both men had been involved in other operations in Baltimore with Webster and had many connections with influential friends in Richmond. No one knew then, however, that Scully harbored a bundle of neuroses and fears that he kept at bay with the bottle.

Interestingly, Pinkerton did not issue orders to these men, per se, but instead asked them if they would be *interested* in *volunteering* for the duty. He did this for a very specific reason. As he explained years later in his book *The Spy of the Rebellion*:

> *I felt very loathe to peremptorily order a man upon an enterprise where there was every possibility of danger, for in the event of fatal result, I should be disposed to reproach myself for thus endangering the lives of those under my command. It is true, that under the terms of service, and by virtue of the authority vested in me, I had the undoubted right to issue such order; but I always preferred that my men should voluntarily, and without urging, signify their willingness to undertake hazardous missions.*

Lewis gladly accepted the challenge but was reticent about serving alongside Scully. He took Pinkerton aside and begged the chief not to send the younger man along. The assignment, according to Lewis, was too risky for two men. "One man can remember a story and stick to it," Lewis explained, "but two will be sure to suffer."

Pinkerton convinced Lewis that Scully would only be used as a courier to deliver Webster's mail, if necessary. Once Webster was rescued, Scully would return to Washington, while Lewis would join Webster and move deeper into enemy territory for further orders.

Lewis relented. Scully was in, and now it was time to prepare for the mission.

Pinkerton gave the agents "new clothes, luggage, a Navy Colt pistol apiece, and a bag of gold coins." He manufactured a fake letter, addressed to Webster, "apparently written by a rebel spy," which introduced the two men as friends of the South. Pinkerton also arranged for an escort—an operative by the name of William H. Scott, who was well acquainted with Federal commanders along the battle lines—to see the men across the Potomac.

Writes James Mackay: "On a beautiful sunny afternoon in late February, Lewis and Scully took leave of their boss."

Despite all the precautions and the well-heeled guide, their journey into Virginia proved arduous. After passing through Union patrols and bidding Scott a grateful farewell, they took a rowboat across the river and encountered a sudden and unexpected squall.

The boat ended up swamped in an estuary, and the men had to wade through icy waters—in an eerie reenactment of Webster's ordeal—to get to land. After reaching the Virginia shore, they buried any incriminating documents or letters in the sandy loam, then wandered the forests until they reached a small village.

It was there that they got more bad news: The Leesburg ferry had been sunk by a Federal gunboat, and another ferry would not be expected until the following day. Dodging rebel patrols, they bided their time until the next ferry put out for Richmond.

They did not reach the Southern capital until late in the afternoon on February 26.

Lewis and Scully had no idea where to find Webster, so they checked into the Exchange Hotel, where they, in Pinkerton's words, "remained quietly for the night," planning their movements. The next day they started their search at the offices of the *Richmond Enquirer*, the proprietors of which had used Webster many times as a courier.

But what Lewis and Scully did not notice as they entered the *Enquirer* building was that a young woman by the name of Morton happened to be passing the newspaper's office at almost the same time. This young lady caught a glimpse of the two agents, and the memory of an unpleasant encounter in Baltimore filled Miss Morton with such repugnance that she decided to report her sighting immediately to the authorities.

The newspapermen at the *Enquirer* had no clue as to Webster's whereabouts. But just as Lewis and Scully were about to leave, an office worker took them aside and explained confidentially that he had heard a rumor that Webster was bedridden at the Monument Hotel.

Writes Pinkerton: "Repairing at once to the place where they were directed, they were shown to Webster's room, and here they found the brave fellow, lying a weak and helpless invalid, attended by Mrs. Lawton, whose attentions to him were unremitting."

Even in his feverish, weakened state, Timothy Webster found the unexpected visit by his fellow counterspies deeply troubling. He feared that their presence might tip off observant authorities. In a tense, formal, almost coded exchange, Webster strongly urged the two rescuers to make themselves scarce.

Lewis and Scully left the hotel after only a few minutes of awkward, hushed conversation.

In retrospect, it is tempting to speculate: Had the two rescuers retreated to their hotel to rethink their mission, all might have gone according to plan. Had they perhaps withdrawn from Richmond at that point and reported back to Pinkerton in order to regroup, disaster might have been averted. But they did no such thing.

Later that day, concerned for the well-being of their stricken comrade, they returned to Webster's room. There they found Webster in the presence of a hard-nosed rebel officer named Captain John McCubbin. Webster, concealing his alarm, made the introductions.

"Have you gentlemen reported in at General Winder's office?" the captain asked Lewis and Scully, reffering to John H. Winder (no relation to Charles Sidney).

"No, sir," Lewis replied. "We didn't think it was necessary, having fully reported to Major Beale, and having received his permission to travel."

"It *is* necessary." The captain let out a flinty laugh, which held very little mirth. "And now I'm giving you official notice of that fact."

"Very well, very well," Lewis backpedaled. "We'll do so as early as possible."

"Any time within a day or two will answer nicely."

Webster, crestfallen on his bed, immediately saw through the casual facade of the captain—the officer's cold smile as menacing as a gun barrel—and Webster knew it was too late. The mistake had been made.

And now it was only a question of how much damage had been done.

***

The next day, at the provost-marshal's office, Captain McCubbin casually grilled the two counterspies under the watchful eye of General Winder. Lewis and Scully told the officers that they were fellow couriers of Webster's, working for the South, that they were natives of England and Ireland, and that Scully had been in America nearly three years, while Lewis had arrived only eighteen months ago. Scully spoke of his connection with a dry-goods house in New York City, and Lewis explained that he represented a London publishing firm. They showed them the fake letter and explained past affiliations with secessionist families in Baltimore, for whom they had smuggled goods in and out of the South.

Writes Pinkerton of the fateful interrogation: "This interview was conducted in a very pleasant manner . . . and after they had fully answered all the questions which had been propounded to them, they took their leave, being politely invited by the general to call upon him whenever convenient."

***

Feeling smugly confident they had passed the test, Lewis and Scully returned to Webster's hotel. There they found Webster in worse condition than the night before. Wracked with pain, Webster listened to their account of the interrogation.

Before the men had finished, a knock on the door interrupted their tale. Hattie Lawton answered it and found a detective from the provost-marshal's office standing there, looking apologetic. Lawton invited the man in the room.

"Please forgive the intrusion," the detective said to Lewis. "I've been asked to follow up on a small detail from the interview with General Winder."

"Certainly," Pryce Lewis said cordially.

"May I ask each of you gentlemen what parts of England and Ireland you hail from originally?"

Lewis and Scully each answered the question, and the detective thanked them and took his leave.

Webster's feverish eyes burned with urgency. "Get away from Richmond immediately!"

Lewis and Scully stared incredulously at the sick man propped up in bed.

"There's danger brewing," Webster went on with fire in his gaze. "You are certainly suspected, and it may go very hard with all of us, unless you leave the city at once!"

"Why do you think so?" Scully looked taken aback. "We certainly can't be suspected of anything. . . . You're alarming yourself unnecessarily."

A spasm of agony rocked Webster, and he stiffened, before managing a hoarse dissent: "I tell you, that man never would have come here with that question unless there was something wrong. You must, indeed, get away . . . or the consequences will be serious—"

Webster had hardly gotten the words out when another rap on the door gave everyone in the room a start. Lawton answered it and came face to face with two men, one of whom was very familiar to Pryce Lewis.

In the early weeks of the war, back in Washington, Lewis and Scully had conducted a series of searches—per Pinkerton's orders—of the sprawling estate of Jackson Morton, the former U.S. senator from Florida. Upon secession, Morton had become an outspoken representative of the Confederacy, and his home in the capital—still occupied at that time by his wife and daughter—had become a target for Federal investigators. Lewis himself had searched the daughter's bags on more than one occasion at the train station during her many trips to the South.

Now, this moment, at the threshold of Webster's room, standing beside a high-ranking official with the Richmond provost-marshal's office, was a young Confederate lieutenant named Chase Morton, scion of the Morton fortune and the youngest son of Senator and Mrs. Jackson Morton.

Lewis kept his cool and did not give away his astonishment at the sight of Morton. But Scully nervously avoided the young lieutenant's burning gaze and hastily tried to excuse himself from the room. He was in such a hurry he left his overcoat behind. Lewis apologized for his companion's rudeness and followed Scully into the corridor, but just as the two agents were hurtling down the stairs, a voice called out from Webster's doorway.

"Are your names Lewis and Scully?!"

Lewis paused, turned, and bravely faced his inquisitor at the top of the stairs. "Yes, sir."

"I have orders to convey you to General Winder's office."

———

"Don't you remember me?" Lieutenant Chase Morton was livid and did most of the talking that day in the imposing office of General Winder, who was absent at the moment, attending other matters.

Surrounded by Confederate officers and detectives, Lewis and Scully were being subjected to unrelenting scrutiny. "I do not," Pryce Lewis calmly replied. "I do not remember ever having seen you at any time before today."

"You don't remember coming to my mother's house in Washington? Searching my sister's bags?"

"No, sir, I do not."

"You don't remember coming there as an agent of the Secret Service of the federal government and making a thorough search of our premises and its contents?"

Scully squirmed.

"You are mistaken, sir," Pryce Lewis intoned, still with little or no betrayal of emotion. "I know nothing of what you are alluding to."

Lieutenant Morton lost his temper then, and started shouting, when all at once General Winder entered the room, and all conversation ceased.

After a series of salutes and deference paid to the older man, Winder came over to Lewis. With an icy smile, the general shook Lewis's hand. "How do you do, Mr. Lewis . . . and how is Mr. Seward?"

———

Lewis and Scully were placed under arrest and confined to the ramshackle Henrico County Jail. A complex of rotting two-story brick piles, surrounded by stockades of ancient timbers, the jail was located just south of town, on the edge of the wetlands. For three days, the pair languished in a cell with six other detainees. Formal charges had not yet been imposed, and no one from the provost-marshal's office communicated with either operative during this time.

In General Winder's words, they were "given time to think the matter over."

Whatever thinking Lewis and Scully did during this period, it is not improbable that their thoughts turned to Webster. With a mixture of shame, regret, panic, and anger, they each considered the possibility that their apprehension would result in danger to Webster.

They passed the hours bolstering each other's resolve, agreeing to stick to their original story. They would say nothing beyond the claim that they were Southern couriers falsely accused of counterespionage, and they would abide by the consequences, no matter how grave.

For Pryce Lewis, the proposition of remaining steadfast was never in question. The stubborn insistence that he was unjustly arrested came less from courage or honor and more from his admiration for Webster.

John Scully, rattled by the arrest, already showed signs of breaking. Perhaps the rebels intuited this dichotomy; on the fourth day, early in the morning, they would systematically begin working at this weak spot.

Scully jumped at the sound of bars clanging. An attaché with the provost-marshal's office stood outside the cell, calling Scully's name.

Evidently General Winder had requested an audience with the young man.

Writes Pinkerton: "Scully prepared himself . . . and taking leave of his companion, followed the officer. He did not return that night, and for days afterwards, Lewis was in ignorance of what had become of him."

Chapter Eighteen

Desperation County

March 16, 1862, 7:00 p.m.

"Time!" The elderly jailer called out to the prisoners, all of whom were scattered around the yard at Henrico for their evening exercise.

Every night, for the last two weeks, the inmates had sheepishly filed out of the cell-house at this time to take their constitutional stroll around the scabrous, trash-strewn exercise yard. Pryce Lewis was among their number, each night becoming more and more anxious, restless, and filled with dread over losing touch with Scully.

But tonight would be different. Tonight one of the prisoners would not return to his cell.

"Time! Time!" called the old turnkey, and like a regimental platoon drilled in countermeasures, the prisoners suddenly turned and, moving as one, converged on the entrance to the cell-house in a wave, mobbing the jailer and pushing into the building.

The plan worked perfectly. The unexpected throng flustered and distracted the old man, who would normally take a head count at this point. But tonight, he merely threw up his hands and got out of the way.

The men marched in lockstep back to their cells, and within minutes the barred doors had clanged shut and the lamps had been extinguished. Silence fell upon the jailhouse like a shroud.

Outside, in the yard, in the darkness, a head pushed its way out of a trash heap.

The errant prisoner, Charles Stanton, had slipped away from the group earlier that evening, according to plan, and had hidden under the refuse. A hard-bitten, leathery sailor from New York, Stanton had been imprisoned after a quixotic attempt at hijacking a Confederate gunboat.

Stanton was about to climb out of his festering nest—and execute the next phase of the planned escape—when the sound of footsteps drove him back under the garbage.

The shadow of the guard loomed. Apparently the old man had noticed something odd about the refuse heap, and he approached the pile to investigate. He drew a wooden match from his pocket. He struck it, the tiny flame flaring in the dark. He held it near the trash for a better look. Underneath the garbage, Stanton's heart chugged. A blast of wind suddenly extinguished the match.

After searching for another match, and finding none, the old man gave up. He slowly turned and walked out of the yard, locking the gate behind him.

Stanton sprang into action. He crawled out of the trash heap and, staying low, he crept quickly across the yard to the inner door. The lock broke easily under the force of a quick nudge—as it had been slowly disabled over the last two weeks by a contraband file—and Stanton slipped into the dark jailhouse on nimble feet.

The other prisoners—including Lewis—moved to their barred cell doors, also weakened from relentless rasping, and prepared to muscle themselves out. Stanton went to Lewis's door first, ready to slam a boot against the lock. But then Stanton paused.

In the stillness any noise out of the ordinary would draw too much attention. They hadn't thought of this little detail in the planning. Any hint of pounding would reach the ears of the guards in the main building across the yard. Stanton realized it immediately.

And by the look of Pryce Lewis's grave expression, as the two men exchanged somber glances, it was clear that the dapper Brit realized it as well.

Then a sound drew Lewis's attention across the corridor to a row of cells on the other side of the guardhouse, and an unexpected solution suddenly presented itself.

It is highly likely that the Henrico County Jail—like many improvised POW camps used by the South during the war—had once been a holding pen for slaves or perhaps an auction house in which people of color were kept for sale. At this moment, in fact, in that dimly lit jailhouse, Pryce

Lewis saw a group of black prisoners staring back at him with strange, expectant expressions on their faces.

Writes Pinkerton: "The colored men, without any solicitation or instruction, came to the rescue in a very important, though unexpected manner. They commenced to sing in concert, at the top of their voices, snatches of plantation songs and camp meeting melodies."

The noise of the black men singing allowed Lewis, Stanton, and five others to smash open their compromised doors and slip free of their captivity.

⁓

They managed to climb the stockade using planks they had hidden in the yard.

They made it to the other side without a sound and hurried into the woods. The moon shone down on them from a cloudless sky, lighting their way.

In whispers and hand gestures, Lewis took the lead, navigating by the stars, heading northward. It was after 8:00. Martial law dictated that anyone in the city after 9:00 must have a pass. Lewis and his band of prisoners hurried across the back roads to make it out of town before curfew fell.

By midnight they reached the Chickahominy River, a snaking tributary northeast of Richmond. They kept on through swamps, quagmires, and deep pools. Pinkerton writes: "The air was cold and frosty, and their wet garments clung to them like ice; their limbs trembled; their teeth chattered with the cold, and their condition was really a pitiable one indeed."

⁓

They crossed miles of rugged backcountry throughout the night, but by daylight the weather had worsened. Lewis and his fellow escapees could barely move by this point, so they decided to hunker down in the deepest part of the woods for some much needed rest. They shared the meager corn cakes that they had smuggled from the prison mess hall, and they even risked building a fire.

But sleep proved impossible. And by nightfall that next evening, they knew they had to continue on, or suffer the consequences of capture. The sky, clouded now, offered no moonlight, as they plodded on through the muck and deadfalls.

They had not gotten far when a storm suddenly unleashed its fury on them. The rains came down in torrents, drenching them. The winds yammered and howled through the pines. Soon the elements drove the men under a canopy of trees, where they huddled against the trunks in futile attempts to shield themselves from the deluge.

Movement now was out of the question, and Lewis struggled to stay alert. But soon exhaustion claimed the hearty Brit, and he collapsed into a cold, wet heap beneath a tree. He slept fitfully.

The storm eventually lifted, and with daylight Pryce Lewis realized that half of his companions had vanished. With the other three men, Lewis struggled to build another fire, but just as the kindling began to catch, the noise of footsteps, many footsteps, shuffled in the trees all around them.

It happened so quickly, so abruptly, that Lewis barely had a chance to stand up.

Within moments, Confederate soldiers surrounded him.

By the time the rebel search party returned to Richmond with Lewis and company in tow, the news of the Yankee jailbreak had made all the papers. Writes Mackay: "The *Times Dispatch* reckoned that the crowds that turned out to see them being led back to prison were larger than those which had greeted the Prince of Wales two years earlier."

As the ringleader of the escape, Lewis was put in leg irons on General Winder's orders and taken to Castle Godwin, "a filthy fortress that had once been a slave pen."

Manacled in solitary confinement, Lewis steadfastly stuck to his story; but what he did not know yet was that the hapless John Scully, over the past three weeks, had been suffering through a ruthless series of interrogations and court-martial proceedings.

The entire Morton family had identified Scully as a Federal agent, and the young man had been found guilty of spying and sentenced to death by hanging—the execution to be carried out on April 4 between 10:00 a.m. and 2:00 p.m. Scully's only hope for a stay, according to his captors, was a full confession, which would ultimately implicate Timothy Webster.

Pryce Lewis would soon face a similar fate—his speedy trial concluding on April 1 with the same results—but what Lewis feared most was not a guilty verdict resulting in the sentence of death by hanging.

What Lewis dreaded more than anything else—even death—was the possibility that his hapless companion would lose his nerve and talk.

—◆—

"You will not tell them what you know—" Lewis whispered with frantic urgency to his friend and colleague, "—will you, John?"

John Scully sat slumped in the corner of his squalid cell, his unkempt appearance that of a degenerate, a reprobate at rock bottom. "I don't know . . . I don't know what I will tell them," he murmured.

It was a day after Lewis's death sentence had been handed down, and somehow, Scully had managed to convince his jailers that he was seriously ill and had begged them to allow a brief visit from Lewis. As a Roman Catholic, Scully wanted Lewis to help him procure a priest.

Scully needed comfort and counsel, and perhaps absolution for what he was about to confess.

"For God's sake, Scully, don't say anything about Webster; we can meet our fate like men, but to mention his name now would be wrong indeed!"

"I don't know what I'm going to say." Scully bowed his head. He seemed delirious, almost intoxicated with dread, his clothing disheveled, his hair mussed. Had the rebels beaten him? Had they fed him moonshine to loosen his tongue? "I don't want to do wrong," he wept. "But I cannot tell you what I may have to do yet."

—◆—

"What's the matter?" Hattie Lawton blurted on the evening of April 3, rising from her chair in the corner of the dimly lit bedroom.

She had been sitting vigil in the private chamber of the Campbell residence while Webster writhed on the bed across the room in fitful, feverish slumber. Now he stirred at the sound of voices.

"One of Winder's men is below," the woman in the doorway nervously informed Lawton. "And I fear his presence indicates misfortune for Webster."

The woman's husband stood behind her in the hallway of the stately old home. The Campbells had been one of the few people left in Richmond who had shown any kindness to Webster after the guilty verdicts had been handed down against his two friends. Mr. Campbell had helped move Webster from the Monument to the Campbells' guest quarters, where Webster could receive better care.

Although Webster's condition had begun to improve in recent days, the last week in March had been a different kind of ordeal for the courier. Forced to testify in the sham proceedings conducted against Lewis and Scully, Webster had been obliged to give his statement from his hotel room. He had told the court that Lewis and Scully were good friends of the South and that they were in no way in the employ of the government. Apparently satisfied with his testimony, the officers of the court had left. After several anxious days, a newspaper was brought to Webster's bedside, revealing the grim verdict for Lewis and Scully. Subsequent news of the death sentences, in Pinkerton's words, "filled the cup of Webster's misery to overflowing, and, sinking upon a chair, he wept like a child."

Now Webster moaned across the room, as he slowly came awake at the commotion. "Who is it?" he said in a choked voice. "What do they want?"

"Cashmeyer," Mr. Campbell replied, referring to one of the head investigators with Winder's detective unit. "He inquired for you, Webster, and says he must see you at once."

"Let him come up at once," Webster said. Later, Hattie Lawton would tell Pinkerton that she thought she saw a glimmer of hope in Webster's reddened eyes at that moment. Perhaps Winder's men brought good tidings regarding Lewis and Scully—a stay of execution perhaps.

Mr. Campbell turned and vanished down the stairs, and a moment later he returned with the Confederate officer named Cashmeyer, who entered the room with, in Pinkerton's words, "a cold and formal manner." The officer looked at Webster and said, "I have the painful duty to inform you, Mr. Webster, that I am directed by General Winder to arrest you, and convey you at once to Castle Godwin."

In the deathly, stunned silence that followed—a silence that weighed down on the room—a pair of Confederate soldiers suddenly appeared in the doorway behind Cashmeyer.

"You cannot wish to take him away in this condition, at this hour of the night," Hattie Lawton protested. "Such an action would be his death and would be the worst of inhumanity!"

Webster climbed from his sickbed and stood shakily yet bravely, meeting the officer's gaze.

"I cannot help it," Cashmeyer said, a trace of sadness in his voice. Until this moment, the officer had treated Webster with respect, and with sympathy and condolence. Now he spoke carefully, almost gently, answering Lawton but not taking his eyes off of Webster. "My orders are to take him, dead or alive, and those orders I must obey."

"Then I will go, too," Lawton defiantly snapped. "He needs care and attention. Without it, he will die. And no one can nurse him so well as I."

Cashmeyer turned his gaze to the brazen little olive-skinned woman, a shade of pity coming over his face. "I am sorry to inform you, madam, that my orders are to arrest you as well, and to search your trunks."

"This is infamous!" Webster boomed. "What can Winder mean by arresting this woman, and what am I charged with that renders your orders necessary?"

The officer replied softly, "Webster, as God is my witness, I do not know. I only know what my orders are, and that I must obey them."

Later that night, in a fetid, rotting cell at Castle Godwin, Pryce Lewis rose from his cot and went over to the barred window to drink in what might very easily have been among his last glimpses of the natural world. He had been reading all night, ruminating on his fate, and around midnight had fallen into "a fitful sort of slumber, full of dreams," when the noise from the prison yard stirred him awake.

He looked down upon the moonlit drive and saw a carriage pulling up.

Three of General Winder's men got out and helped a fourth figure out of the coach. The fourth gentleman was, in Mackay's words, "well dressed but pale and ill"—Webster—followed closely by a very dejected-looking Hattie Lawton.

Lewis slumped with despair.

So Scully had talked after all.

Inside the receiving area of Castle Godwin, General Winder greeted the arresting officers with handshakes and smiles, and then, upon seeing Webster, the general brusquely ordered the ailing courier to be searched.

Webster was too weak to protest. After the cursory examination, Webster was, in Pinkerton's words, "remanded to a room, in which a number of Union prisoners were already confined, and the atmosphere of which was reeking with filth and disease."

As Webster stumbled into the room, pale and emaciated and scarcely able to walk, the other prisoners gathered around him, staring with silent pity.

One prisoner marveled, "My God, they will send the dead here next."

Chapter Nineteen

The Whisper of the Gallows

April 6, 1862

Part of Allan Pinkerton's genius—aside from his preternatural cunning and innate investigative skills—was his enormous heart. He felt a tremendous empathy for his fellow human beings, even for the fallen souls whom he helped bring to justice over the years. Perhaps this sensitivity— this kindness and warmth—helped him as an investigator, helped him judge character and understand human nature. But no greater expression of the man's tenderness can be found than in his reaction to the news that John Scully, in the early days of April, confessed to Timothy Webster's complicity in the counterespionage ring.

Pinkerton was in the field, near Yorktown, organizing scouts for McClellan, when he first heard that Lewis and Scully had been captured and sentenced to die. McClellan had just begun his Peninsular Campaign, leading more than 120,000 troops into position outside the historic port town for the first phase of his scientific assault on the heart of the Confederacy. There he met up with unexpected resistance from the forces of General J. B. Magruder—and the campaign immediately bogged down.

Yorktown, a sort of inaugural for McClellan's grand strategy, was the same place George Washington had defeated the forces of British General Cornwallis eighty years earlier, effectively ending the Revolutionary War.

Now, on the evening of April 6, 1862, Allan Pinkerton, head of McClellan's Secret Service, sat in a camp outside Williamsburg, scanning the Richmond newspapers for crumbs of intelligence, when he saw a small paragraph, which filled him with dread:

YANKEE SPIES!

Two Lincoln spies, giving the names of John Scully and Pryce Lewis, were arrested at the Monument Hotel and are now in prison. The proof of their connection with the Secret Service of the enemy is most positive. They were recognized on the street by a young lady, whose baggage they searched in Baltimore, while she was on her way to the south. Suspecting that they were detective officers sent by the Yankee government to Richmond, she communicated her suspicions to a young man, who gave information of the presence of the strangers at General Winder's office.

Pinkerton's blood "seemed to freeze in his veins." His heart stood still. He immediately relayed the terrible news to General McClellan.

In his memoir, Pinkerton recalls McClellan's reaction: "His sympathy and sorrow were as acute as though the men had been joined to him by ties of blood." But the most telling reaction came later, after all the facts of the debacle in Richmond were known, when Pinkerton learned that John Scully, in his darkest moment, had implicated Webster.

Writes Pinkerton:

Who can blame this man? Who, that has stood before the frowning scaffold, and with a free world before him, can utter words of censure? Only those who have suffered as he did, prostrated as he was, can know the terrible agony through which he passed, ere the fatal words were forced from his trembling lips. For myself, I have no judgment to utter. Now, as when the news was first communicated to me, I cannot express an unjust sentence . . . and who, in our day, can claim their possession in the very face of death and dishonor?

Morning seeped across the window ledge, the dull yellow light bringing little relief to the furrowed brow and heavy heart of Pryce Lewis, alone and forlorn in his claustrophobic limbo. When the cell door clanged open at 11:00, he hardly moved from his somber perch in the corner.

"I have good news for you, Lewis," Father McMullin said, stepping into the cell with a hopeful expression. The priest had been attempting to help the two condemned spies for days now.

Since Lewis and Scully were officially British subjects, not born in this country, a plea had been lodged at the British Consulate. But the request had gone nowhere. The acting British consul, described by Pryce Lewis as a "short, fussy, ineffectual" man named Frederick Cridland, had tried to persuade Winder to be lenient. But the general claimed, according to Mackay, that "he had enough evidence to hang a hundred Pinkerton agents."

Now the priest looked at Lewis and said, "President Davis has respited you for two weeks!"

Lewis looked up but said nothing. The stay of execution would most certainly come with conditions.

Sure enough, the priest added, "It still looks dark for you, though. . . . I think you should tell the authorities all you know."

Lewis did not.

For two weeks, he stuck to his cover story and denied knowing any Federal agents in Richmond. In the meantime, Winder's detective continued working on Scully. It was an agonizing period for Lewis, who was worried that Scully had already talked and implicated Webster. And in the end—even though General Winder could hardly imagine a man as well connected as Webster turning out to be a spy—it was indeed Scully's confession that sealed Webster's fate.

Around the middle of April, a guard casually mentioned to Lewis, in passing, that Timothy Webster had been found guilty and would hang.

———

On April 18, 1862, the news reached Allan Pinkerton that Timothy Webster had been sentenced to die on the morning of April 28.

In his memoir Pinkerton writes: "This was the crowning burden of all, and I was almost prostrated by the blow. Hurried consultations were held, every conceivable plan was suggested and discussed, which would avail in the slightest degree to avert so terrible a fate from the faithful patriot who was now in such deadly danger."

Panic and desperation in equal measures drove Pinkerton's frantic activities over those next few days.

He went to McClellan and suggested sending a "flag-of-truce" boat to Richmond to bargain for the lives of the three men. McClellan refused, claiming that a deputation of this kind would be a tacit admission that

Lewis, Scully, and Webster were indeed spies and would probably result in their instant execution.

Pinkerton decided to return immediately to Washington, where he could access the highest levels of government in his race against the clock. Accompanied by Colonel Thomas Key, a senior officer in McClellan's inner circle, Pinkerton arrived in the capital on April 21, and proceeded posthaste to the White House for an emergency audience with Lincoln, who agreed to summon a special cabinet meeting that night to consider the case.

Meanwhile, Pinkerton went to the War Department to make a special plea to Edwin Stanton, who was now Lincoln's secretary of war. "I will do everything in my power to save Webster's life," Stanton told Pinkerton, but then added, "I am little disposed to assist the others who betrayed their companion to save their own lives."

⚊⚊

That night, at the special cabinet meeting, Pinkerton made an impassioned plea for moving heaven and earth to save his operatives. Lincoln decided that the best course of action would be to communicate with the rebel authorities through official channels. He directed Stanton to draft a letter to Jefferson Davis, conveying several key points:

1. The Federal government had traditionally been lenient and forbearing toward rebel spies; and in many cases such persons had been released after a short confinement.

2. In no instance had anyone so charged by the Federal government been tried for his life or sentenced to death.

3. If the rebel government proceeded to carry out its sentence of death for these individuals, the Federal government would "initiate a system of retaliation which would amply avenge the death of the men now held."

Lincoln directed Stanton to authorize General John E. Wool—now occupying Fort Monroe, Virginia—to send the message by flag-of-truce boat or by telegraph. Stanton spent the rest of that night carefully wording the message.

By morning, Stanton had completed the letter and showed it to Pinkerton.

"Mr. Secretary, we cannot afford to imply," Pinkerton said, crestfallen, after reading the message. The letter hedged too much for Pinkerton's taste. "We must threaten. This is no time for diplomacy!"

Stanton was offended. "I do not tell you how to write your letters, sir," he said icily. "Do not tell me how to write mine."

In Arthur Orrmont's words: "Though a brilliant, able man, Stanton had a formidable weakness—he took criticism badly."

On the morning of April 23, Pinkerton and Colonel Key set out for Fort Monroe with the cabinet's dispatch. They found General Wool, who immediately forwarded the dispatch—marked top priority—to General Huger at Norfolk. The full text went out via telegraph from Norfolk to Jefferson Davis at the rebel capital that very afternoon.

The agonizing wait followed. Pinkerton paced the confines of the encampment well into the night, brooding, second-guessing himself, and lamenting the fact that he might have misread the dangers present in Richmond.

Years later he recalled those nail-biting moments at Fort Monroe: "Feeling that all had now been done that was possible to save the lives of my men, and believing that the hate and malignity of the rebel officers would not carry them to such a murderous extent as this, I awaited the result of our mission with painful solicitude."

As dusk closed in on the north side of Richmond, the sounds of sawing and hammering pierced the stillness of twilight in a grove of hickories.

In happier times this wooded meadow served as fairgrounds for such genial activities as pie eating contests and livestock shows, but in November 1860 fifteen companies of the First Regimental Cavalry of the Southern militia moved into the area and established the grounds as "Camp Lee."

"We anticipate a display of 'troopers,'" the *Richmond Dispatch* enthused at the time, "the likes of which we have never seen."

Over the next eighteen months, the sylvan pasture would be flooded with soldiers and materiel. The following May, the Twenty-third Virginia

Infantry Regiment would begin drilling here, and the grounds would become a major attraction in wartime Richmond. Citizens flocked to Broad Street on a regular basis to watch the troops prepare for battle.

But tonight, as darkness gathered around the Colonial-style barracks with their white pillars and steeples of Revolutionary heroes, the timbers of a new structure rose above the trees. The hangman's platform, hewn from pine, took shape as the gallows materialized like an apparition.

The banging and sawmill noises drifted on the evening breeze. With a shift in winds, would the sound have reached Carey Street, a couple of miles away, where the ugly, scorched-brick pile of Castle Godwin stood?

Would a whisper of the noise have penetrated the squalid cell where Hattie Lawton and Timothy Webster waited, hoping against hope for a reprieve?

There was a terrible logic behind the gallows being erected in such a conspicuous public arena, and Allan Pinkerton learned the reason the next day. Jefferson Davis sent a response back to the Union leaders—via General Huger—that he had considered the matter carefully. Davis agreed to commute the death sentences on Lewis and Scully, but that was as far as he would go.

In Timothy Webster's case—Davis reasoned—an example would have to be made. The execution would be carried out as originally planned, on April 28, which was less than a week away.

Pinkerton spent a sleepless night on April 24 at Fort Monroe. Wracked with despair, guilt, and rage, he could barely conceive of losing his best man to such appalling circumstances. Touched by tragedy more than once in his life, he still groped for a solution. It is likely he would have single-handedly pushed McClellan's troops onward toward Richmond, carrying the battle flag himself, if he thought it was possible.

Writes Arthur Orrmont: "Had McClellan moved faster toward Richmond, he might have been able to capture both the city and Timothy Webster. But 'Little Mac' was forced to fall back, and retreat in a masterly fashion to Harrison's Landing."

Until April 24, all contact between Timothy Webster and Hattie Lawton at Castle Godwin had been strictly supervised and limited to that of a medical nature. Now, with the execution set—and all potential reprieves declined—the guards relaxed their stance and allowed the two companions to be together around the clock.

Writes Pinkerton: "The meeting between Webster and Mrs. Lawton was a most affectionate one. Tears filled the eyes of the faithful woman, as she gazed at the pale and emaciated form of the heroic patriot."

For a time, the twosome simply comforted each other. They held each other's hands, and Lawton offered words of sympathy between her choked sobs. Webster, ever the stalwart professional, soothed and reassured Lawton, probably more than she comforted him.

The days passed in a blur, and Lawton rarely left Webster's side during this time. She straightened and cleaned his cell and made the grim surroundings as cheerful as possible. She cooked for him and made him delicacies with ingredients procured through the sympathetic staff. Lawton never gave up hope that Webster's terrible destiny, now looming in a matter of days, could be averted.

Lawton sought a meeting with Jefferson Davis but found the Confederate president otherwise engaged with General Robert E. Lee, and in no mood to hear further pleas. In a stunning act of Pinkertonian brazenness, Lawton managed to persuade Davis's wife, Varina, to accommodate a brief meeting.

In a tearful meeting, under guard at the presidential mansion, Hattie Lawton earnestly appealed to Varina Davis's humanitarian side. Lawton spoke of Webster's infirmities and pleaded with the First Lady of the Confederacy—a highly religious, intelligent woman—to have mercy on the poor soul, whose life hung in the balance.

It was all in vain.

Recalls Pinkerton: "While fully sympathizing with the fate of the unfortunate man, Mrs. Davis declined to interfere in matters of state, and Mrs. Lawton left the house utterly hopeless of being able to avert the dreadful fate which impended over Webster."

Over the last couple of days leading up to the execution, Webster most likely experienced a subtle yet very powerful shift in mind-set. Both Pinkerton and Lawton have suggested that Webster held a slim hope—albeit an unspoken one—that McClellan would reach Richmond before the fateful hour. But as Pinkerton writes: "As the days passed, and this result seemed further from accomplishment than ever, even that flickering ember of hope died out, and [Webster] prepared to meet his fate like a man."

All of which led to one last request, which Webster made on the day before his execution.

CHAPTER TWENTY

Death Be Not Proud

APRIL 27, 1862

Brigadier General John H. Winder, his lantern jaw triumphantly jutting, his mane of iron-silver hair swept back from his chiseled features, entered the prisoner's cell with a bounce to his step.

He expected to hear a full confession, a death's-door revelation from the prisoner who had summoned him that day. But when he saw Timothy Webster and Hattie Lawton sitting across the chamber, their backs rigid with purpose, something in their body language told the general that things were not necessarily as they first seemed.

"Webster, you have sent for me," the general said, standing on the threshold. "What is it that you desire?"

"General Winder, I have sent for you to make an appeal to your manhood." Webster spoke from the edge of his bed, his face wan with fever. "My fate is sealed—I know that all too well. I am to die, and I wish to die like a man."

"That's fine, Webster, but what is it that I can do for you?"

"I know there is no hope for mercy, but, sir, I beseech you to permit me to be *shot*, not be hanged like a common felon—anything but that."

"I am afraid that cannot be done," the general replied, after a brief moment's consideration.

"It is not much to ask," Webster pleaded. "I am to die, and am prepared, but, sir, for God's sake, let me not die like this. Change but the manner of my death, and no murmur shall escape my lips."

"I cannot alter the sentence that has been ordered."

At this point, Hattie Lawton—who had been standing nearby, trying to keep her raging emotions in check—could no longer hold her tongue.

"General, as a woman I appeal to you—you have the power and can exercise it. Do not, I pray you, condemn this brave man to the odium of a felon's death. Think of his family, and his suffering. It is not much that he asks. He doesn't sue for pardon. He doesn't seek to escape your judgment, harsh and cruel as it is. He only prays to be allowed to die like a brave man in the service of his country. You certainly have nothing to lose by granting this request; therefore, in the name of justice and humanity, let him be shot instead of the dreadful death you have ordained for him."

John Winder had a hard, square face, with a patrician nose that protruded over his thin, stern lips. While Lawton spoke, he made no attempt to interrupt, but his lips grew sterner, stiffer. When she finished, he turned on his heels and went to the door. "His request and yours must be denied," he said. "He hangs tomorrow."

The general started to leave.

"Then he will die like a man!" Lawton's words flew at the officer like darts. "And his death will be upon your head—a living curse until your own dark hour comes!"

Winder huffed out the door, slamming it violently, leaving the condemned in awful silence.

—◆—

Webster's last night passed with the agonizing, glacial slowness of a waking dream.

Hattie Lawton never left his side, and despite her own devouring sorrow, she did her best to strengthen and sustain him. She took down on paper his messages to friends and family, his expressions of love for his family and his statements of unwavering devotion to his country. She prepared his last meal and ministered to his needs, dabbing his fevered brow with damp cloths.

In the small hours of that night—the deepest nadir of darkness before dawn—Webster turned to Lawton and said, "And be sure to tell Major Allen that I met my fate like a man. Thank him for his many acts of kindness to me. I've done my duty, and I can meet death with a brave heart and a clear conscience."

Through her tears Lawton made sure she got every word just right.

—◆—

Pinkerton would not hear these words until many months later, but that night, back in Washington, tormented by the horrible cogs of fate that he had failed to stop, he most likely found sleep as problematic as did his hapless subordinates in Richmond. This moment—on a personal level on par with the loss of his daughters, as well as his mother's death in 1854— would haunt the sturdy detective for the rest of his life.

In fact, it is instructive to consider the passage in Pinkerton's Civil War memoir, written more than twenty years later, which postulates what might have been running through Timothy Webster's mind in that lonely cell on that last, horrible, endless night. The contents of the passage, reproduced here in its entirety, reveal more about Pinkerton than perhaps any other artifact or document that has survived the century and a half since these events occurred:

How many times the gaunt, repulsive form of the fatal scaffold appeared to the vision of the condemned man, as he sat firm and rigid in his dark cell, we may not know. How many times he lived over again the bright scenes of his past life! The happy, careless days of childhood, when the fond eyes of a loving mother beamed upon him in his sporting gambols. His school days, the lessons conned by the evening lamp in the dear old home of long ago. The merry days of youth, which glided away amid scenes of mirth and jollity. The first dawnings of the passion of his life, when a soft hand nestled lovingly in his, and earnest eyes, full of love and trust, seemed to speak a world of affection. Then the stirring scenes of active life, he a man among men, battling with the world, performing his daily duties, mingling honorably with his fellows, and upheld by a pride of honor and self-respect—all these thoughts came upon him with a distinctness which brought their actual presence near. Now he was listening to the sweet lullaby of his mother's voice, now he stood in the hall of the "Sons of Liberty," in the midst of affrighted conspirators and blue-coated soldiers—anon he strayed by a purling stream, with a loved one upon his arm—and again he breasted the dashing waters and deluging storm on the bay, as he rescued the women and children from the stranded boat. So vivid were these pictures of his mind that he lived again a hundred scenes of his past life, partook of a hundred pleasures, shared in a hundred sorrows. Suddenly in the midst of some thrilling vision of by-gone days,

the flickering of his lamp or the tread of the sentry outside would recall
him from a delightful reverie to the dark and dreadful present.

⁓

The first rays of dawn filtered through the barred window—heralding, in a merciless coincidence, a lovely spring day—as Webster lay, in Pinkerton's words, "calm and wakeful on his cot, his hand clasped tenderly in Lawton's." Neither spoke a word.

All at once there came the sound of hurried boot-steps outside the door in the corridor. The footsteps paused outside the cell. The bolts shot back, and the door jacked open to reveal the beefy form of a Confederate officer, Captain A. G. Alexander, in full dress grays.

The clock on the wall read a quarter past 5:00.

"Come, Webster, it's time to go."

Webster could barely sit up. "Go where?"

"To the fairgrounds."

"Surely not at this hour," Webster exclaimed, momentarily perplexed. "The earliest moment named in my death warrant is six o'clock."

"It's the order of General Winder, and I must obey it," Alexander told him. "You must prepare yourself at once."

Webster managed to climb to his feet. Although feeble with illness, his hands did not shake as Lawton helped him dress and groom himself as if for church. When he was ready, he turned to his longtime female companion. "Goodbye, dear friend," he murmured softly, taking both her hands in his. "We shall never meet again on earth. . . . God bless you and your kindness to me. I will be brave, and die like a man. Farewell, Hattie."

As the soldiers helped Webster totter out the door, Hattie Lawton collapsed.

Her tortured shriek might have been heard as far away as the steaming banks of the James River.

⁓

Writes James Mackay: "Not since September 1776, when Nathan Hale had been hanged as a spy by the British during the War of Independence, had an American been executed for espionage, and the Richmond crowds were determined to make the most of the entertainment."

By the time Webster arrived at the fairgrounds via carriage, the morning sun had risen, and a throng of thousands ringed the encampment, as though waiting for the livestock show or the pie eating contests to begin. There was a nip in the air, and Virginians had come from far and wide—from countless farms and villages up and down the James—to see the spectacle. They called out and hollered as Webster was slowly, arduously shuffled along the gauntlet to a building on the north side of the camp.

There, in a spartan room, he remained for nearly five hours, joined by a clergyman, who had been requested to accompany Webster in his last moments. At ten minutes past 11:00, the guards came and fetched Webster.

By this point, he could barely walk, and the attendants had to prop him up by each shoulder to get him across the distance to the gallows. Still, even in his wobbling condition, the doomed man wore a look of "calm composure" (Pinkerton's phrase). His pale face betrayed little emotion, and his eyes were clear. In the aftermath, the Richmond press would print all manner of biased and contradictory reportage on Webster's behavior. One account had him snarling and cursing the guards, while another claimed he wept and begged for mercy.

He did neither.

Timothy Webster simply trundled along as best he could, until he reached the steps of the gallows and then ascended slowly yet steadily to the platform. The hangman, a man named Kapard, awaited with the noose. Kapard, a warden from Castle Godwin, was not an official executioner—Richmond had no such practitioner at this time—and as he placed the noose around Webster's neck, his actions were tentative at best. Webster girded himself.

Writes Pinkerton: "Amid a breathless silence, he stood for a moment and gazed about him. The bright, blue sky overhead, the muskets of soldiers glistening in the rays of the sun, the white, eager faces, which surrounded him."

Somehow Webster managed to stay upright as the guards tied his hands behind his back and bound his legs. Then the black hood went over his head.

⸺

Darkness. Silence. The huff of a man's final breaths magnified by rough fabric.

Blinded and practically insensate, Webster may have very well heard his own heart pumping its last beats. An eerie silence had fallen across the fairgrounds, as though the entire assembly had ceased to breathe.

The signal rang out.

The trap door sprang.

And then something completely unexpected happened.

———

In 1890, author Ambrose Bierce, the great fictionalizer of the Civil War, wrote what is arguably his best-known story, included in the book *Tales of Soldiers and Civilians*.

"An Occurrence at Owl Creek Bridge" tells the fable of a condemned Confederate prisoner dropping through the gallows, only to find himself temporarily saved by a broken noose. A great and exciting chase ensues, as the soldier manages to escape the hanging party.

But alas, at the end of the yarn, the reader realizes it's all an elaborate delusion—conjured by the prisoner's traumatized brain, as he plunges inexorably through space—abruptly ending with the snap of the rope around his neck.

On April 28, 1862, amid the teeming masses of Camp Lee, Timothy Webster might have manufactured a similar hallucination as he struck the hard-packed ground beneath the gibbet with a thud (apparently the rope had been too slack to do its job properly).

Lying in a "confused heap" (Pinkerton's phrase), still blind and bound hand and foot, limp and motionless, Webster heard the noise of frantic voices all around him. All manner of illusory thoughts may have bombarded his mind at that point. Had he passed through some horrible portal?

Was this heaven or hell?

He probably decided upon the latter as he felt the hands of his captors upon him, roughly lifting him off the turf, then muscling him back up the steps of the gallows. The trap was readjusted, and the noose was once again wrapped around Webster's injured neck—this time, so tightly it caused excruciating pain.

Webster could barely get the words out, his voice muffled by the hood. "I suffer a double death," he uttered.

One of the guards shouted up at Kapard from beneath the gallows. "The rope's too short now!"

Kapard took his time casually measuring the rope as Webster suffered. "It'll do," Kapard said casually, then gave a nod to an assistant.

The door kicked open.

Webster fell a second time, now snapping hard and swinging for a moment in midair, then settling.

———

The body was left dangling for a full thirty minutes before being cut down.

The *Richmond Examiner* later observed, "There was not a motion of the body or a quiver of a muscle."

Pinkerton sadly recalls: "Rebel vengeance was at last satisfied, the appetite for human blood sated. Treason had done its worst, and the loyal spy was dead."

Later in the day, Winder's men cut up pieces of the hangman's noose as souvenirs.

———

"May I see him before he is taken away?" Hattie Lawton asked a sheepish Captain Alexander, who had just returned to Castle Godwin to give her the news.

"There is no objection to that," the rebel captain said softly.

Alexander accompanied Lawton downstairs to the makeshift morgue on the ground floor. There, in a dark room, Webster's remains lay in a metallic coffin.

Lawton approached slowly. She looked down at her dead comrade. His face looked oddly tranquil, not discolored or contorted in the least. Lawton took it as a sign he had died as he had lived—a brave man.

A group of rebel officers stood a respectful distance away, holding their hats.

Emotion surged within Hattie Lawton, and she turned to the men. "Murderers! This is your work! If there is vengeance or retribution in this world, you will all feel it before you die!"

Alexander, as if pierced by her words, came forward. He stepped up to the coffin and laid a hand on Timothy Webster's cold forehead. Speaking softly, his voice quavering with emotion, Alexander said, "As sure as there is a God in heaven, I am innocent of this deed. I did nothing to bring this about, and simply obeyed my orders in removing him from the prison to the place of execution."

It was the oldest excuse known to man, and on that day, it fell on deaf ears.

—◦—

Pinkerton petitioned General Winder for permission to send Webster's body back to the North for a proper burial. Permission was denied. Pinkerton tried to persuade the rebels to at least allow the body to be put in a vault at Richmond until the end of the war.

This request was also rebuffed.

Late at night on April 28, Winder ordered Webster's body to be carried away, to be buried in a pauper's grave outside Richmond.

CHAPTER TWENTY-ONE

Theater of Blood and Regret

MAY 1862

The devastating loss of Timothy Webster stole a piece of Allan Pinkerton's spirit.

In trademark fashion, the husky Scot sublimated his grief by immersing himself in the continuing labors of the war. General McClellan was on the move, and "Little Mac" needed his spymaster to scout the backwaters of eastern Virginia. Writes Arthur Orrmont: "Crushed by the blow, Allan Pinkerton threw himself desperately into work, hoping to avenge Webster's death by amassing more and more intelligence of the enemy who had killed his best man and taken from him a valued friend." But for the remainder of his tenure as head of the Secret Service, Pinkerton felt a diminution of his authority—a sense of being edged out of power by the flamboyant, devious Lafayette Baker.

Baker, whose own Union Intelligence Service began to overshadow Pinkerton's operation, spent much of his time attempting to discredit McClellan, sending reports of his alleged blunders to Lincoln. In cahoots with Secretary of War Edwin Stanton, Baker became notorious for utilizing strong-arm techniques adopted from his days as a professional vigilante in San Francisco. He terrorized, threatened, and blackmailed suspects, and he often bragged that there was no single Confederate spy or agent behind Union lines who was unknown to him.

The rivalry between Baker and Pinkerton would continue beyond the war, with Baker convincing many, including future historians, that *he* was the sole progenitor of the Secret Service.

By May 21, 1862, McClellan's forces had pushed to within eight miles of Richmond.

Unfortunately, at the edge of the Chickahominy River, the Army of the Potomac encountered treacherous swampland. Progress ground to a halt. Meanwhile, Lincoln decided to remove General McDowell's forces from McClellan's army—nearly forty thousand men—to guard Washington. This left McClellan in the dangerous position of launching an attack on the rebel capital with numbers equal to—or perhaps even less than—those opposing him.

Dreadful weather only added to the quagmire. Relentless rains flooded the river and made bridge building impossible. The Union advance was held up for days. Eventually McClellan inched his way forward, seizing Mechanicsville, only five miles outside of Richmond, on May 24.

In the meantime Robert E. Lee took command of the Confederate army and immediately launched fierce attacks on the Union's right wing. This drove McClellan back to the James River in a violent skirmish that came to be known as "The Infernal Week" (June 26 to July 2). Lee's eighty-five thousand clashed hard with McClellan's one hundred thousand, the sky raining cannonballs and each side holding its ground. In the grip of battle, on the morning of June 28, McClellan dashed off an angry telegram to Stanton at the War Department.

"If I save this army now," McClellan raged, "I tell you plainly that I owe no thanks to you or any other persons in Washington. You have done your best to sacrifice this army." Stanton was livid.

Pinkerton found himself caught in the middle of clashing egos. Perhaps disillusioned himself with the "carpet warriors" in Washington, Pinkerton started keeping track of the backroom maneuvering and fractious infighting. He wasn't exactly *spying* on his political masters, but he was paying very close attention.

On July 7, in an ill-advised gesture, McClellan drafted a long letter to President Lincoln, urging a more statesmanlike attitude toward the conduct of the war, as well as a more conciliatory approach to the Southern states in general. Ambivalent over slavery, McClellan had never been shy about expressing his mixed feelings toward the purpose of the war.

The general personally handed the letter to Lincoln on July 8, when the president paid a visit to McClellan's headquarters at Harrison's Landing.

It was the beginning of the end for George McClellan.

⸻

During this period Allan Pinkerton remained steadfastly loyal to his insolent, misunderstood general, who had already suffered the humiliation of being replaced as general-in-chief of the entire Union forces by Major General Henry Halleck. Looking back on these days, Pinkerton recalls, "I followed the fortunes of General McClellan, never doubting his ability or his loyalty, always possessing his confidence."

Pinkerton spent much of the summer months shuttling back and forth from the battlefield to Washington on his trusty sorrel horse. The steed had been with the beefy detective since before the war, and the two of them—man and beast—had formed a strong bond. The chestnut horse, with its massive hocks and thick neck, seemed as stubbornly impervious to fatigue as its master.

As August rolled on, Pinkerton busied himself with the business of interrogating prisoners, deserters, Union sympathizers, and runaway slaves. In Washington he found himself often testifying at court-martial hearings. He also continued grappling with racketeers, black-market operators, crooked contractors, and corrupt politicians. The more he learned, the more disillusioned he became with the power structure at the center of government.

When not struggling with Washington intrigue, Pinkerton followed McClellan's field headquarters southward, sometimes serving as the general's unofficial attaché and running interference between the army and the War Department.

Writes Mackay: "Allan's old loyalties were sorely tested and divided between the powerful personalities of the two men with whom he had worked before the war."

In fact, on one occasion, President Lincoln made an unannounced visit to one of McClellan's encampments. When told of the surprise guest, McClellan conveniently vanished. Hosting duties were left to Major Allen, who proceeded to entertain the president, reminiscing about the old days on the Illinois Central Railroad.

On another occasion, while encamped at McClellan's field headquarters, Pinkerton received an unexpected guest: his eldest son, William.

Now nearly sixteen, and prone to wear the slouch hats and worn tunics of the working-class artisan, Willie persuaded his father to let him stay on with the army and join the scouting parties for reconnaissance missions. William's "baptism of fire" came during the Battle of Malvern Hill. Engaged as a dispatch-rider, he raced back and forth through the barrage of zinging mini-balls, barely avoiding serious injury.

If Joan Pinkerton had caught wind of what was going on, she would have had both her son's *and* her husband's heads on a plate.

The truth of the matter, however, was that her husband was proud of his boy's courage and energy. In the early weeks of August, in fact, Willie proved his mettle even further by becoming an observer in one of Professor Thaddeus Lowe's giant weather balloons. It was the first time in history that aerial reconnaissance was used in warfare, and because of his modest weight, William Pinkerton was the first occupant of such a contraption.

By mid-August, the Army of the Potomac had retreated back to the York Peninsula. Ten major battles had been fought, and the losses on both sides were ghastly. McClellan's troops, battered and weary, needed encouragement. A message that McClellan wired to Halleck at this point provides an interesting window into McClellan's personality, a devotion to his troops that must have resonated with Pinkerton:

> *Please say a kind word to my army, that I can repeat to them in general orders . . . no one has ever said anything to cheer them but myself. Say nothing about me; merely give my men and officers credit for what they have done. They deserve it.*

No response came from Halleck. Animosities deepened between McClellan and Washington. Pinkerton watched the infighting with disgust, consistently taking McClellan's side. And regardless of the debate that has raged over the years among historians and scholars regarding

McClellan's effectiveness, it cannot be denied that "Little Mac" cared deeply for his soldiers.

The general petitioned the War Department endlessly for "fresh footwear, uniforms, blankets, greatcoats, and other stores" before the onset of winter that year. But the politicians refused practically every request—even though thousands of troops were barefoot and pack horses were starving.

On August 21, Halleck wired orders for McClellan to provide reinforcements to General John Pope's forces, who were being hemmed in by Lee. This did not sit well with McClellan. He despised Pope, not only for Pope's incompetence in the field, but also for Pope's infamous orders to his men, "giving them a free hand to rape and pillage."

In a letter to his wife, McClellan groused: "I will not permit this army to degenerate into a mob of thieves, nor will I return these men of mine to their families as a set of wicked and demoralized robbers."

Allan Pinkerton bore down harder on his fieldwork at this point. He smelled blood on the winds, a great battle looming between the forces of McClellan and Lee. Assigning a new team of operatives, headed by George Bangs, Pinkerton began closely monitoring Lee's movements. And in early September, a glimmer of good fortune shone on the spies.

One of Lee's aides had accidentally dropped a small parcel at a temporary encampment. The package contained three cigars—Lee's brand—wrapped in field orders. Discovered by a Union patrol, the parcel made its way to Pinkerton, who immediately showed the package to McClellan.

The general took one look at the documents and exclaimed, "Here is a paper with which if I cannot whip Bobbie Lee, I will be willing to go home."

On September 17, around dawn, in a vast meadow behind Antietam Creek, near Sharpsburg, Maryland, McClellan and Union General Joseph Hooker suddenly opened fire on Lee's left flank. Cannon blasts filled the air over Miller's cornfield, and the opposing ranks marched into a head-on collision. Mini-balls shredded the proud colors flying on either side, and the bodies of young men pirouetted in mists of blood.

The action intensified when Union Major General Ambrose Burnside entered the fray, capturing a stone bridge over the creek and slamming hard into Lee's right flank. But at a crucial point, Confederate General A. P. Hill's division arrived to launch a counterattack. Now the air filled with smoke and thunder, and chaos roared over the tattered cornstalks and bloody wild grass.

⸺⸺

At the height of battle, Pinkerton rode along the periphery of the action on his sturdy sorrel. The horse knew no fear and entered the rumble of artillery without complaint. Pinkerton, who was accompanying a cavalry squadron, needed to get to the other side of the stream, where deep woods would provide cover from Confederate snipers.

As he passed a rocky shoal, Pinkerton gave a yank on the reins, and the horse complied. Charging into the water, the steed dutifully carried its stocky rider across the sluggish creek.

Without warning a mortar blast shattered the clear sky and arched out over the creek. Pinkerton heard the sickening zing in the air, and all at once the cannonball smashed into the faithful horse, instantly killing the animal and launching Pinkerton out of the saddle.

Landing hard in the water, Pinkerton smashed his head against a small boulder. He most likely suffered a concussion, but somehow he managed to stagger to his feet, half stunned, and called out to a passing cavalry officer. The officer scooped him from the water, and Pinkerton climbed onto the man's horse.

Riding double in a hail of gunfire, the two men stole away to the far banks—and into the forest. Pinkerton, heartbroken once again, bowed his head at the loss of his mount.

⸺⸺

The Battle of Antietam would turn out to be the bloodiest single-day skirmish in American history: twenty-three thousand young men either dead, wounded, or missing in the muddy rural pasturelands. Worst of all, the tactical outcome was inconclusive. Although technically a Union victory, Lee was allowed to retreat in relatively good condition.

In the aftermath of the battle, McClellan sent Pinkerton back to Washington to gauge Lincoln's reaction.

After a lengthy meeting with Lincoln, Pinkerton wired back to McClellan: "I must confess that he impressed me more at this interview with his honesty towards you and his desire to do you justice than he has ever done before."

It was a false sense of security, however, as the tide of the war was about to change, along with the fortunes of McClellan and Pinkerton.

———

Two days after Pinkerton's visit to the White House, on September 22, 1862, Abraham Lincoln published his Emancipation Proclamation.

Flush with strategic victory at Antietam, Lincoln now changed the complexion of the war. The executive order declared the freedom of all slaves in the Confederate states. It did not address border states, but it did, in effect, provide the legal framework to free more than four million slaves. It also posited a higher purpose for the Civil War.

The dynamic in the South immediately shifted. As Northern regiments slowly closed in on enemy states, slaves began running away in droves, heading for Union lines, at which point they would legally be free.

Reactions in Washington to the proclamation were mixed at best.

A bitterly divided cabinet argued over the best resolution to the slave issue. Some favored conscription of all freed Southern blacks into the Union army. Others proposed forced exile of the slaves to colonies in Liberia, Haiti, or Panama. The proclamation rattled the nation, and rumors of plots against the government spread across the land on both sides of the Mason-Dixon Line.

Pinkerton did not know it then, but the seismic shifts in the government's prosecution of the war had only just begun.

———

October brought agonizing frustrations for Pinkerton. In Washington, he battled recalcitrant War Department accountants who refused to pay his operatives in a timely manner. Assistant Secretary Peter Watson demanded the full names of Pinkerton's spies.

Until this point, Pinkerton had simply provided the paymasters with initials, and now Pinkerton was angrily refusing to comply with Watson's demands. "The very nature of this service," he sharply informed the bureaucrat, "requires me to keep my men unknown."

Complicating matters were signs—observed by Pinkerton but mostly kept to himself—that Stanton and his minions were engineering further changes in the high command. While McClellan consolidated his position—strengthening defenses around Harper's Ferry on the Shenandoah and building great pontoon bridges to transport wagons and artillery over that river—wheels were in motion in Washington to reshuffle the hierarchy of command.

———

Much has been written over the years of George McClellan's Achilles' heel as a field general—his hesitancy to attack, his delaying tactics, his punctilious insistence on caution and stacking the odds in his favor. At Antietam, McClellan's final sin of omission (in the eyes of his superiors in Washington) was allowing Lee to retreat and not pursuing the Confederate forces into Richmond.

With the benefit of hindsight, as well as the knowledge of Timothy Webster's onetime overestimate of rebel troop strength in the Southern capital, historians have fixated on Allan Pinkerton as a convenient scapegoat for McClellan's downfall. For generations, Pinkerton biographers, Civil War scholars, and historians have perpetrated the canard of Pinkerton's alleged faulty intelligence as the reason for McClellan's strategic gaffs. To this day—even though modern scholars have reached a different consensus—the Internet is rife with Pinkerton-bashing.

"Intelligence is not the word," gripes one anonymous chat room participant. Another blogger wisecracks, "Not recognizing Pinkerton as the Confederate operative he so obviously was had to be McClellan's greatest failing." Author and historian Thomas Allen, writing on the CIA website, remarks, "McClellan, who himself was naturally inclined to embellish troop strength estimates, believed Pinkerton's numbers."

Even Pinkerton's own grandniece, Margaret Pinkerton Fitchett, writing in an unpublished memoir, parrots the prevailing wisdom of the mid-twentieth century, claiming her great-uncle "failed dismally as an intelligence agent."

But perhaps the strongest condemnation of Pinkerton's work as a spymaster comes from biographer James Horan in his 1967 book, *The*

Pinkertons: The Detective Agency That Made History, in which he devotes an entire chapter ("Too Many Bayonets") to Pinkerton's shortcomings as an intelligence officer:

> *In the spring and summer of 1862 Allan Pinkerton's headquarters was in the field with the Army of the Potomac. Here he failed miserably both as a front lines intelligence officer and as a political infighter. The best that can be said of him is that he should have remained in Washington, chasing spies.*

Horan's sweeping condemnation—one of the principle sources of this pervasive "faulty intelligence" theory—is apparently just the beginning. Horan had problems with Pinkerton's entire modus operandi. Among many other critiques, the biographer writes of the detective's alleged naïveté in believing that slaves had something to offer:

> *In the field, Pinkerton, in his sympathy, was uncritical of the excited, uneducated slaves who stood before him in his tent, twisting a ragged hat, shuffling their feet in the excitement of knowing that at last they were among friends and in sight of food and freedom. Though they were incapable of giving realistic information about what was happening on a grand scale behind Confederate lines, it is evident that Pinkerton believed everything they told him.*

Countering these tenuous arguments are more recent works on the subject, which all but disprove Horan's postulations. "Horan makes much of the fact that [Pinkerton] imported to the battlefield the working methods of his Chicago detective agency, with disastrous results," writes James Mackay, "although no actual reports are cited in support of this view."

Another one of the central pillars of the controversy—besides the mistakes made in the Webster case—revolves around a report McClellan sent to Stanton on June 25, 1862, in which the combined forces of Lee and Stonewall Jackson were estimated to be near two hundred thousand men. In reality, the Confederate troop strength was approximately half that figure. Horan places the blame for this inaccuracy squarely—and unfairly—on Pinkerton's shoulders. But, as Mackay writes, "[The] mass of reports and dispatches quoted so extensively by McClellan in his own story gives the lie to this."

McClellan augmented Pinkerton's intelligence with myriad reconnaissance missions and follow-up reports from his staff. He did not rely exclusively on Pinkerton's analysis, hence his reports cannot be attributed solely to Pinkerton's intelligence (which, by numerous accounts, appears mostly sound). Moreover, the historical record shows that as late as July 1862, McClellan was unsuccessfully lobbying his masters in Washington for only ten thousand fresh troops—which belies the myth that Pinkerton single-handedly spooked McClellan into requiring fifty thousand to a hundred thousand more men.

Contemporary scholars place the blame elsewhere. The fluid nature of troop movements in the early years of the war, combined with overwhelming evidence of Pinkerton's comprehensiveness in his reports to McClellan, inform the modern reassessment of Pinkerton's effectiveness as a pioneering intelligence chief. But perhaps the best argument for reconsideration is found in the very nature of George McClellan as a tactician. Naturally cautious, relentlessly analytical, McClellan did not need faulty intelligence in order to founder in the field.

As historian Edward Bonekemper writes in his 2007 book *McClellan and Failure*, "[McClellan] was unlikely to have taken the offensive on the Peninsula until absolutely compelled to do so—regardless of how many troops he had."

~~

At 11:30 on the night of November 7, General Ambrose Burnside and General C. P. Buckingham rode into McClellan's field headquarters with stunning news. Stanton was ordering McClellan to hand over his command to Burnside. McClellan would be demoted to a job behind the lines in Trenton, New Jersey, for the duration.

Pinkerton was infuriated—if not surprised—by the decision. McClellan's men were thunderstruck, threatening to march on Washington to take over the government. McClellan, exhibiting his trademark professionalism and poise, stayed on long enough to calm the situation and hand the command over to Burnside in an orderly fashion.

On November 10, in Warrenton, Virginia, the Army of the Potomac gave "Little Mac" an emotional send-off. Raw recruits and grizzled veterans alike "wept uncontrollably, as their favorite general, desperately struggling to maintain his self control, rode along their ranks."

In his emotionally charged farewell address, McClellan told his men: "In parting from you I cannot express the love and gratitude I bear you. As an army you have grown up under my care. In you I have never found doubt or coldness. The battles you have fought under my command will proudly live in our nation's history. The glory you have achieved, our mutual perils and fatigues, the graves of our comrades fallen in battle and by disease, the broken forms of those whom wounds and sickness have disabled—the strongest associations which can exist among men—unite us still by an indissoluble tie."

In sympathy with McClellan, Pinkerton officially resigned his commission as head of the Secret Service and withdrew all his operatives from the Army of the Potomac. He mistrusted Burnside, who made no effort to retain Pinkerton's services.

On his last day at Warrenton, after packing his personal items, he wrote a letter to Pryce Lewis, who was still in prison at Castle Godwin.

Pinkerton told Lewis he was resigning from the army and "returning to the old stand in Chicago."

Chapter Twenty-Two

Under the Providence of God

SEPTEMBER 29, 1863

The prison boxcar slowed in a scream of metal and a whirlwind of steam.

Inside the dark compartment, the emaciated prisoner, dressed in ragged tatters, peered through the slats and saw the pier, the gray reaches of the Chesapeake in the distance, and the exchange boat moored there with its star-spangled banner flying proudly on its mast.

Pryce Lewis wept for joy. Upon his release from Castle Godwin—accompanied by John Scully in a prisoner exchange—Lewis writes in his memoir: "If before this moment I had any English feelings left, I was turned into a complete American at that time."

Lewis and Scully arrived in Annapolis the next morning, expecting a heroes' welcome. Instead, they found themselves greeted by no one. Pinkerton was now in Chicago, McClellan in New Jersey. Lewis didn't even have enough money for transport fees into Washington and had to pawn his once-elegant suit coat for three dollars. This bought the former prisoners two tickets and a little bread and cheese for the trip.

Upon arriving in Washington that night, the two men sought the comfort of the only high-ranking official they could remember meeting: William Wood, superintendent of the Old Capitol Prison.

Stirred from his bed, Wood went down to the prison gates and stared in disbelief at the ragged souls standing on the threshold. But when Wood heard the unmistakable British accent of Pryce Lewis, he gasped. Wood immediately took the wayward spies in, fed them, and had them examined by the prison doctor.

Wood could barely hold back his tears as he watched the two men devour the food like ravenous dogs. "My God," Wood kept saying. "Why didn't you telegraph me? I would have sent a special locomotive for you."

The next day, Wood found the War Department completely apathetic about the former spies. Stanton wanted nothing to do with the two men. Finally Wood telegraphed Pinkerton, who was en route to Philadelphia for a case. Pinkerton wired back:

> *Many thanks for your kind information. Tell Scully and Lewis to come here. I cannot possibly leave just now. Should they require money to come please let them have it. I will return it to you. Give them my address here and tell them to avoid all publicity of their affairs until they see me.*

Very little is known about the meeting in Philadelphia between Pinkerton and the two spies. It is clear that Lewis and Scully—after languishing for nearly a year and a half in the hellish confines of Castle Godwin—felt betrayed by their boss. It is also likely that Pinkerton was still stinging from the loss of Webster. In Lewis's memoir, the dapper Brit alludes to "a hot interview with the old man."

Neither Lewis nor Scully would ever work for Pinkerton again.

———

Washington's Old Capitol Prison—run with an iron hand by the volatile Wood—had been home to another key player in the Pinkerton saga since January 1862. Rose Greenhow had spent seventeen months at the facility, housed with her daughter Rose, defiantly continuing to speak out against her captors. Charming her guards, cavorting with officials, secretly sending messages to rebel authorities, and lobbying influential Washingtonians for her parole, she finally managed to secure her release in June 1863.

Under armed escort—after promising in writing not to return to the North for the remainder of the war—Greenhow was taken to the front lines and handed over to rebel officials. She was given a hero's welcome by the South and treated like royalty.

In August 1863, she went abroad as an unofficial ambassador of the Confederacy. Her memoir, *My Imprisonment and the First Year of Abolition Rule in Washington*, was published in November of that year and became an overnight best seller. She dined with Queen Victoria and Napoleon III.

In September of the following year, she took passage on the British steamship *Condor*, ostensibly to return to America to present a diplomatic report to her old friend Jefferson Davis. On September 30, 1864, the ship encountered a tremendous storm off the coast of Wilmington, South Carolina, and ran aground.

In an effort to avoid Federal gunboats, Greenhow insisted that the captain lower a lifeboat so that she and other agents could escape. Near the shore, the lifeboat capsized, and Greenhow's two male companions managed to swim to safety. But the grande dame was not as fortunate.

Apparently Greenhow had sewn hundreds of gold sovereigns (the royalties from her book) into the lining of her corset and underclothing, and the weight caused her to sink and drown in the raging waters off Wilmington.

Writes Pinkerton: "No trace of her was ever afterwards discovered."

In 1864, John Scully returned to Chicago and spent the rest of his working life as a security guard at City Hall. He died in obscurity, his death date unknown. Pryce Lewis, on the other hand, experienced a far more notable—if not tragic—destiny.

Serving out the remainder of the Civil War working for Wood as a bailiff at the Old Capitol, Lewis never truly shed the guilt and angst over the Timothy Webster debacle. The common belief among Northerners was that Lewis had spilled his guts in Richmond.

In 1866, when Wood took over as head of the Secret Service (replacing Lafayette Baker), Pryce Lewis joined Wood's staff and served in good stead for many years as an operative for the fledgling agency. Later in his life, Lewis went to work for the Equitable Life Assurance Society in New York.

In 1903, the Pinkerton National Detective Agency—then run by Pinkerton's sons—published a small pamphlet setting the record straight on Timothy Webster's capture and execution. The publication fully vindicated Pryce Lewis, who had fought long and hard to clear his name. According to the pamphlet, "Lewis remained staunch and did not confess." But apparently the gesture came too late for Pryce Lewis.

Secretly haunted by the stigma of betrayal, Lewis committed suicide in 1910 in New York by jumping off the top of the Pulitzer Building.

Lafayette Baker, Pinkerton's nemesis in Washington, would ultimately see his own career end in disgrace. Accused by President Andrew Johnson of spying on the White House (a charge Baker would admit to in his memoirs), Baker was relieved of his duties as government spymaster in 1866.

He would go to his grave, in 1868, the victim of arsenic poisoning.

His murderer was his brother-in-law, Wally Pollack, an employee of the U.S. War Department.

⸺

Allan Pinkerton spent the remainder of the war years—1862 to 1865—commuting between Washington and Chicago, resuming much of the old casework that had been shelved back at the agency's headquarters. Most of his civil work during this period involved the railroads. He successfully tracked down and secured the prosecutions of a dozen conductors on the Philadelphia and Reading rail lines for brazen acts of large-scale larceny.

In the spring of 1864, Pinkerton and his team of operatives—including a feisty Willie Pinkerton, now seventeen—responded to a request from Secretary Stanton to go to New Orleans to investigate massive cotton frauds. And it was there, in the Crescent City—as Pinkerton uncovered damning evidence of corruption on a grand scale—that the burly detective received the horrible news that his seven-year-old daughter, Belle, who had been in poor health most of her life, had died. This tragedy, in some ways, was the final shock that would steal what was left of Pinkerton's spirit.

Now Pinkerton watched the events around him spiral toward historic, and sometimes heartbreaking, conclusions.

⸺

George Brinton McClellan, the brilliant, mercurial military strategist known by many as "Little Mac," never again assumed a command of any military force. His ambivalence over the Emancipation Proclamation—he told his wife back in 1862 that he felt "no sweeping measure of emancipation should be carried out"—would ultimately lead him to the political arena.

In August 1864, with the war raging toward its bloody denouement, McClellan pursued the presidency on the Democratic ticket by wooing disgruntled Republicans. The former general-in-chief ran on a platform of "unswerving fidelity to the Union under the Constitution," and he roundly condemned the Lincoln administration for "its lack of sympathy toward prisoners-of-war." McClellan promised "care, protection, and regard" for all soldiers and sailors.

As one historian puts it: "[McClellan] was *too* successful in this respect, for some of his most enthusiastic supporters were notorious Copperheads."

Pinkerton found himself embroiled in an unexpected controversy at this time when one of McClellan's aides, Colonel E. H. Wright, called a secret meeting with the detective to present evidence of a plot by some of McClellan's friends to murder Lincoln. Pinkerton's reaction was characteristically prophetic. He believed that the election "was already settled," that McClellan had no chance of winning, and that the tide of history would bury the conspiracy.

Pinkerton was correct on almost all counts. In November, McClellan carried only three states—Delaware, Kentucky, and New Jersey—and lost in a landslide favoring Lincoln. The final electoral tally was twenty-one for McClellan and 212 for Lincoln.

The day after the election, McClellan sent to Lincoln the resignation of his commission as a major general in the regular army.

———

Pinkerton was in New Orleans when the war that had claimed six hundred thousand lives came to a somber close. On April 9, 1865, General Robert E. Lee surrendered his army at Appomattox Courthouse to Lincoln's greatest asset, the forty-three-year old former West Point cadet and battle-scarred veteran of the Mexican-American War, Ulysses S. Grant.

Five days later, on Good Friday, amid the festive, celebratory atmosphere in Washington, Mary Todd Lincoln, who had just recently come out of a deep depression over the loss of her youngest son, William, urged her husband to accompany her to a play.

Ford's Theatre was showing *Our American Cousin*, playwright Tom Taylor's farce about an awkward, boorish American who goes to England to claim his family's estate from his aristocratic relatives. The play, which had done huge business in New York at Keene's Theater, was a light-hearted romp full of laughs and wordplay—just the kind of medicine for melancholy that the Lincolns needed at this point.

Lincoln thought it might be nice to take Ulysses Grant along, but the general had plans to take his wife to Philadelphia that night and politely declined. After attempting to persuade several other couples to come with similar results, the Lincolns invited Major Henry Rathbone and his fiancée, Clara Harris, who enthusiastically accepted.

Mrs. Lincoln was very fond of Clara and had invited her to attend numerous White House functions in the past. Having her along at the play would be a pleasant distraction.

The Lincolns ran late that night. The curtain was scheduled for 8:00, but the presidential carriage didn't arrive at the theater until 8:25, the first act of the play well under way. The coachman, Francis Burns, pulled the carriage up to the front of the theater, while the valet, Charles Forbes, opened the doors for the fashionably late quartet. Lincoln's bodyguard, John F. Parker, led the way up to the theater's second floor, where the private presidential box awaited its famous occupants.

Parker, as a security agent, had a somewhat spotty record. He had a weakness for drink and prostitutes, and had been disciplined on various charges over the years. But on this night, he had a chance to redeem himself by steadfastly remaining at his post outside the door to Lincoln's private box seats for the duration of the performance. If he had done so, the annals of history would have recorded the events of April 14, 1865, very differently.

As it happened, Parker got bored by the second act and left his post. He went downstairs, found Burns and Forbes, and the three of them adjourned to Peter Taltavul's saloon next door for an evening of drinks and fellowship.

Back at the theater, the play continued. The second act curtain fell, and the third act started up moments later in a swell of whimsical music.

Up in the dark cubicle of the bunting-draped presidential box, Lincoln and his companions enjoyed the arch humor of Taylor's play. Rathbone and Harris held hands. Mary Todd Lincoln chuckled softly, as her husband gently rocked in his upholstered bent-wood rocker.

Halfway through the third act, in scene two, the main character of the play, Henry Hawk, utters the line considered the showstopper. When accused by the British dowager of not knowing the manners of good society, he says, "Well, I guess I know enough to turn you inside out, old gal—you sockdologizing old man-trap!"

That night, the line got a tremendous wave of laughter that drowned the noise of John Wilkes Booth slipping unnoticed into Lincoln's compartment.

The .44-caliber blast that rang out in the wake of that laughter changed history, changed the Reconstruction, changed the balance of power in the wounded land for generations. Writes historian James L. Swanson: "The ball ripped through [Lincoln's] chestnut colored hair, cut the skin, perforated the skull, and, because of the angle of Lincoln's head at the moment of impact, drove a diagonal tunnel through Lincoln's brain from left to right. The wet brain matter slowed the ball's velocity, absorbing enough of its energy to prevent it from penetrating the other side of the skull and exiting through the president's face. The ball came to rest in Lincoln's brain, lodged behind his right eye. Lincoln never knew what happened to him."

Among the innumerable lives transformed by the assassination, Allan Pinkerton—still in New Orleans, still recovering from the shock of his daughter's death—experienced the loss of Lincoln as a sort of nightmarish inversion of the inaugural passage through Baltimore only four years earlier. "Under the providence of God," he wrote to the War Department on April 19, "in February 1861 I was enabled to save him from the fate he has now met. How I regret that I had not been near him previous to the fatal act. I might have had the means to arrest it."

CHAPTER TWENTY-THREE

High Lonesome

RECONSTRUCTION AND BEYOND: 1865–1884

Over the next few turbulent, acrimonious, chaotic years—commonly known as the Reconstruction Era—Pinkerton cemented his place in history as the quintessential gumshoe. While carpetbaggers, scalawags, and violent opposition groups such as the Ku Klux Klan terrorized the beleaguered South, Allan Pinkerton turned his attentions to the west.

With the advent of the first transcontinental railroad, a new kind of criminal had emerged: the proverbial armed outlaw. And Pinkerton was there with his ever-expanding roster of steel-nerved "Pinks" to catch them.

During this period, Pinkerton's sons, William and Robert, rose in prominence as managing partners, and the number of cases closed by the Pinkertons over the next decade staggered the imagination. They tracked down the infamous Reno Brothers—the nation's first iconic band of train robbers—by kidnapping the Reno patriarch. They caught the homicidal Farringtons—a pair of murderous twins from Tennessee—by infiltrating their tiny rural community. They guarded innumerable payrolls, and they investigated countless holdups across the Wild West.

The new robber barons needed the services of private police forces, and the Pinkertons were the gold standard. The agency had opened branch offices in Philadelphia, New Orleans, and Denver, and business boomed. Other detective agencies began to spring up across the nation, copying Pinkerton's business model and innovative techniques.

Pinkerton had reached the height of his powers, and his hubris shows in a letter he wrote to George Bangs from this period:

*I feel no power on earth is able to check me, no power in Heaven or
Hell can influence me when I know I'm right. I think it cannot be long
ere our enemies flee—that they are vanquished, it cannot be long if we
persevere in the right and they are continually wrong.*

Kate Warne, the matronly heart and soul of the Pinkerton Female Detective Bureau, the woman who had enjoyed the honor of accompanying Abraham Lincoln on his inaugural passage to Washington, continued to provide exemplary service as a detective until a consumptive illness slowed her down late in 1867.

On January 28, 1868, as church bells rang outside her window, Mrs. Warne died quietly in her sleep. She was thirty-five years old.

Pinkerton was at her bedside. Later he wrote of her extraordinary service: "She exceeded far beyond my utmost expectations. Mrs. Warne never let me down."

The next day, delivering the sad news to George Bangs in a telegram, Pinkerton noted gloomily, "The old group is slowly dying off."

Pinkerton sent George Bangs to Richmond to locate Timothy Webster's unmarked grave. At some length, Bangs found the site and had the coffin disinterred and shipped back to the North for a proper funeral, as well as a gravestone befitting Webster's prolific and heroic accomplishments.

Webster was buried in Onarga, Illinois, in a lovely cemetery lined with larch trees, near Pinkerton's summer home. Years later a memorial to Webster was erected in Chicago's Graceland Cemetery—on the Pinkerton family plot—with an elaborate, moving epitaph:

IN THE MEMORY OF
TIMOTHY WEBSTER
THE PATRIOT AND MARTYR
BORN IN 1821 IN NEW HAVEN
SUSSEX CO. ENGLAND
EMIGRATED TO AMERICA IN 1833
AND ENTERED

PINKERTON'S
NATIONAL DETECTIVE
Agency of Chicago in 1856

On the night of Febr. 22, 1861
ALLAN PINKERTON,
TIMOTHY WEBSTER
And KATE WARNE
safely protected
ABRAHAM LINCOLN
a conspiracy having been discovered
for his assassination from
Philadelphia to Washington
where he was inaugurated
President of the U.S.
on
March 4th, 1861

———

He enjoyed the confidence of
ABRAHAM LINCOLN
And sealed his fidelity with his blood.

———

Hattie Lawton, registered at the dismal Castle Godwin as "Mrs. Timothy Webster," spent a little more than a year in Confederate prison.

On December 13, 1862, she was one of four Federals released in a prisoner exchange. Pinkerton would never see Lawton again. Writes historian Priscilla Rhoades: "Like the professional operative she was, she vanished without a trace."

———

Harry Davies, the polished young Frenchman who had infiltrated the Palmetto Guards back in Baltimore in 1861, left the Pinkerton organization at the start of the war. He enlisted in a Union cavalry regiment and served as an officer for the remainder of the conflict. No record exists of his postwar life.

In April 1869, the long hours and inhuman stress finally caught up with Allan Pinkerton. As he sat at his desk in his Chicago headquarters, a sudden blinding headache drove him to the floor. He had suffered a massive stroke. He was rushed home, and after visits from physicians, was told he would never walk again.

Completely paralyzed on one side and virtually unable to speak, Pinkerton refused to succumb. His iron will confounded the best doctors in Chicago and New York. He spent months soaking in medicinal salt springs in Michigan, and gradually he regained the use of his legs. He forced himself to take excruciatingly painful morning walks, each day going a little farther, until he was walking twelve miles a day. Although he never fully recovered physically, his mind was as sharp as ever, and he was back at work—albeit behind a desk—in the early months of 1871.

By this point, William and Robert were effectively running the business.

On the evening of October 8, 1871, a fire broke out in Chicago's lumber district and caught on the lake winds. The blaze vaulted over the river and devoured the ranks of wooden structures lining the north side. By the time the conflagration was brought under control, nearly eighteen thousand buildings were gone.

Among the properties lost in the Great Chicago Fire was Pinkerton's headquarters, its priceless cache of case files and Civil War history reduced to ash. Later, the *Chicago Tribune* carried a banner headline: THE MOST COMPLETE AND EXTENSIVE RECORDS OF CRIMINAL HISTORY IN AMERICA DESTROYED.

By 1877, William and Robert Pinkerton had officially taken over control of the agency. The old man, however, did not go gently into that good night. Pinkerton spent his final years furiously churning out memoir after memoir, spinning numerous yarns of lurid derring-do, and, some would say, an embroidery of embellishments. He also continued to micromanage the business from his armchair, meddling in every detail of the agency, driving his sons to distraction. After one particularly messy feud, Pinkerton presented his son, Robert, who was contemplating resignation, with a letter, which, in the words of James Mackay, "pulled out every stop, applied every last ounce of emotional blackmail and ended with the anguished proclamation, 'You are my children . . . I love you . . . soon you will have everything.'"

———

George H. Bangs, Pinkerton's devoted superintendent—and perhaps the closest thing to a best friend the brawny detective ever had—retired from the agency in 1881.

On September 14, 1883, William Pinkerton brought a telegram to his father, which carried news that Bangs had died suddenly at his summer home in Roselle, New Jersey. Later, William Pinkerton recalled his father's reaction: "[He] sat staring straight ahead, hands gripped tightly over the head of his cane, tears rolling silently down his cheeks."

———

The last known letter dictated by Allan Pinkerton before his death was sent in October 1883 to a black man named C. E. Chapman. A former slave, Chapman had written to the agency to express his admiration for Pinkerton's fight against slavery and to ask if Mr. Pinkerton might be willing to provide an autograph.

Pinkerton replied in writing: "I am not in the habit of giving my autograph to any persons, for particular reasons to myself, but in this instance for the purpose you wish it, I forward it to you. I have always been a friend to the colored man and will do anything to secure him his rights."

In Memoriam

Glory is that bright tragic thing
That for an instant
Means Dominion—
Warms some poor name
That never felt the Sun,
Gently replacing
In oblivion.

—EMILY DICKINSON

SUNDAY, JUNE 8, 1884

The old man trundled down a sidewalk, past the gargantuan, gilded, iron-reinforced buildings that had risen from the ashes of the Great Chicago Fire. Once a bull of a man with broad shoulders and a barrel chest—his dark Scottish features set off by a lush beard—he now hunched as he walked, his beard cobweb-gray, his portly body infirm and trembling with the palsy of a past paralytic stroke.

Eleven weeks short of his sixty-fifth birthday, he would have given the impression of a man a decade older.

Yet even in his feeble condition, the old man would have exhibited a certain stubbornness in his gait. Through close observation one might detect the faint remnants of an indomitable life force. The old man refused to be shut in—even after a series of illnesses. He insisted on walking, and therefore, on this mild summer day, he hobbled on, alone, obstinate, Sisyphus in a bowler hat.

No one knows the cause of his fall. The impediment that made him trip is unknown, lost in the annals of historical minutiae. But what *is* known is that the old man, at some point that day, tumbled to the pavement and bit his tongue hard enough to contract gangrene within days, and eventually a severe case of septicemia.

Sure-footed and as steady as bedrock throughout most of his career, he had fallen only a handful of times in the past. In Chicago, on a blustery night in 1853, pierced by an assassin's bullet, he had toppled to the paving stones. In the pandemonium of the battlefield, at Antietam, his mount blasted out from under him, he had plunged to the rocky river bottom. But on *this* occasion, with his stroke-ravaged nervous system shutting down, the blood welling up in his mouth, he may very well have realized that gravity was now claiming him for the duration.

He may very well have known that he would not stubbornly walk away from *this* collapse.

In those endless moments before help arrived—perhaps from a passerby or from a citizen who recognized the old man—did Allan Pinkerton struggle to remain conscious? Did he find his thoughts casting back over the epic trajectory of his life? Like the valiant condemned man facing the gallows, did he flash back to the Glasgow slums of his boyhood, his sainted mother Isabella proudly bringing home a single egg for the family? Did he see the soulful brown eyes of his beloved Joan, or hear her lovely soprano voice crooning "The Rose of Allandale"—the words coming back to the old man on a Great Highland bagpipe's mournful call? *"The flowers be-decked the mountainside/And fragrance filled the vale."* Or did he remember those bonny days on the Fox River as he fashioned barrels in his little workshop in Dundee, the river purling down the valley, a glistening ribbon of silver in the sunshine? Did he envision the faces of his long departed family and friends . . . did he see Timothy Webster's slender visage, or Kate Warne's soft curls, or his little baby Joan, or his poor sweet sickly Belle? Did he hear the sound of laughter and song at Robbie Fergus's place . . . or feel the rough clasp of Abraham Lincoln's gentle calloused hand . . . or smell the wood smoke on the wind of a Baltimore winter . . . or taste the tang of copper on his tongue as he hid in the lightning and shadows of Rose Greenhow's gardens . . . or see the breath puffing in cold vapor from the foaming bit of his faithful chestnut steed . . . and all the miles and milestones traveled as Major Allen . . . and McClellan's weather balloons floating dreamlike above the blood-soaked battlefields . . . and all the fallen soldiers and loved ones and innocent souls like cord wood on the hard ground? For what? For what purpose? All the death and love and joyous life snuffed in the space of a mere instant.

Allan Pinkerton lingered for three weeks following this accident. Gripped in excruciating pain, his gangrenous tongue making the mere act of swallowing torturous, he finally passed away at his home on July 1, 1884. He left his estate—valued at a half a million dollars—to his wife.

Emotionally ravaged by her husband's passing, Joan Pinkerton sank into a deep depression. Writes Mackay: "The gentle lady who had made that terrible voyage from Scotland with her firebrand of a husband, who had survived shipwreck and untold hardships, who had risen from humble housewife in Dundee to chatelaine of an imposing mansion in Chicago, simply gave up the will to live."

Joan Pinkerton, bedridden for months after her husband's death, summoned her sons to her bedside on May 13, 1886. Shortly before dawn she whispered to William that she was going to join his father.

She closed her eyes and silently slipped away.

Allan Pinkerton left his business to his sons, the copyright on all his books to his one surviving daughter, and his phenomenal achievements as America's first private detective to the ages.

Notes and Acknowledgments

ONE OF THE MYRIAD ASPECTS OF ALLAN PINKERTON'S LIFE THAT SUNK a hook into me as a writer was the discrepancy between the layperson's perception of Pinkerton's legacy and the true origins of the iconic trademark. It seemed to me that Pinkerton's story had been subsumed over the years into the larger legacy of the Pinkerton organization (not to mention the sour taste that the name leaves in the mouths of many of my lefty friends). Admittedly, toward the end of the nineteenth century, long after the patriarch and founder had quietly passed away at his Chicago home, Pinkerton agents saw their ranks grow into a virtual paramilitary organization. Often engaged in strikebreaking and the escorting of scabs across picket lines, the "Pinks" were viewed by some as thugs and pawns of the robber barons.

Incredibly, at one point in its history, the Pinkerton organization employed more personnel than the standing army of the United States. Concerns over abuses of such organizations led to the "Anti-Pinkerton Act" of 1893. The ruling forbade the U.S. government from employing these kinds of police organizations for any reason. The law is still on the books today. As recently as 2006, in fact, the Anti-Pinkerton Act was cited in official protests against the use of contractors in the Iraq war.

But tempering all this—perhaps even proving it one of the great paradoxes of history—was Allan Pinkerton's humanity, vision, and progressive ideals. The man was far from perfect; he was somewhat of a curmudgeon, a despot with his family and underlings, and the manufacturer of lurid fictions regarding his casework. But his compassionate, enlightened views toward his fellow human beings became a compass for the creation of this work.

Because of the dearth of primary sources—other than Pinkerton's own vainglorious first-person narratives—I endeavored to triangulate secondary sources whenever possible, using biographies, letters, transcripts, and newspaper articles as "correctives" to Pinkerton's accounts. The definitive biography is James Mackay's meticulous *Allan Pinkerton: The First Private Eye* (1996, John Wiley and Sons), from which I mined much of the background here. In my view, the three other indispensable biographies spanning the twentieth century are: *The Pinkertons: A*

Detective Dynasty by Richard Wilmer Rowan (1931, Little Brown and Company), *Allan Pinkerton: America's First Private Eye* by Sigmund A. Lavine (1963, Dodd and Mead), and *Master Detective Allan Pinkerton* by Arthur Orrmont (1965, Julian Messner Books).

My process here bears further explanation. It is conceivable that an entire book could be culled solely from Pinkerton's various memoirs, as they are—among many other things—extremely comprehensive. A partial list of autobiographical works generated during those last contemplative years of his life reveals a man brimming with secrets to tell, an oeuvre amounting, at the time of his death, to nearly three million words:

The Gypsies and the Detectives

A Double Life and the Detectives

Bucholz and the Detectives

Claude Melnotte as a Detective

The Spiritualists and the Detectives

The Mississippi Outlaws and the Detectives

The Bank-Robbers and the Detectives

The Railroad Forger and the Detectives

Criminal Reminiscences and Detective Sketches

The Expressman and the Detectives

The Somnambulist and the Detectives

The Model Town and the Detectives

The Burglar's Fate and the Detectives

The Molly Maguires and the Detectives

Thirty Years a Detective

Chock-full of dialogue, dramatically structured, and in many places beautifully written, the two key sources informing this book are as wide-ranging as their titles are ridiculously long: 1) *Professional Thieves and the Detective: Containing Numerous Detective Sketches Collected from Private*

Records by Allan Pinkerton (1880, G. W. Carleton) and 2) *The Spy of the Rebellion: Being a True History of the Spy System of the United States Army During the Late Rebellion Revealing Many Secrets of the War Hitherto Not Made Public Compiled from Official Reports Prepared for President Lincoln, General McClellan, and the Provost-Marshal-General* by Allan Pinkerton (1883, Samuel Stodder Books). These formed the foundation of the book's narrative, as well as the factual standard by which I measured all other accounts.

In many instances I found myself mired in almost *Rashomon*-like quandaries, as I endeavored to shore up discrepancies. (*Rashomon*, the classic Japanese film, directed by Akira Kurosawa, revolves around a crime witnessed by four individuals who recall the event in four mutually contradictory ways.) The middle section of this book, for example, which deals with Rose Greenhow, is built upon two incongruous accounts: one by Greenhow herself and one by Pinkerton. Each first-person account steeps the events in his or her own melodramatic, self-serving perspective. My solution was to employ secondary sources, as well as good, old-fashioned logic, in order to arrive at an educated synthesis.

The dialogue in the book is another fascinating conundrum. I opted to use *only* dialogue that could be sourced—either primarily or secondarily—even though much of it rings slightly false, slightly stiff, and expositional. It is unlikely that nineteenth-century detectives and criminals, in the heat of their struggles, spoke with such flat, unaffected King's English—despite the fact that virtually every word of dialogue cited here was recounted in a letter, a biography, a news item, or a memoir. I chose to stay true to the record, and even the *summaries* of exchanges were rendered practically verbatim. In the rare instance that I altered documented dialogue—a dozen or so words inserted here or there, a few edits—I annotated each and every crumb of narrative license in the endnotes.

No such liberties, though, were ever taken with the spoken words of Abraham Lincoln. On this subject I defer to a footnote written by Richard Rowan in *The Pinkertons: A Detective Dynasty*: "The author has not accepted biographical license to create dialogue for a dramatic episode in the career of a national hero."

Pinkerton's story echoes across the ages. Doris Kearns Goodwin's astonishing feat of scholarship, *Team of Rivals* (2005, Simon & Schuster)—a gold mine of detail for this work—speaks to the kind of adversarial politics and general nastiness that resonates eerily with today's national scene. Barack Obama, another former Illinois legislator facing a polarized electorate, is a great admirer of Goodwin's book. "He talks about it all the time," a top aide once reported to Joe Klein.

On January 18, 2009, as if channeling the spirit of the Great Emancipator, President-Elect Obama retraced the fateful whistle-stop inaugural journey undertaken by Lincoln—the ghost of Allan Pinkerton most assuredly becoming restless as Obama passed through Baltimore.

Two venerable institutions that I would like to acknowledge as indispensable—not only to this author but to anyone who endeavors to crack open the history of Illinois—are the Chicago History Museum and the Abraham Lincoln Presidential Library and Museum in Springfield, Illinois. Specifically I would like to thank James Cornelius, Jennifer Ericson, and Mary Michals at the Lincoln Museum for their inordinate generosity and interest in this project.

Many thanks to my brilliant editor at Lyons Press, Keith Wallman, who took the sheet music and made it sing. Also, a *huge* thank you to the meticulous and brilliant line editors who worked on this project, Kristen Mellitt and Steven Talbot, for inhumanly fine detail work on the line edit. Special thanks to the irrepressible Peter Miller for never giving up and to James J. Wilson for the Pinkerton first edition. And lastly, I would like to express my heartfelt gratitude to my intrepid, faithful, tireless research assistant, Rachel Walker, for her uncanny ferret-like ability to find innumerable kernels of gold, many of which can be found in the endnotes.

Page Notes

Prologue: Incident at Eaton Walker's

vii. "Before you, looking upstream . . ." Allan Pinkerton, "How I Became a Detective," *Professional Thieves and the Detective* (New York: G. W. Carleton, 1880), 17.

viii. "Our time in that little shop . . ." James Mackay, *Allan Pinkerton: The First Private Eye* (New York: John Wiley and Sons, 1996), 57.

viii. *Squarely built, compact* . . . Mackay, et al., photographic evidence.

viii. "Said it was important, sir. . . ." Pinkerton, *Professional Thieves and the Detective,* 23–24.

viii. *The sun was high* . . . Pinkerton, *Professional Thieves and the Detective* 24. (Note: The sweat, odors, and angle of the light are my extrapolations from the detective's journals.)

ix. "We want you to do a little job . . ." Pinkerton, *Professional Thieves and the Detective,* 24–54. (Most, if not all, of the dialogue here and throughout is derived from either Pinkerton's own accounts or the accounts of eyewitnesses and participants.)

xi. "I had become an outlaw . . ." Mackay, *Allan Pinkerton,* 50.

xi. "The Atlantic crossing . . ." Ibid., 53.

xii. *The building's façade* . . . Pinkerton, *Professional Thieves and the Detective,* 28 (Illustrative evidence.)

xii. "There was the usual . . ." Pinkerton, *Professional Thieves and the Detective,* 27.

xiv. "There I was . . ." Ibid., 32.

xv. *By his own admission. . .* , Mackay, *Allan Pinkerton,* 64.

xvi. "Telegram today from the Sheriff . . ." Arthur Orrmont, *Master Detective Allan Pinkerton* (New York: Julian Messner Books, 1965), 43–44. (Note: The conversation is mostly from Orrmont, who learned of it from the Pinkerton organization years after the founder's death.)

xvii. "Those who waded . . ." Theodore J. Karamanski and Dean Tank, *Maritime Chicago* (Chicago: Arcadia, 2000, 14.

xvii. "There was no pavement . . ." Ibid., 32.

xviii. *Early settlers relied* . . . Richard C. Lindberg, *To Serve and Collect: Chicago Politics and Police Corruption from the Lager Bear Riot to the Summerdale Scandal 1855–1960* (Carbondale: Southern Illinois University Press, 1998), 1. (Note: Richard Lindberg is one of the greatest living historians of Chicago crime and punishment, which is saying quite a lot, since this is a city known for its transgressions; most of what appears in this early chapter on police history comes courtesy of Mr. Lindberg's scholarship.)

xviii. "When a burglary was committed . . ." Ibid., 2.

Chapter One: Tinderbox

3. *Around 5:30 p.m. on a muggy Chicago summer* . . . *Chicago Daily Tribune,* September 1, 1857, p. 1. (Note: This rather long article in the *Tribune* contains Pinkerton's own sworn account of this incident, from which all the dialogue is either taken directly or from summaries of exchanges.)

4. *His steely nerves could be observed* . . . *Daily Democratic Press,* September 9, 1853, p. 1.

4. *In fact this idiosyncrasy had actually saved* . . . *Chicago Daily Tribune,* September 7, 1853, p. 3.

5. *On a regular basis Pinkerton would disguise* . . . Dresser, Clarence P., *The Detective Magazine,* "Pinkerton," March 1887.

5. "His early record of running . . ." Richard Rowan, *The Pinkertons: A Detective Dynasty* (Boston: Little Brown & Company, 1931), 25.

5. *As his daughter Joan would recall* . . . Sigmund Lavine, *Allan Pinkerton: America's First Private Eye* (New York: Dodd, Mead, 1963), 20.

6. *The clapboard cottage on Adams Street* . . . Mackay, *Allan Pinkerton*, 81.
6. "The institution of human bondage . . ." Ibid., 82.
6. *The Commercial House hotel was a squat, brick edifice* . . . Photographic evidence, Chicago Historical Society, *Special Archives*, Chicago, Illinois.
7. *In 1811, Vidocq organized* . . . Eugène F. Vidocq, *Memoirs of Vidocq: Master of Crime* (Edinburgh: AK Press, 2003), 1–50.
8. *The myth that Pinkerton* . . . Mackay, *Allan Pinkerton*, 71.
8. "I've got it!" Orrmont, *Master Detective Allan Pinkerton*, 47.
9. "This boy is a free indentured ward . . ." *Chicago Daily Tribune*, September 1, 1857, p. 1 (dialogue reconstructed by author from Pinkerton's summary account).
10. "STOP!" *Chicago Daily Tribune*, September 1, 1857, p. 1. (Note: Although this word is never mentioned in the article, and it is speculation, Pinkerton's testimony summarizes this moment as the strongest command for them to cease.)
11. "Both were obsessive . . ." Mackay, *Allan Pinkerton*, 79.
12. *He was a skilled litigator* . . . Thomas J. DiLorenzo, *The Real Lincoln: A New Look at Abraham Lincoln, His Agenda, and an Unnecessary War* (New York: Three Rivers Press, 2002), 15.
12. "'They each were typical . . .'" Mackay, *Allan Pinkerton*, 80.
12. "I have never spoken with intentional disrespect . . ." *Illinois Gazette*, August 15, 1846, p. 1.
13. *No charges were levied* . . . *Chicago Daily Tribune*, September 1, 1857, p. 1.
14. "We cannot blame the colored men . . ." Ibid.

CHAPTER TWO: BLOOD ON THE WIND

15. *Harper's New Monthly Magazine described* . . . Marcy, James, "Detective Pinkerton," *Harper's New Monthly*, circa 1860s, p. 712.
16. "The states, jealous of their rights . . ." Mackay, *Allan Pinkerton*, 72.
16. "That's fairly good circumstantial . . ." Orrmont, *Master Detective Allan Pinkerton*, 58. (Note: Most of the dialogue here, and throughout the remainder of the chapter, is from Orrmont's narrative reconstruction of Pinkerton's case file. Interestingly, Pinkerton's various biographers differ on the details here: Lavine, for instance, posits an entirely different cast of operatives in the Columbia case. Orrmont's version, though, was chosen for its resonance with Pinkerton's own patterns of behavior and use of black operatives.)
16. *Pinkerton puffed his Cuban* . . . (Hypothesis on the author's part for narrative purposes; according to Pinkerton's own admission, he was a heavy cigar smoker by this point.)
18. *A impressive man named George Bangs* . . . Mackay, *Allan Pinkerton*, 73.
18. *In the 1853–54 Chicago City Directory* . . . Hael & Smith's *Chicago City Directory for 1853–'54*, (Chicago: Robert Book Printers, 1853), 153.
19. "I am overwhelmed with business . . ." Voss, Frederick S., and Barber, James G., "Pinkerton Brought Law and Order—19th Century Style," *Smithsonian Magazine*, August 1981, 61.
19. *Lewis, in the words of Mackay* . . . Mackay, *Allan Pinkerton*, 73.
19. "The detective should be . . ." Allan Pinkerton, *The Molly Maguires and the Detectives* (BiblioLife, 2009 [1877]), 2.
19. *With striking, angular features* . . . Photographic evidence, from a public domain portrait (author's phrase).
20. "The year 1856 did not offer much . . ." Margaret Bzovy, "First Female Pinkerton Detective: Kate Warne," *American Western Magazine*, January 2004, 7.
21. "I'm here to inquire about a job . . ." Ibid., 7–9. (Note: Dialogue here is reconstructed from two accounts: Bzovy's summary of what was said that day, and Mackay's.)
22. "The more he considered it . . ." Mackay, *Allan Pinkerton*, 74.
22. *He loved Dickens* . . . Lavine, *Allan Pinkerton*, 33.
23. "True," Pinkerton said, chewing . . . Orrmont, 58–59.
23. *Chicago had become, according to* . . . Ibid., 27.

24. *An early glass "Ambrotype" photograph* . . . Mackay, *Allan Pinkerton,* and Chicago History Museum (photographic evidence).
24. *Columbia, Tennessee, in the late 1850s* . . . "Hood's Virtual Driving Tour," americancivilwar.50megs.com, Columbia pages.
25. "And that's only part of it," Webster said . . . Orrmont, 61.
25. "The initials 'J.C.' might also be traced . . ." Ibid. , 61–62.
26. *"Yessir," Mary Littleton piped in* . . . Ibid., 61. (Note: In the interests of narrative flow, the author has attributed some dialogue from the historic account to Jock Littleton and some to Mary, although no such delineation appears in either Orrmont's or Pinkerton's accounts.)
26. *The couple had rigged the tube* . . . Lavine, *Allan Pinkerton,* 43.
27. "We keep him awake half the night . . ." Ibid., 43. (Note: This dialogue, attributed by Lavine to an undercover butler named Binney, is spoken here by Jock Littleton, the more likely speaker.)
27. *"The devil you say . . ."* Rowan, *The Pinkertons,* 75. (Note: The words spoken here by Pinkerton are a combination of two accounts, Orrmont's and Rowan's.)
28. "The conductor, a new man . . ." Ibid., 76.
28. "Let's have the cologne . . ." Orrmont, *Master Detective Allan Pinkerton,* 62.
28. "So sure was (Slocum) . . ." Rowan, *The Pinkertons,* 76.
29. "In the small, almost airless smoker . . ." Orrmont, *Master Detective Allan Pinkerton,* 63.
30. "He was fearfully injured . . ." Rowan, *The Pinkertons,* 78.
30. "That—perfume—" Slocum uttered . . . Ibid., 78.
31. "I know I'm—dying—justice . . ." Ibid., 78.
31. "He sighed once, and lay still . . ." Ibid., 78.
32. "I must admit that among the thousands . . ." Pinkerton, *Professional Thieves and the Detective,* 147.

CHAPTER THREE: AN EXTREMELY GRAVE AND URGENT MATTER

33. JOHN BROWN'S RAID AT HARPER'S FERRY . . . Orrmont, *Master Detective Allan Pinkerton,* 64.
34. "Of this there is absolutely no proof . . ." Mackay, *Allan Pinkerton,* 85.
34. *He even persuaded George McClellan* . . . Ibid., 85.
34. "Had it not been for the excessive watchfulness . . ." Ibid., 85.
35. "He was a man who could get by . . ." Ibid., 92.
36. *The president of Adams Express* . . . Ibid., 87.
36. "Mrs. Maroney is planning a trip . . ." Lavine, *Allan Pinkerton,* 35.
36. "The choice of the open eye . . ." Mackay, *Allan Pinkerton,* 91.
37. *Warmed by an Indian-summer dusk* . . . Bryner, B.C., "Abraham Lincoln in Peoria, Illinois," 1924, self-published booklet (portions available online at *atlaspodcasts.org*).
37. "His voice was unmusical . . ." Richard Carwardine, *Lincoln: A Life of Purpose and Power* (New York: Vintage Books, 2003), 51–52.
39. *In the picture, taken just before* . . . Photographic evidence, Brady, Library of Congress.
39. "Your purpose, plainly stated . . ." Harold Holzer, *Lincoln at Cooper Union: The Speech That Made Abraham Lincoln President* (New York: Simon & Schuster, 2004), 275–276.
39. "The Republican party in its early days . . ." Mackay, *Allan Pinkerton,* 95.
40. *Lincoln responded with another fiery* . . . Ibid., 95.
41. "In many portions of the South . . ." Allan Pinkerton, *The Spy of the Rebellion: Being a True History of the Spy System of the United States Army During the Late Rebellion, Revealing Many Secrets of the War Hitherto Not Made Public, Compiled from Official Reports Prepared for President Lincoln, General McClellan* (New York: Samuel Stodder, 1883), 39. (Note: This book, with its unprecedented tongue twister of a title, was published one year before Pinkerton's death and is a detailed personal account of not only Pinkerton's most important work but also of the birth of modern intelligence agencies. It forms the basis of much of what follows in this work.)

41. "Men thronged the streets ..." *New York Tribune,* November 9, 1860.
41. The narrow, gas-lit streets ... Photographic evidence, courtesy of Enoch Pratt Free Library, Baltimore, MD (smartlink.pratt.lib.md.us/exhibits).
42. "My dear Pinkerton ..." William Wise, *Detective Pinkerton and Mr. Lincoln* (New York: E. P. Dutton, 1964), 9.
42. He called the office boy ... Ibid., 10.

CHAPTER FOUR: INTO THE BREACH

44. *Northeasterly winds whipped* ... "Register of Meteorological Observations, Under the Direction of the Smithsonian," January 21, 1861 (Andsager, Midwest Regional Climate Center, Champaign, Illinois).
44. "We are about to be deprived ..." William C. Davis, *Jefferson Davis: The Man and His Hour* (New York: HarperCollins, 1991), (www.senate.gov/artandhistory/history/minute/Jefferson_Davis).
45. "Absolute silence met the conclusion ..." Ibid., (www.senate.gov).
45. *The headquarters of the Philadelphia* ... (Derived from illustrations) Wise, *Detective Pinkerton and Mr. Lincoln,* 11.
45. "In the event of war ..." Ibid., 10. (Note: All of the dialogue in this section is from Wise, with corroborative summaries from Pinkerton's account.)
46. "Serious damage might be done ..." Pinkerton, *The Spy of the Rebellion,* 48.
46. *In his document Pinkerton stressed* ... Ibid., 51.
46. *In Springfield, Abraham Lincoln* ... Gruber, Ruth, "Abraham and Mary Lincoln," *The American Experience,* PBS, 2001.
47. *In mid-January, Mary Lincoln innocently* ... Doris Kearns Goodwin, *Team of Rivals* (New York: Simon & Schuster, 2005), 306.
47. *The small black brooch* ... Lavine, *Allan Pinkerton,* 50.
49. "I found the same excitable condition ..." Pinkerton, *The Spy of the Rebellion,* 48.
49. "No damned abolitionist ..." Ibid., 49.
50. "If I live ..." Goodwin, *Team of Rivals,* 306.
50. *By day, the men fireproofed* ... Mackay, *Allan Pinkerton,* 98.
51. "Webster's talent for sustaining ..." Lavine, *Allan Pinkerton,* 51.
51. *Davies checked into a first-class hotel* ... Pinkerton, *The Spy of the Rebellion,* 60.
52. *The Relay House sat at a wide, graveled intersection* ... *The Baltimore Sun,* April 2, 1860, p. 1. (Note: The year before this scene, J. H. Luckett was mentioned in an article about renovations to the road and structure at this location: "... the diversity of view cannot be excelled ...")
53. *The terse message, written by the master mechanic* ... Pinkerton, *The Spy of the Rebellion,* 54.
54. "Wait a minute ..." Lavine, *Allan Pinkerton,* 50–51. (Note: The dialogue here is verbatim from Lavine.)

CHAPTER FIVE: A STRANGE AND ALMOST WEIRD PRESENTIMENT

57. *A chilly drizzle* ... Goodwin, *Team of Rivals,* 306.
57. "His face was pale ..." Ibid., 307.
57. *Lincoln stood on the running rail* ... Pinkerton, *The Spy of the Rebelion,* 52. (Note: The complete text of Lincoln's farewell, truncated in many other sources, is found in *The Spy of the Rebellion.*)
58. "A strange and almost weird ..." Ibid., 53.
58. "Three cheers were given ..." Ibid., 307.
58. *Judge David Davis, a three-hundred-pound* ... Goodwin, *Team of Rivals,* 306–307.
59. *Built in 1825, situated in the heart* ... Notes from Cantor Print #91, Enoch Pratt Free Library, Baltimore, MD.
59. "The most comfortable of all hotels ..." Ibid., captions.
60. "Their leader was pronouncedly in favor ..." Pinkerton, *The Spy of the Rebellion,* 50.
60. "This hireling Lincoln shall never ..." Ibid., 63.

61. *Thirty-four large-caliber blasts* . . . Goodwin, *Team of Rivals*, 307.
61. *Dark furniture* . . . Ibid., 307.
62. "You're talking about murder . . ." Mackay, *Allan Pinkerton*, 98, and Pinkerton, *The Spy of the Rebellion*, 64–67. (Note: This opening line is a speculation, one of the few in this book, of the author, for narrative purposes. It is probable, however, that Pinkerton said this to elicit the response from the infamous barber, which is indeed in the historic record, as is the remainder of the conversation at Guy's that afternoon.)
62. *Even Pinkerton found himself vulnerable* . . . Mackay, *Allan Pinkerton*, 98.
63. *The mousy young Lieutenant Hill* . . . Pinkerton, *The Spy of the Rebellion*, 66–67.
64. *One observer noted* . . . Goodwin, *Team of Rivals*, 307.
64. *The brief message, sent by Allan* . . . Mackay, *Allan Pinkerton*, 99.
65. "This information Mr. Judd did not divulge . . ." Pinkerton, *The Spy of the Rebellion*, 74.
65. "I've discovered what the plotters . . ." Wise, *Detective Pinkerton and Mr. Lincoln*, 21.
65. *That day, after the regiment* . . . Pinkerton, *The Spy of the Rebellion*, 70–72.
66. "On the twenty-third of February . . ." Wise, *Detective Pinkerton and Mr. Lincoln*, 21.
66. "Boss, unfortunately I don't know . . ." Ibid., 21–22.
67. "You will have to get to the inner circle . . ." Rowan, *The Pinkertons*, 88.

CHAPTER SIX: THE DRAWING OF THE RED

68. *Earlier that day, Lincoln had received* . . . Goodwin, *Team of Rivals*, 309.
68. "The image of Lincoln dancing . . ." Ibid., 309.
69. *The author of the short epistle* . . . Artifact: "Scurrilous Letter" courtesy of the Chicago History Museum, Permanent Collection. (Note: The text of the letter has been abridged here for comprehensibility.)
70. *Davies, a man who, according to one historian* . . . Lavine, *Allan Pinkerton*, 52.
70. "At dinner they have boiled pastes . . ." Marc McCutcheon, *Everyday Life in the 1800s* (Cincinnati, Writer's Digest Books, 1993), 173.
70. "Your nomination has been approved!" Pinkerton, *The Spy of the Rebellion*, 76; Rowan, *The Pinkertons*, 89–90. (Note: The dialogue here is an amalgam of the two sources.)
70. *For the last forty-eight hours* . . . Ormmont, *Master Detective Allan Pinkerton*, 68.
71. "It looks as if the plan . . ." Ibid., 90. (Note: This dialogue is a slight variation on Orrmont's. According to Richard Rowan, what Davies said was, "It really looks as if our plan to kill Lincoln couldn't go wrong." Considering the fact that this exchange, according to more than one source, took place at a public restaurant, it is more likely that Davies uttered the slightly more cryptic version, which is closer to Orrmont's version.)
72. *The private parlor at the Barnum* . . . Pinkerton, *The Spy of the Rebellion*, 76. (Note: The description of the room is from an illustration in Pinkerton's memoir.)
73. *The most vulnerable moment in Lincoln's passage* . . . Allan Pinkerton, "An Unpublished Letter to William Herndon," *The American Magazine*, 1868, 17–22.
73. *The time had come to draw the lots* . . . Pinkerton, *The Spy of the Rebellion*, 76–80 (Note: The events at the Barnum that night are reconstructed mostly from Pinkerton's 1883 memoir, corroborated by Rowan, Mackay, and Orrmont.)
74. *Later Davies would remark to Pinkerton* . . . Rowan, *The Pinkertons*, 92.
74. "We have to keep close watch . . ." Wise, *Detective Pinkerton and Mr. Lincoln*, 29–30. (Note: Nothing has been added to this dialogue—which is mostly from Wise's account—although certain words have been contracted and omitted for flow.)
75. *The next day, February 17, a smartly dressed woman* . . . Lavine, *Allan Pinkerton*, 52–53. (Note: Accounts vary here, with more than one stating that Pinkerton rode to New York alongside Warne, before turning around and traveling to Philadelphia; however, Lavine's account seems more in keeping with logic and expediency, not to mention Pinkerton's urgent need to speak with Felton.)

76. *Felton listened closely* ... Ibid., 53.
77. *Over the last two weeks in Baltimore* ... Pinkerton, *The Spy of the Rebellion,* 75.
77. "Mr. Judd, I presume ..." (Note: The scene is accounted in "A Letter from Hon. N. B. Judd, November 3, 1867, to Mr. Allan Pinkerton," first collected in *Rare Lincolniana No. 5,* New York: William Abbatt Publishers, 1914.)
78. "The contents alarmed Judd ..." Mackay, *Allan Pinkerton,* 100.

CHAPTER SEVEN: COUNTERPLOT
80. "The streets were alive ..." Pinkerton, *The Spy of the Rebellion,* 81.
81. "I saw a young man walking on the outside ..." Judd, *Letter to Pinkerton,* November 3, 1867.
82. "Come in, sir ..." Rowan, *The Pinkertons,* 94.
82. *Judd insisted on seeing* ... Judd, *Letter to Pinkerton,* 1867.
82. *At last Judd "slumped in a chair"* ... Lavine, *Allan Pinkerton,* 54.
83. "The trio pushed, shoved, lost their hats ..." Ibid., 54.
84. "I went in," Lincoln wrote ... Lossing, Benson J., "Mr. Lincoln's Statement," *Lossing's History of the Civil War—Vol. 1* (New York: The War Memorial Association), 1912, p. 278.
84. "What have you men been doing ..." Lavine, *Allan Pinkerton,* 54.
84. *Measuring his words very carefully* ... Rowan, *The Pinkertons,* 95–100. (Note: The dialogue throughout this set-piece scene is mostly from Richard Rowan's account, with backup corroboration from Pinkerton's memoir, as well as Judd's salient letter of 1867 and the works of Lavine and Wise. It is interesting to note, though, that Rowan—who is one of the principal secondary sources of dialogue for this book—felt strongly about getting it right. In his 1931 book, *The Pinkertons: A Detective Dynasty,* published only forty-seven years after the detective's death, Rowan wrote, "The author has not accepted biographical license to create dialogue for a dramatic episode in the career of a national hero (Lincoln)." Rowan goes on to cite numerous providers of cross-references for dialogue and sequences of events: Pinkerton, Judd, Lamon, Felton, Curtin, Kenney, Franciscus, Stearns, Lewis, Thayer, Dunn, Wynn, and Pitcairn. For these reasons, the book you are reading weighs the Rowan version of actual dialogue spoken second only to Pinkerton's own published accounts.)
84. "A shade of sadness fell ..." Pinkerton, *The Spy of the Rebellion,* 84.
85. "The plotters believe that if you were killed ..." Wise, *Detective Pinkerton and Mr. Lincoln,* 36.
86. *What the Dix woman had revealed* ... Rowan, *The Pinkertons,* 98–99.
86. "You will therefore perceive ..." Pinkerton, *The Spy of the Rebellion,* 84–85.
87. *Then he "gravely shook hands* ..." Rowan, *The Pinkertons,* 100.
88. *Earlier that day, in Washington, D.C.* ... Goodwin, *Team of Rivals,* 311.
88. *A wiry, almost emaciated-looking* ... Photographic evidence, Library of Congress, "F. W. Seward," ca. 1860, #LC-BH824-5347.
88. "I know of no reason to doubt it ..." "Conspirators Frustrated," *New York Times,* February 21, 1902, p. 1. (Note: The dialogue in this sequence, including Lincoln's, was taken from Fred Seward's eyewitness account published in the *New York Times.*)
89. "The street was crowded with people ..." Ibid.
89. *I had never before seen him* ... Ibid.
90. *Working deep undercover in the guise* ... Mackay, *Allan Pinkerton,* 101.
90. "... all things were fixed, doomed in one way or another ..." Carwardine, *Lincoln,* 39.
91. *Lincoln often told his law partner* ... Ibid., 39. (Note: The parentheses are mine.)
92. *"Why?" Norman Judd wanted to know* ... Lavine, *Allan Pinkerton,* 56.

CHAPTER EIGHT: CUTTING THE WIRES
93. *The overflow audience* ... Wise, *Detective Pinkerton and Mr. Lincoln,* 40.
93. *The* New York Times *later remarked* ... *New York Times,* February 24, 1902.
94. "It was their hope that in due time ..." Wise, *Detective Pinkerton and Mr. Lincoln,* 40–41.

94.   *He handed the papers to Judd* . . . Lavine, *Allan Pinkerton*, 57.
95.   *She proceeded directly to the ticket counter* . . . Bzovy, "First Female Pinkerton Detective," 1–6.
96.   "I reckon they will laugh at us, Judd . . ." Judd, *Letter to Pinkerton*, November 3, 1867.
97.   *The plan was for the president-elect to discreetly* . . . Rowan, *The Pinkertons*, 104–105.
97.   "The banqueting Pennsylvanians were not allowing . . ." Rowan, *The Pinkertons*, 104–105.
97.   "Ladies and gentlemen," Curtin said . . . Lavine, *Allan Pinkerton*, 57.
97.   *Curtin recalled years later* . . . Curtin, Letter to Pinkerton, *Rare Lincolniana*, December 8, 1867.
99.   As Lincoln approached the side exit . . . Judd, *Letter to Pinkerton*, November 3, 1867.
99.   "Drive to the executive mansion!" Wise, *Detective Pinkerton and Mr. Lincoln*, 45.
100. *Satisfied that the brief jaunt of a few blocks* . . . Ibid., 45–46.
100. *The reins cracked, plumes of vapor* . . . Lavine, *Allan Pinkerton*, 58. (Note: The references to the horses' breath showing and the dusky cold atmospheric impressions here all are speculations, due to consistent references across numerous eyewitness accounts to the weather that night.)
101. The last man to emerge . . . Lewis, Letter to Pinkerton, *Rare Lincolniana*, November 7, 1867.
101. *Judd, who had remained at the hotel* . . . Lavine, *Allan Pinkerton*, 58–59.
101. *Wynn—hand-picked by his superiors* . . . Rowan, *The Pinkertons*, 108.
102. Back at the Jones House, as Lincoln's absence . . . Pinkerton, *The Spy of the Rebellion*, 99–101.

Chapter Nine: On the Night Train

104. *As the clock approached half past 9:00* . . . Rowan, *The Pinkertons*, 109.
104. *He removed the shawl* . . . Pitcairn, Letter to Pinkerton, ca. 1867.
105. *Lincoln, ever the dry Kentucky wit* . . . Orrmont, *Master Detective Allan Pinkerton*, 74.
105. "We're to meet the 10:50 train, on the PW&B . . ." Wise, *Detective Pinkerton and Mr. Lincoln*, 51.
105. *Around 10:45 that night, about twenty blocks away* . . . Lavine, *Allan Pinkerton*, 59–60.
106. As they approached the PW&B depot, Kenney instructed . . . Letter of H. F. Kenney, Esq., *Rare Lincolniana*, ca. 1867.
107. In the "cold, drafty shed, with its acrid reek . . ." Mackay, *Allan Pinkerton*, 102.
107. *He clenched his fists—an involuntary tic* . . . Wise, *Detective Pinkerton and Mr. Lincoln*, 61. (Note: Although Pinkerton's habit of clenching his fists in stressful situations is a speculation on the part of both William Wise and the author of this book, the notion is bolstered by photographic evidence, as well as numerous citations in many sources of the man's eccentric way of moving, with a clenched fist behind his back.)
107. "Brother William!" Orrmont, *Master Detective Allan Pinkerton*, 75.
108. "The poor chap mustn't be disturbed . . ." Lavine, *Allan Pinkerton*, 60.
109. *The agents used bull's-eye lanterns* . . . Ibid., 61.
110. Unbeknownst to Pinkerton, one other passenger . . . Rowan, *The Pinkertons*, 110–111.
110. "Lincoln was pushed up into a sleeping berth . . ." Kunhardt, Phillip (et al.), *Lincoln*, (New York: Alfred A. Knopf, 1992), 19.
111. *Pinkerton once again marveled at Lincoln's calm* . . . Pinkerton, Unpublished Letter to William Herndon, August 23, 1866.
111. "He had almost no sleep . . ." Wise, *Detective Pinkerton and Mr. Lincoln*, 55.

Chapter Ten: Nocturne on a Lonely Platform

113. *In the distance, Webster's bull's-eye* . . . Lavine, *Allan Pinkerton*, 61.
114. *They crossed the outskirts of Baltimore* . . . Pinkerton, *The Spy of the Rebellion*, 96.
115. *The city was in profound repose* . . . Ibid., 96.
115. *His heart practically stopped* . . . Wise, *Detective Pinkerton and Mr. Lincoln*, 58.
116. "Did you anticipate this delay, too, Mr. Pinkerton?" Ormmont, *Master Detective Allan Pinkerton*, 76–77.
116. "Does this waiting make you nervous . . ." Wise, *Detective Pinkerton and Mr. Lincoln*, 61.

117. *The unidentified figure—only inches away* . . . Ibid., 60–62.
117. *Written in high-comic style by Daniel Emmett* . . . Howard L. Sacks and Judith Sacks, *Way Up North in Dixie: A Black Family's Claim to the Confederate Anthem* (Washington: Smithsonian Institution Press, 1993), 158.
118. *The Natchez Courier would eventually crown* . . . E. Lawrence Abel, *Singing the New Nation: How Music Shaped the Confederacy, 1861–1865* (Mechanicsburg, PA: Stackpole Books, 2000), 36.
118. "No doubt there will be a great time in Dixie . . ." Pinkerton, *The Spy of the Rebellion,* 97.
118. "Such impressive songs . . ." Orrmont, *Master Detective Allan Pinkerton,* 76.

CHAPTER ELEVEN: IN THE KILN OF PROPHECY

119. "Thank God this prayer meeting's over. . . ." Pinkerton, "Allan Pinkerton's Unpublished Letter," *The American Magazine,* circa unknown, p. 22.
120. Surrounded by Pinkerton men, the president . . . Ibid., 77.
120. "No talking here!" Pinkerton, *The Spy of the Rebellion,* 98.
121. *On his arrival at the hotel* . . . Ibid., 99.
121. *Upon hearing the news, Ward Lamon* . . . Mackay, *Allan Pinkerton,* 103–104.
121. *The pro-secession newspaper,* The Charleston . . . Holzer, Harold, "Abraham Lincoln and Jefferson Davis: Rivals in Popular Prints," *The Journal of Mississippi History,* an abstract, *mdah. state.ms.us/pubs/rivals.pdf.*
121. *Even Pinkerton noted how Lincoln later* . . . Pinkerton, *History and Evidence of The Passage of Abraham Lincoln from Harrisburg, PA, to Washington, D.C.* (Privately Printed, 1882), 22.
122. *Minutes later, Mary Lincoln and the boys* . . . Mackay, *Allan Pinkerton,* 104.
122. "There was a very large trunk or two . . ." *Baltimore Sun,* February 25, 1861, p. 1.
123. *To Kate Warne, Lincoln softly said* . . . Richad W. Rowan, "Lincoln's Sister," *The American Weekly Magazine,* February 11, 1951. (Note: The dialogue at this meeting is amalgamated from two principle sources: Rowan and Orrmont. Other sources, such as Pinkerton's account, summarize the meeting, corroborating the gist of the words spoken.)
124. *Arriving at the Baltimore station at dusk* . . . Mackay, *Allan Pinkerton,* 104.
124. *According to Davies, the conspirators learned* . . . Rowan, *The Pinkertons,* 116.
125. "Stop, Harry . . ." Orrmont, *Master Detective Allan Pinkerton,* 78.

CHAPTER TWELVE: THAT WHICH IS MOST DANGEROUS

126. *On March 4, Abraham Lincoln marked his inauguration* . . . David Herbert Donald, *Lincoln* (New York: Simon & Schuster, 1995), 282–283.
126. *Reaction to the address* . . . Ibid., 283.
127. *On March 9, Lincoln's cabinet met* . . . Mackay, *Allan Pinkerton,* 106–107.
128. *At 3:20 a.m., on April 12, Confederates sent* . . . Ibid., 107.
129. *On April 15 President Lincoln issued* . . . Orrmont, *Master Detective Allan Pinkerton,* 79.
129. *A lone traveler moved through the Pennsylvania dusk* . . . Pinkerton, *The Spy of the Rebellion,* 114–130. (Note: Accounts vary as to whether Pinkerton was initially asked by Lincoln to provide intelligence services during the war—which is Pinkerton's assertion—or whether Pinkerton offered his services. James Mackay, probably the foremost authority, claims that Pinkerton sent a written proposal, but the facts of Webster's service as a courier, as described in Pinkerton's memoir, seem fairly incontrovertible. An effort is made here to keep the two issues separate.)
130. "I hear you are hard on clothes . . ." Lavine, *Allan Pinkerton,* 67.
130. "You have brought quite a bit of mail . . ." Pinkerton, *The Spy of the Rebellion,* 128. (Note: Page numbers from Pinkerton's memoirs, which contain profuse dialogue, vary from edition to edition, due to that fact that they are in the public domain, and the only extant copies, as far as this author is aware, are digital prints from different on-demand presses.)

130. *This was an immense task* . . . Mackay, *Allan Pinkerton*, 109.

131. *Webster was nearly lynched in Pennsylvania* . . . Ibid., 110.

131. *The first letter, from Norman Judd* . . . American Memory (online) www.memory.loc.gov. (Note: The exact wording of Pinkerton's and Judd's letters are found in the transcriptions provided by the Lincoln Studies Center, Knox College, Galesburg, Illinois, of the original artifacts.)

132. "If you would like one of these . . ." Orrmont, *Master Detective Allan Pinkerton*, 80.

132. *The United States Secret Service—as it exists today* . . . www.secretservice.gov/history.

133. "Come to Washington as soon as possible . . ." Pinkerton, *The Spy of the Rebellion*, 129.

CHAPTER THIRTEEN: A NEST OF LOVELY SNAKES

137. "From her first appearance in Washington . . ." Ishbel Ross, *Rebel Rose* (New York: Harper & Brothers, 1954), 4–5.

138. *Drunken bluecoats wandered* . . . Mackay, *Allan Pinkerton*, 121.

138. *In this chaotic* . . . Ibid., 122.

139. "Sir, I wish you could prove . . ." Orrmont, *Master Detective Allan Pinkerton*, 81.

139. *Have heard of your achievement* . . . Ibid., 81.

140. *McClellan told the detective* . . . Ibid., 84.

140. *The chestnut gelding, in its own way* . . . Photographic evidence, "Allan Pinkerton on horseback at Antietam," Public Domain, Library of Congress. (Note: The loyal and steadfast horse, on which Pinkerton rode during the Civil War, is mentioned in numerous sources. Mackay calls it a "splendid bay," and Rowan refers to it as a "sorrel"—which are two different horses. The photograph reveals the telltale light-colored tail of a sorrel or "chestnut." The speculation that it was a gelding—a neutered male—is also due to the photographic evidence, as well as the unlikelihood of a spy riding a hot-tempered—in tact—stallion through war zones.)

140. *The Rebels have sunk two boats* . . . Mackay, *Allan Pinkerton*, 114.

141. *The chaotic battle with General Beauregard's army* . . . Bruce Catton, *The Civil War* (New York: American Heritage, 1960), 36–51.

141. *Five days earlier, Greenhow had sent* . . . Ross, *Rebel Rose*, 113–114.

141. *They had come for a pleasant afternoon* . . . Catton, *The Civil War*, 50.

142. "The West Virginia campaign may have been . . ." Mackay, *Allan Pinkerton*, 117.

143. "I find myself in a new and strange position . . ." Stephen Sears, *George B. McClellan: The Young Napoleon* (New York: Ticknor and Fields, 1988), 95.

143. *McClellan declared the city out of bounds* . . . Mackay, *Allan Pinkerton*, 121.

144. "I would rather you worshipped President Lincoln . . ." Orrmont, *Master Detective Allan Pinkerton*, 92–93.

145. *His agents would have the entrée* Pinkerton, *The Spy of the Rebellion*, 247–248.

145. "I mean to make a modern army . . ." Orrmont, *Master Detective Allan Pinkerton*, 93–94.

146. "Hello, Dad . . ." Ibid., 94–95.

147. *Pinkerton didn't write President Lincoln* . . . Ibid., 95.

147. "Webster! You're *here*, are ya?!" Pinkerton, *The Spy of the Rebellion*, 275–279. (Note: This encounter is meticulously detailed in Pinkerton's memoir.)

149. "Webster, it must be admitted, was wholly unprepared . . ." Ibid., 276.

CHAPTER FOURTEEN: DARKENING SKIES

151. "In our part of the world, there were no secrets . . ." Harry Thompson, from *Secrets of the Civil War*, © 2008, A&E Television Networks.

152. "I was then quite a stranger in Washington . . ." Pinkerton, *The Spy of the Rebellion*, 254.

152. "Many of these ladies were extremely fascinating . . ." Ibid., 250.

153. "McClellan, in truth, had a voracious appetite . . ." Rowan, *The Pinkertons*, 130.

153. *Historians have alluded to Pinkerton's* . . . Mackay, *Allan Pinkerton,* 121–136. (Note: Although James Mackay never articulates this in a literal sense, the text during the "Rebel Rose" section of Mackay's biography drips with unrequited attraction—as do other sources containing between-the-lines allusions to Pinkerton's repressed feelings. The temptation is great to read more into Pinkerton's fascination with these seductive female spies—especially his feelings for Greenhow—than is present in the historic record, not to mention any account. "Over the years," Mackay writes, "the myth has developed of the puritanical lawman falling under the spell of the Southern siren." Even Kate Warne has not escaped the hindsight of suggestive biographies. But perhaps Mackay should have the last word on the subject of Allan Pinkerton's fidelity to Joan, which this author believes was 100 percent true throughout his marriage: "The many references to [Warne] in his letters indicate the affection he felt for her, but this sprang from admiration for her skill and dedication rather than from any sexual feelings.")

153. "She knows my plans better than Lincoln . . ." Ross, *Rebel Rose,* 121.

153. *The brick house—"while not at all imposing . . ."* Pinkerton, *The Spy of the Rebellion,* 253.

154. In Pinkerton words, "Lewis wore a full beard . . ." Ibid., 211.

154. *Pinkerton later would call Bridgeman* . . . Ibid., 211.

155. *Pinkerton started to whisper something* . . . Ibid., 256.

155. *At this point in her career* . . . Mackay, *Allan Pinkerton,* 125.

156. *Born in 1817 in Port Tobacco, Maryland* . . . Ross, *Rebel Rose,* 3–18.

156. *Notwithstanding her stunning, patrician* . . . Photographic evidence, Ross, *Rebel Rose,* 115.

157. *On the other side of the door stood* . . . Pinkerton, *The Spy of the Rebellion,* 257.

157. "Boss!" Ibid., 258.

157. *Pinkerton could hear fragments* . . . Ibid., 259.

158. "My blood boiled with indignation . . ." Ibid., 259.

159. "Halt, or I fire!" Ibid., 260.

159. *For quite a while the captain paced* . . . Ibid., 261.

159. "I wasn't really following you, sir . . ." Lavine, *Allan Pinkerton,* 92–93.

160. *Time crawled for Pinkerton* . . . Pinkerton, *The Spy of the Rebellion,* 261–265. (Note: As is the case with several events described in Pinkerton's first-person accounts, there is no way to corroborate moments like these—solitary experiences—but the amount of detail provided by the detective, especially in this case, suggests reliability of recall.)

161. *A gray-haired, professorial-looking man* . . . Photographic evidence, "Thomas Alexander Scott," Project Gutenberg eText 17976.jpg.

162. "I had gone to visit some friends . . ." Pinkerton, *The Spy of the Rebellion,* 266–267. (Note: Pinkerton's wartime memoir is effusive with dialogue, although, in this section, the ellipses and italics have been added for dramatic emphasis.)

162. *The next day, before Pinkerton had a chance* . . . Mackay, *Allan Pinkerton,* 126.

162. "Mrs. Greenhow must be attended to . . ." Ross, *Rebel Rose,* 139.

CHAPTER FIFTEEN: THE DEVIL IS NO MATCH FOR A CLEVER WOMAN

163. *Rays of morning sunlight bathed* . . . Ross, *Rebel Rose,* 140. (Note: Accounts differ as to the time of day of Rose Greenhow's arrest. Many defer to daytime. Greenhow's own account pinpoints the time of her arrest at 11:00 a.m., which jibes with Mackay's assertion that the warrant was issued "on the morning of 23 August.")

163. *She had sensed someone following her* . . . Rose O'Neal Greenhow, *My Imprisonment and the First Year of Abolition Rule at Washington* (London: Richard Bentley, Publisher, 1863), 53.

164. "She studied the men openly . . ." Ross, *Rebel Rose,* 140.

165. *Among these agents was Hattie Lawton* . . . Mackay, *Allan Pinkerton,* 127. (Note: The presence of Hattie Lawton, although accounts vary, is maintained strongly by Mackay. This makes sense on one level: A police matron is routinely present in the apprehension of a woman. The remark on Lawton's face is from Greenhow's own account, which refers to Lawton as a policewoman named "Ellen"—but it seems reasonable to assume that "Ellen" may have been Lawton's cover.)

165. *The olive-skinned Lawton particularly irritated* . . . Greenhow, *My Imprisonment,* 62.

166. "*There is nothing yet that can come under* . . ." Ross, *Rebel Rose,* 143.

166. Writes Ross: "A high wall surrounded . . ." Ibid., 144.

166. "I did not know what they had done . . ." Greenhow, *My Imprisonment,* 58.

167. *The correspondences from Wilson* . . . Ross, *Rebel Rose,* 143. (Note: Photographic evidence also informs this section, as Wilson's love letters are widely available.)

167. *Pryce Lewis would have seemed* . . . Mackay, *Allan Pinkerton,* 127.

168. *The oppressive heat had pressed* . . . Greenhow, *My Imprisonment,* 61.

168. *Greenhow made her move* . . . Mackay, *Allan Pinkerton,* 127.

169. *By nightfall, he had recovered* . . . Ibid., 127.

169. *She got an idea* . . . Ross, *Rebel Rose,* 144–146.

170. *The guards did allow the Mackall sisters* . . . Greenhow, *My Imprisonment,* 67.

171. *Pinkerton even found evidence* . . . Mackay, *Allan Pinkerton,* 127–128.

172. *Toward the end of August* . . . Ibid., 122–123.

172. *Born in 1826 in Stafford, New York* . . . Ibid., 123.

173. *The detective described Thompson as* . . . Ibid., 129.

173. *In mid-September Webster commenced* . . . Pinkerton, *The Spy of the Rebellion,* 335–337.

174. *Only one of the plotters managed* . . . Orrmont, *Master Detective Allan Pinkerton,* 101.

175. "The Endless Time . . ." Tom Stoppard, *Rosencrantz and Guildenstern Are Dead* (New York: Grove Press, 1968). (Note: I lifted the ominous title of Part IV from Stoppard.)

CHAPTER SIXTEEN: SEALED IN A FEVER

177. *Icy winds drowned the cheerful harangue* . . . Pinkerton, *The Spy of the Rebellion,* 468.

177. *In one massive report* . . . Mackay, *Allan Pinkerton,* 139.

178. *With a warm clasp of the hand* . . . Pinkerton, *The Spy of the Rebellion,* 470.

179. *By the time he reached the southern port* . . . Ibid., 471.

179. *Established in 1708, situated in a prime* . . . Village Website: http://leonardtown.somd.com/ history, "The 19th Century" page.

180. "We can't cross here at all . . ." Pinkerton, *The Spy of the Rebellion,* 471.

181. "All right, Tom . . ." Ibid., 473.

181. *The wind through the low pines* . . . Ibid., 473.

182. *The effects of the misadventure* . . . Ibid., 474–475.

183. *In the middle of the nineteenth century* . . . MayoClinic.com, "Rheumatic Fever" page.

184. *Often posing as Webster's wife* . . . Photographic evidence, Library of Congress, "Allan Pinkerton and Kate Warne," American Civil War, Selected Images (Public Domain). (Note: It is this author's belief that Hattie Lawton is misidentified in this famous daguerreotype as "Kate Warne"—mostly due to the repeated references in an array of sources to Lawton's "male" persona in the field.)

185. *Jones was a naturally suspicious* . . . Mackay, *Allan Pinkerton,* 140–141.

186. I often recall, and with an emotion . . . Pinkerton, *The Spy of the Rebellion,* 485–486.

CHAPTER SEVENTEEN: THE WORM TURNING

187. "*Pickets!*" Ibid., 489.

188. *Around midnight they came* . . . Ibid., 489–490.

189. "Let Webster go where he pleases . . ." Ibid., 491.

190. *For months he had been planning* . . . Orrmont, *Master Detective Allan Pinkerton,* 109.
190. *On February 23, 1862* . . . Mackay, *Allan Pinkerton,* 141. (Note: The timeline comes from extrapolations, as neither Pinkerton nor my secondary sources keep strict track of dates in their respective narratives. This particular date is derived by back-timing from the day Lewis and Scully checked into the Ballard House in Richmond.)
191. "One man can remember a story . . ." Ibid., 141.
192. Pinkerton gave the agents . . . Ibid., 141.
192. *But what Lewis and Scully did not notice* . . . *Richmond Enquirer,* March 4, 1862, p. 1.
193. "Have you gentlemen reported in . . ." Pinkerton, *The Spy of the Rebellion,* 503.
194. "Please forgive the intrusion . . ." Ibid., 505. (Note: The dialogue attributed to the Confederate detective is reconstructed from Pinkerton's summary of the exchange.)
195. *In the early weeks of the war* . . . Jackson Morton citations, William and Mary Alumni Association (www.alumni.wm.edu/).
195. *Upon secession, Morton had become* . . . http://bioguide.congress.gov/.
196. "Are your names Lewis and Scully?!" Pinkerton, *The Spy of the Rebellion,* 507.
196. "Don't you remember me . . ." Ibid., 508.
196. *A complex of rotting two-story brick* . . . Pinkerton, *The Spy of the Rebellion,* 513.
197. *Scully jumped at the sound* . . . Ibid., 512. (Note: Scully's reaction is a speculation due to Pinkerton's vivid description of the young man's jittery state of mind.)

CHAPTER EIGHTEEN: DESPERATION COUNTY

198. *"Time!" The elderly jailer* . . . Ibid., 515. (Note: The word *"Time!"*—uttered by the turnkey—is from Pinkerton's summary.)
198. *The errant prisoner, Charles Stanton* . . . Ibid., 514–515.
200. "The colored men, without any solicitation . . ." Ibid., 517–518.
200. *In whispers and hand gestures* . . . Ibid., 518. (Note: The bulk of the prison escape is exhaustively detailed by Pinkerton, most likely from Lewis's first-person account, provided years later in Philadelphia; only a few phrases used here, such as this one concerning hand gestures, are author embellishments provided as connective tissue, for the purposes of narrative clarity, derived from Pinkerton's own details (e.g., in this instance, his phrase, "The men issued silently forth."))
201. *As the ringleader of the escape* . . . Mackay, *Allan Pinkerton,* 143.
202. "You will not tell them . . ." Pinkerton, *The Spy of the Rebellion,* 526.
202. "One of Winder's men is below . . ." Ibid., 537–539.
204. *Now he spoke carefully, almost gently* . . . Ibid., 538. (Note: Pinkerton speaks to Cashmeyer's sympathy in detail here: "A shade of pity came over his face.")
204. *Later that night, in a fetid, rotting* . . . Mackay, *Allan Pinkerton,* 144.
204. *Inside the receiving area of Castle Godwin* . . . Pinkerton, *The Spy of the Rebellion,* 539.

CHAPTER NINETEEN: THE WHISPER OF THE GALLOWS

207. YANKEE SPIES! . . . *Richmond Enquirer,* March 4, 1862.
207. *Pinkerton's blood 'seemed to freeze* . . . Pinkerton, *The Spy of the Rebellion,* 544.
207. *Who can blame this man* . . . *?* Ibid., 528–529.
207. "I have good news for you . . ." Mackay, *Allan Pinkerton,* 144.
208. *On April 18, 1862, the news reached* . . . Ibid., 145.
209. *Pinkerton decided to return immediately* . . . Ibid., 546–547.
209. "I will do everything in my power . . ." Mackay, *Allan Pinkerton,* 146.
209. *He directed Stanton to draft a letter* . . . Pinkerton, *The Spy of the Rebellion,* 547.
210. "Mr. Secretary, we cannot afford . . ." Orrmont, *Master Detective Allan Pinkerton,* 111.
210. *In happier times this wooded meadow* . . . *Richmond Dispatch,* October 30, 1860, p. 1.
211. *But tonight, as darkness gathered* . . . Artist rendering, "Civil War Richmond," mdgorman.com /images/ca29.JPG.

211. *In Timothy Webster's case—Davis reasoned* . . . Mackay, *Allan Pinkerton*, 146.
212. *They held each other's hands* . . . Pinkerton, *The Spy of the Rebellion*, 554.
212. *In a tearful meeting, under guard* . . . Ibid., 549–550.

Chapter Twenty: Death Be Not Proud

214. *Brigadier General John H. Winder, his lantern jaw* . . . Photographic evidence, "The Photographic History of the Civil War Volume 7—Prisons and Hospitals," pddoc.com /photohistory/v7/102.htm.
214. *"That's fine, Webster, but what is it* . . . *"* Pinkerton, *The Spy of the Rebellion*, 550–551. (Note: This single line of dialogue does not exist in Pinkerton's account; it is inserted for dramatic logic, rhythmic flow, and readability. According to Pinkerton, Webster gave Winder an earful with no breaks in his plea.)
215. *Hattie Lawton never left his side* . . . Ibid., 550.
216. *How many times the gaunt, repulsive form* . . . Ibid., 552–554.
217. *"It's the order of General Winder* . . . *"* Ibid., 555.
217. *Her tortured shriek* . . . Ibid., 556. (Note: According to Pinkerton—"[Her] piercing shriek rent the air . . ."—so that it could be heard, considering the physical location of the prison, across the streets facing the river.)
218. *There was a nip in the air* . . . Mackay, *Allan Pinkerton*, 147.
218. *Days later, the Richmond press* . . . Ibid., 147.
219. *In 1890, author Ambrose Bierce* . . . enotes.com/occurrence-owl-creek-bridge.
219. *"I suffer a double death* . . . *"* Pinkerton, *The Spy of the Rebellion*, 557–558.
220. *The Richmond Examiner later observed* . . . Mackay, *Allan Pinkerton*, 147.
220. *Later in the day, Winder's men cut* . . . Ibid., 147.
220. *"May I see him before he is taken* . . . *"* Pinkerton, *The Spy of the Rebellion*, 558–559.

Chapter Twenty-One: Theater of Blood and Regret

223. *By May, 21, 1862, McClellan's forces* . . . Mackay, *Allan Pinkerton*, 151.
223. *"If I save this army now* . . . *"* Ibid., 152.
224. *In Washington he found himself* . . . Ibid., 153.
225. *Now sixteen, and prone to wear* . . . Ibid., 155.
225. *Please say a kind word to my army* . . . Pinkerton, *The Spy of the Rebellion*, 576.
226. *This did not sit well with McClellan* . . . Mackay, *Allan Pinkerton*, 156.
226. *The general took one look* . . . Ibid., 159.
227. *The action intensified* . . . Catton, *The Civil War*, 96.
227. *At the height of battle, Pinkerton rode* . . . Pinkerton, *The Spy of the Rebellion*, 569. (Note: The death of the trusty sorrel is rendered from Pinkerton's own recollections, as well as Mackay's description of the incident. Pinkerton bowing his head is purely speculation.)
228. *After a lengthy meeting with Lincoln* . . . Mackay, *Allan Pinkerton*, 160.
228. *In Washington, he battled recalcitrant* . . . Ibid., 163.
229. *"Intelligence is not the word* . . . *"* (This and the other fragments were taken from a message board string on July 14, 2009 at http://boards.straightdope.com; they are merely meant as a sampling of how the myth of placing blame on Pinkerton for McClellan's failures has survived the decades.)
229. *Even Pinkerton's own grandniece* . . . Margaret Fitchett, from an unpublished memoir, which can be found at http://freepages.Genealogy.rootsweb.ancestry.com/~Pinkerton/the_early_pinkertons_main.htm.
230. *In the spring and summer of 1862* . . . James D. Horan, *The Pinkertons: The Detective Agency That Made History* (New York: Crown, 1967), 114.
230. *Horan makes much of the fact* . . . Mackay, *Allan Pinkerton*, 153.
231. *Moreover, the historical record* . . . Ibid., 154.

231. *At 11:30 on the night of November 7* ... Ibid., 165.
232. *In his emotionally charged farewell* ... Pinkerton, *The Spy of the Rebellion*, 577.
232. *On his last day at Warrenton* ... Mackay, *Allan Pinkerton*, 167.

CHAPTER TWENTY-TWO: UNDER THE PROVIDENCE OF GOD

233. "If before this moment I had any English ..." Ibid., 171 (Note: Mackay uses many quotes from Pryce Lewis's memoirs, which appear to be out of print. The greatest single source for Pryce Lewis correspondences, biographical works, and memorabilia, however, is New York's St Lawrence University, an invaluable resource for this work [http://www.stlawu.edu/library/node/576]. Plus Gavin Moritmer's *Double Death* [Walker, 2010] is also a comprehensive wellspring of Lewisiana.)
233. *Stirred from his bed* ... Mackay, *Allan Pinkerton*, 171.
234. *In Lewis's memoir, the dapper Brit* ... Ibid., 172.
235. "No trace of her ..." Pinkerton, *The Spy of the Rebellion*, 270.
235. *Lafayette Baker, Pinkerton's nemesis* ... Signal Corps Association website (http://scard.buffnet.net), "Lafayette Baker" page.
235. "Lewis remained staunch and did not ..." Pinkerton National Detective Agency, Administrative File, 1857–1999, From the UPA Collection, Research Collections in American Legal History, Reel 3, 0619.
236. *His ambivalence over the Emancipation Proclamation.* ... Mackay, *Allan Pinkerton*, 161.
236. *The former general-in-chief ran* ... Sears, *George B. McClellan*, 376–379.
237. *Pinkerton found himself embroiled* ... Mackay, *Allan Pinkerton*, 168–169.
237. *Lincoln thought it might be nice* ... James Swanson, *Manhunt: The Twelve-Day Chase for Lincoln's Killer* (New York: HarperCollins, 2006), 12.
238. *Parker, as a security agent* ... Mackay, *Allan Pinkerton*, 174.
238. *Halfway through the third act* ... Swanson, *Manhunt*, 42–43.
239. "The ball ripped through ..." Ibid., 45.

CHAPTER TWENTY-THREE: HIGH LONESOME

240. *They tracked down the infamous* ... Rowan, *The Pinkertons*, 199–209.
241. *Pinkerton was at her bedside* ... Bzovy, "First Female Pinkerton Detective," 6.
241. "She exceeded far beyond ..." Mackay, *Allan Pinkerton*, 74.
241. *Webster was buried in Onarga* ... Photographic evidence, Graceland Tombstone, Courtesy of Rachel Walker.
242. "Like the professional operative she was ..." Priscilla Rhoades, "The Women of Castle Thunder," *The Kudzu Monthly*, an e-zine, August 2, 2004.
242. *Harry Davies, the polished young Frenchman* ... Donald Markle, *Spies and Spymasters of the Civil War* (New York: Hippocrene Books, 1994), 150–151.
243. *He had suffered a massive stroke* ... Mackay, *Allan Pinkerton*, 201–202.
243. THE MOST COMPLETE AND EXTENSIVE ... *Chicago Tribune*, October 9, 1871.
244. *After one particularly messy feud* ... Mackay, *Allan Pinkerton*, 234.
244. *Later, William Pinkerton recalled* ... Ibid., 236.
244. "I am not in the habit of giving ..." Ibid., 236.

EPILOGUE: IN MEMORIAM

247. *He left his estate* ... Mackay, *Allan Pinkerton*, 237.
247. *Emotionally ravaged by her husband's passing* ... Ibid., 237.

Sources

Abel, E. Lawrence. *Singing the New Nation: How Music Shaped the Confederacy, 1861–1865*. Mechanicsburg, PA: Stackpole Books, 2000.

Bonekemper, Edward H. *McClellan and Failure: A Study of Civil War Fear, Incompetence, and Worse*. Jefferson, NC: McFarland, 2007.

Carwardine, Richard. *Lincoln: A Life of Purpose and Power*. New York: Vintage Books, 2002.

Catton, Bruce. *The Civil War*. New York: American Heritage, 1960.

Chicago Historical Society. *Special Archives: Documents and Letters*. Chicago, Illinois.

Davis, William C. *Jefferson Davis: The Man and His Hour*. New York: Harper Collins, 1991.

DiLorenzo, Thomas J. *The Real Lincoln: A New Look at Abraham Lincoln, His Agenda, and an Unnecessary War*. New York: Three Rivers Press, 2002.

Donald, David Herbert. *Lincoln*. New York: Simon & Schuster, 1995.

Duis, Perry R. *Challenging Chicago: Coping with Everyday Life, 1837–1920*. Urbana: University of Illinois Press, 1998.

Dundee Illinois Historical Museum, Special Collections.

Durie, Bruce. *The Pinkerton Casebook: Adventures of the Original Private Eye*. Edinburgh: Mercat Press, 2007.

Fox River Valley Herald

Garrison, Webb. *True Tales of the Civil War*. New York: Gramercy Books, 1988.

Goodwin, Doris Kearns. *Team of Rivals*. New York: Simon & Schuster, 2005.

Greenhow, Rose O'Neal. *My Imprisonment and the First Year of Abolition Rule at Washington*. London: Richard Bentley, Publisher, 1863.

Harold Washington Library Center, Special Collections, Chicago, Illinois.

Holzer, Harold. *Lincoln at Cooper Union: The Speech That Made Abraham Lincoln President*. New York: Simon & Schuster, 2004.

Horan, James D. *The Pinkertons: The Detective Agency That Made History*. New York: Crown, 1967.

Karamanski, Theodore J., and Dean Tank. *Maritime Chicago*. Chicago: Arcadia Publishing, 2000.

Kunhardt, Phillip B. *Lincoln*. New York: Alfred A. Knopf, 1992.

Lavine, Sigmund. *Allan Pinkerton: America's First Private Eye*. New York: Dodd, Mead, 1963.

Lindberg, Richard C. *Chicago by Gaslight: A History of Chicago's Netherworld, 1888–1920*. Chicago: Academy Chicago Publishers, 1996.

Lindberg, Richard C. *To Serve and Collect: Chicago Politics and Police Corruption from the Lager Beer Riot to the Summerdale Scandal 1855–1960*. Carbondale: Southern Illinois University Press, 1998.

Lossing, Benson J., *Lossing's History of the Civil War—Vol. 1*, New York: The War Memorial Association, 1912.

Mackay, James. *Allan Pinkerton: The First Private Eye*. New York: John Wiley and Sons, 1996.

Markle, Donald. *Spies and Spymasters of the Civil War*. New York: Hippocrene Books, 1994.

Mayer, Harold M., and Richard C. Wade. *Chicago: Growth of a Metropolis*. Chicago: University of Chicago Press, 1969.

McCutcheon, Marc. *Everyday Life in the 1800s*. Cincinnati: Writer's Digest Books, 1993.

Newton, Michael. *Armed and Dangerous*. Cincinnati: Writer's Digest Books, 1990.

Olesky, Walter, ed. *Lincoln's Unknown Private Life*. Mamaroneck, NY: Hastings House, 1995.

Orrmont, Arthur. *Master Detective Allan Pinkerton*. New York: Julian Messner Books, 1965.

Pinkerton, Allan. *History and Evidence of the Passage of Abraham Lincoln from Harrisburg to Washington, D.C., 1861*. Chicago: Pinkerton National Detective Agency, 1892.

Pinkerton, Allan. *The Molly Maguires and the Detectives*. New York: BiblioLife, 2009 (1877).

Pinkerton, Allan. *Professional Thieves and the Detective: Containing Numerous Detective Sketches Collected from Private Records*. New York: G. W. Carleton, 1880.

Pinkerton, Allan. *Reminiscences*. New York: G. W. Carleton, 1879.

Pinkerton, Allan. *The Spy of the Rebellion: Being a True History of the Spy System of the United States Army During the Late Rebellion, Revealing Many Secrets of the War Hitherto Not Made Public, Compiled from Official Reports Prepared for President Lincoln, General McClellan, and the Provost-Marshal-General*. New York: Samuel Stodder, 1883.

Ross, Ishbel. *Rebel Rose*. New York: Harper & Brothers, 1954.

Rowan, Richard Wilmer. *The Pinkertons: A Detective Dynasty*. Boston: Little Brown & Company, 1931.

Sacks, Howard L., and Judith Sacks. *Way Up North in Dixie: A Black Family's Claim to the Confederate Anthem*. Washington: Smithsonian Institution Press, 1993.

Sandberg, Carl. *Chicago Poems*. New York: Dover Publications, 1994.

Sears, Stephen. *George B. McClellan: The Young Napoleon*. New York: Ticknor and Fields, 1988.

Segal, Charles. *Conversations with Lincoln*. New York: G. P. Putnam's Sons, 1961.

Swanson, James. *Manhunt: The Twelve-Day Chase for Lincoln's Killer*. New York: HarperCollins, 2006.

Vidocq, Eugène F. *Memoirs of Vidocq: Master of Crime*. Edinburgh: AK Press, 2003.

Wise, William. *Detective Pinkerton and Mr. Lincoln*. New York: E. P. Dutton, 1964.

Young, David M. *Chicago Transit: An Illustrated History*. DeKalb: Northern Illinois University Press, 1998.

Index